Mark Killick is a senior producer with BBC TV's *Panorama* programme. His many television credits include *The Numbers Game*, which first revealed that Richard Branson had been offered a bribe by a Camelot director in an unsuccessful attempt to stop him bidding for the National Lottery; *The Max Factor*, which exposed Robert Maxwell's share support operation; and *Lady Porter – The Pursuit of Power*, which broke the story of Westminster Council's homes for votes scandal. During his career Mark Killick has won a host of national and international television awards including the Royal Television Society Award for best home current affairs programme and the Broadcasting Press Guild Award for best single documentary. He also writes for newspapers and magazines and specializes in financial investigation. His first book, *The Sultan of Sleaze*, an account of the sex and media empire built by David Sullivan, was published in 1994.

MARK KILLICK

Fraudbusters

The Inside Story of the Serious Fraud Office

INDIGO

An Indigo Paperback
First published in Great Britain by Victor Gollancz in 1998
This paperback edition published in 1999 by Indigo
an imprint of Orion Books Ltd,
Orion House, 5 Upper St Martin's Lane, London WC2H 9EA

A CIP catalogue record for this book
is available from the British Library.

ISBN: 0 575 40138 9

Printed and bound in Great Britain by
The Guernsey Press Co. Ltd, Guernsey, C.I.

Contents

Acknowledgements

EVER SINCE George Staple, the former head of the Serious Fraud Office, said that the SFO couldn't be fairly judged until it had been in existence for ten years, I knew that I was going to write this book. And, to George Staple's credit, when I pointed out to him in May 1996 that the SFO's tenth anniversary was coming up and that I intended to take up his challenge, he agreed to help me. His co-operation and subsequently that of Ros Wright, his replacement as director of the SFO, has made this book possible and I am deeply grateful to both of them.

This is the first time that so many senior members of the SFO have spoken out and the first time that the organisation has opened its files to an outsider in this way. As well as George Staple and Ros Wright, both Dame Barbara Mills and John Wood, the only other two people to have headed the SFO, have given interviews for this book. Additionally, Lord Mayhew and Sir Nicholas Lyell, the two Attorney-Generals who supervised the Serious Fraud Office for the vast majority of its first ten years, have given generously of their time to answer a whole series of difficult questions. Finally, almost all of the case controllers responsible for the SFO's major cases have talked to me candidly over the past year and I am grateful to them all. In particular, I would single out Chris Dickson and Robert Wardle, without whom it would not have been possible to write this book. The same, it has to be said, is also true of James O'Donoghue, Sue Heard and the rest of the SFO press office, who on several occasions saved the project from imminent disaster.

But it would have been wrong for me to rely exclusively on the SFO for material for this book, and I have not done so. I have spoken to some of the most high-profile defendants in cases brought by the SFO, including George Walker, Kevin Maxwell and Lord Spens. Their insights into the SFO have proved as useful as the comments of their defence teams. Finally, I have talked to a large number of third parties, including barristers, police officers and MPs, who have all watched the SFO over the years. I hope that, by assimilating the views of everyone involved in the story, I have produced what will be considered a fair, reasonable and definitive view of the SFO's first decade.

I have also been the senior producer of a BBC Television series of the same name, and I would like to take this opportunity to thank my colleagues in BBC News for their help and assistance. Top of the list must be Mark Hedgecoe, who has done a magnificent job co-producing the series. We have both been very ably supported by Jenny Frayn who, like Mark, has made a significant contribution to the research for this book. I would also like to acknowledge Sally Foster's efforts and, in particular, her contribution to 'The Final Score', which was substantial. Additionally, I should mention BBC *Panorama*'s Manchester team, in particular Harry Dean and Gerry Northan, who generously passed on their research files on Polly Peck. Finally, I would like to thank Mark Damazer, Head of BBC Current Affairs, who approved the whole SFO project; and Tim Suter, the Deputy Head of Current Affairs, and Steve Hewlett, the former Editor of *Panorama*, who both helped me a great deal, particularly in the early stages.

Last, but by no means least, I should like to thank my agent, Vivienne Schuster of Curtis Brown, who backed this book with her legendary zeal, and Sean Magee of Victor Gollancz, who agreed to publish it. I hope they both think the project has been worthwhile. But most of all, I want to thank CK, DK and GK, just for being there.

Mark Killick
December 1997

Introduction

THE SERIOUS FRAUD OFFICE is probably Britain's most controversial crime-fighting organisation. During its short life it has generated admiration and contempt in almost equal measure. It has known triumph with the Guinness convictions, disaster with the acquittal of the Maxwell brothers and ridicule with Roger Levitt's derisory community service sentence. This book goes behind the headlines to examine the full history of the SFO's performance over its first decade.

The public perception of the SFO is of an organisation which loses more cases than it wins. But the reality is very different. Over the first ten years of its existence since becoming operational in April 1988, the SFO has handled over 160 cases and has achieved a conviction rate of 65 per cent. Indeed, over the last three years, this rate has risen steadily towards, and then exceeded, 90 per cent. And yet it is the acquittal of Kevin and Ian Maxwell that has stayed firmly fixed, and uppermost, in the public mind.

The SFO was set up when the government finally realised that the activities of white-collar fraudsters, particularly in the City of London, had become so widespread as to endanger the United Kingdom's reputation for financial probity. Yet, despite the fact that the SFO is currently investigating frauds involving over £2 billion, it still has a budget of only £15.9 million and employs just 175 people. It remains one of the smallest of all government departments.

But while the SFO may be small, it has an extraordinarily high profile, and this has been both its blessing and its curse. In the early days, just two trials, Guinness and Barlow Clowes, convinced the world that it could virtually do no wrong; four years later, following the acquittals of George Walker and Kevin Maxwell, the release on appeal of the County NatWest defendants and the ludicrous sentence of 180 hours' community service meted out to Roger Levitt, it had hardly any friends at all. Now it is on a more even keel and is quietly getting on with the job of prosecuting suspected fraudsters while actively discouraging the hysterical publicity of the early 1990s. The SFO is slowly turning its public image around – but it is acutely aware that one major failure could undo several years of hard work.

This book examines all of the SFO's most public cases and also looks at some facets of its work which have not been so widely reported. The SFO's international desk has assisted numerous foreign authorities in solving important fraud cases and yet has received scarcely any credit at all for this. Even the Davie Report, commissioned by the Attorney-General in 1994 specifically to examine the SFO, was virtually ignored when it concluded that the SFO was doing a good job and should have both its funding and its workload increased.

Above all, this book is intended to give a unique insight into the world of serious fraud in Britain and beyond. The SFO has taken on many of this country's richest and most resourceful people, most of whom are more than capable of meeting the challenge head-on. The resulting clashes have been battles royal, and this book chronicles them all. For the first time, it is possible to see what went on from both sides of the courtroom. It is a truly astonishing story.

Part I

'Get the Handcuffs On'

I

Hallowe'en Night

H ALLOWE'EN MIGHT SEEM a strange occasion for over one hundred of the people most closely associated with Britain's Serious Fraud Office to gather together. It was certainly dark and wet outside, but there was no black magic going on in the Law Society's magnificent old council chamber in London's Chancery Lane. Instead, on 31 October 1997 some of the best-known names in the police, accountancy and the criminal bar were congregating to say farewell to Chris Dickson, perhaps the most successful of all the SFO prosecutors.

Dickson, a softly spoken Ulsterman with a ready smile and a slightly chubby frame, had been with the SFO since it was founded in 1988. He had been recruited from the tough world of the prosecutor's office in Northern Ireland and, as many defendants have found to their cost, his charm and good humour hide a determination to win that some would say borders on the ruthless. Certainly Chris Dickson himself has no doubts as to the role of the Serious Fraud Office. 'The SFO's duty is to prosecute the rich and powerful', he once told me forcefully, 'as aggressively as the poor are prosecuted.'

It's an attitude that has always put Dickson in a minority within the Serious Fraud Office. Everyone at Elm Street, the home of the SFO, knows that the politically correct answer is to say that the job of the prosecution is to present its case fairly and accurately. The result is not meant to be important. But the Elm Street investigators also know that they target some of the richest, brightest and most unscrupulous people in Britain, and that the public expects the SFO to bring them to book. As Dickson has repeatedly said at conferences and elsewhere, 'We have to ask ourselves a very fundamental question. Are we here simply to present cases or are we here to secure convictions? In my view, we've got to get much more aggressive in our attitude. The defence plays to win and so should we.'

One of the reasons why Chris Dickson is able to state his views so openly is that his methods have generally got results. Just the day before his leaving party, he led a dawn raid on a flat in London's Eaton Square, one of the most prestigious addresses in the capital. Dickson was after documents relating to an insider dealing ring in Amsterdam. The first the occupant knew of the raid was when Dickson shook her awake. He politely but firmly explained the position, showed her the warrant and then searched the whole flat with relentless diligence. By 8 a.m. it was all over and the SFO team left the building carrying a number of vital documents.

That dawn raid, moreover, wasn't part of an SFO investigation. It was mounted following a request for assistance from the Dutch police. Dickson is one of a growing number of people at the SFO who believe that serious fraud is becoming increasingly international in scope and that this type of co-operation is now the only way to solve many of the most world's most important fraud cases. To this end, the SFO has set up a Mutual Legal Assistance desk which services requests from fraud squads all over the world. Among the high-profile cases the MLA unit has already assisted with have been the investigations by the Italian police into the affairs of the media magnate Silvio Berlusconi and by the Australian police into those of the corporate raider Alan Bond. This ability to help foreign investigators is just one of a number of extra-ordinary powers possessed by the SFO, which also include the right to compel anyone to answer its questions. In Chris Dickson's view, Parliament has given the SFO these powers for a reason, and he doesn't flinch from using them.

Over his ten years at the SFO, Dickson has handled a number of its biggest cases. He led the investigation into the Bank of Credit and Commerce International, the biggest fraud the world has ever seen. BCCI stole billions of pounds from its customers and it was Dickson's job to investigate and prosecute those responsible for the

British end of the fraud. He eventually brought six cases to court and got six convictions. Like most prosecutors, Dickson doesn't judge success by conviction rates alone; but, as he says, it helps.

It was during the BCCI investigation that Dickson personally authorised what was probably the most audacious arrest ever made by the SFO. In July 1994 he learned that Abbas Gokal, the head of the Gulf Shipping Group and one of the key conspirators in the BCCI fraud, was planning to leave his safe house in Pakistan and fly to New York via Frankfurt. The US federal authorities had granted Gokal immunity from prosecution in exchange for his testimony to a Grand Jury about Pakistan's secret nuclear weapons programme and his knowledge of corruption in US public life. Dickson realised that, for the short period that Gokal was on German soil, he was technically within reach of British justice. He immediately instructed City of London Police officers seconded to the SFO to obtain a warrant for Gokal's arrest and fly to Germany. To Abbas Gokal's horror, he was unceremoniously removed from the first-class compartment of the Pakistani Airlines 747, arrested and flown directly to Britain. The huge diplomatic row that ensued was silenced only by the fourteen-year gaol sentence meted out to Gokal, the longest ever given to a fraudster by a British court. It's a story that, up to now, has never been fully told.

As Chris Dickson circulated around the party, he could see a number of colleagues who had taken part in that extraordinary event. One man he stopped to chat with was former Detective Superintendent Jerry Ohlson, who had just left the City Police to join the new Financial Services Authority. Ohlson had worked alongside Dickson for most of the BCCI inquiry and had been intimately involved in the Gokal snatch. Indeed, it was one of Ohlson's junior officers, Detective Sergeant Doug Reeman, who had first discovered Gokal's plan to make the hazardous journey from Pakistan to New York. No one who knows the BCCI story would ever claim that the Dickson–Ohlson alliance had been a marriage made in heaven, but the overwhelming success of the case made it easy for them to remember only the good times.

Nor was it just the more senior police officers who turned up to say goodbye to Chris Dickson. Detective Inspector Andrew Noad, one of the officers at the sharp end of serious fraud investigation, also came along with a number of his colleagues from both the City and Metropolitan Police fraud squads. Noad has worked with the SFO on a number of its most important cases, but one assignment was particularly gripping. He was the officer who went to Germany in September 1994 to interview Nick Leeson, the rogue trader who single-handedly lost £700 million and destroyed Barings Bank. Noad wanted to assure himself that Leeson was just a trader out of his depth and not part of an organised conspiracy which had managed to benefit from the British bank's enormous losses. Once Noad had established this to his complete satisfaction, he recommended that the SFO should not seek to extradite Leeson to the United Kingdom but instead should allow him to return to Singapore where the crime had been committed. A year later Nick Leeson received a six-and-a-half-year gaol sentence which he is currently still serving.

The fact that so many police officers were present in the Law Society's high-ceilinged room with its huge chandeliers and understated paintings could be attributed in part to the efforts of Michael Chance, another of Dickson's guests. Chance, a big, solid man of about sixty with silver hair, was the first deputy director of the Serious Fraud Office. He had been recruited from the Crown Prosecution Service by John Wood, the SFO's first director, back in 1987, and was responsible for the whole logistical set-up of the SFO. Chance was also the man who had secured Elm House as the organisation's first permanent home. But his most important achievement by far was to convince a highly sceptical police force that the multi-disciplinary approach of the SFO was the way to tackle serious fraud. Ten years later, the SFO has the active support of both the Metropolitan and the City Police Commissioners, although the relationship between the police and the SFO remains a sensitive issue.

Michael Chance left the SFO in 1990, shortly after John Wood retired. He then went on to become head of the Joint Disciplinary Scheme of the Accountancy Standards Council, the body that investigates major complaints against accountants. Now Michael Chance is retiring in his turn and is being replaced, in what is becoming an SFO tradition, by his old friend Chris Dickson. The work of the Joint Disciplinary Scheme is regarded as increasingly important and Chance is convinced that Dickson's inquisitorial skills will prove as invaluable to the JDS as they were to the SFO.

Nor was it just the prosecutors who came to wish Chris Dickson well as he departed the SFO. Keith Oliver, the solicitor who so successfully defended Kevin Maxwell, was one of a number of defence lawyers who turned up to say goodbye. Keith Oliver's firm, Peters & Peters, represents a large number of people prosecuted by the Serious Fraud Office and its partners see the SFO in action on an almost daily basis. Oliver himself, a slim, good-looking man in his early forties, believes that the SFO already takes an overly aggressive view when it comes to prosecuting cases and that it actively encourages the media to present defendants in the most negative way possible.

One particularly good example of this increasingly aggressive stance towards defendants, says Keith Oliver, was the SFO's decision to press ahead with a second Maxwell prosecution following the acquittal of all the defendants in the first trial in January 1996. Oliver argued at the time that a second trial would be deeply unfair and said that it amounted to an abuse of process. After a week of argument Mr Justice Buckley, the trial judge, ruled in his favour and dismissed the charges. But there is another side to this story that has never been told. One of the reasons why the SFO was so keen to have a second trial was that one of the original defendants had confessed to behaving dishonestly and implicated others. This confession wasn't admissible in the first trial but it could have made a very significant impact in the second case. The SFO had always known that it would lay itself open to charges of vindictiveness in pushing for a second trial; but it certainly had its reasons.

As the evening wore on and the wine flowed, Chris Dickson dutifully worked his way round the room, thanking people for taking the trouble to come along on a bitterly cold October night. Perhaps not surprisingly, he spent most of his time talking to those who had been his closest colleagues for the last ten years, his fellow assistant directors at the SFO. Robert Wardle was one with whom he stopped for a while, sharing a number of jokes. Following

Dickson's departure, Wardle is now considered the most senior of the SFO assistant directors and the one to whom Ros Wright, the current director, turns first for help and advice. People who don't know Wardle well tend to think of him as slightly unapproachable, but he is in fact an extremely amusing and likeable man. For a number of years he has handled the Asil Nadir case, an assignment which, with its extraordinary twists and turns, would have taken its toll on a lesser person; but Wardle, with his zest for life, seems to have borne up remarkably well.

Wardle talks with a surprising lack of rancour about the allegations made in Parliament by Michael Mates, the former Cabinet minister, that the SFO behaved improperly in the Nadir case. Wardle admits that the SFO has made some mistakes but laughs out loud at the suggestions, which were recently made on television, that it was somehow involved in an attempt to implicate Nadir in a conspiracy to bribe a judge. Wardle also denies categorically that the SFO was responsible for destroying Polly Peck International, the FTSE 100 company that Asil Nadir ran. The Polly Peck story is an amazing one but, as Wardle says, it doesn't reflect particularly badly on the SFO.

Another of Dickson's close colleagues who attended the party was Philip Henry. A big man with a black moustache, he is Antiguan by birth; like many of his countrymen, he has a passion for cricket, and like Chris Dickson, he believes that winning is important. Currently Henry is running the Morgan Grenfell/Peter Young investigation, which is one of the most sensitive SFO inquiries of recent years and is shrouded in mystery. Peter Young ran Morgan Grenfell's extremely successful European investment funds before it was discovered that he was not investing in blue-chip stocks but had spent tens of millions of pounds making highly speculative investments, not all of which were even in Europe. Philip Henry's job is to decide whether or not there was any criminal activity and, if there was, whether Peter Young knew what he was doing at the time.

The stories of Young's bizarre behaviour have become legendary in the City. A tabloid newspaper tried to publish pictures of him wearing fancy dress with several women friends, but was prevented by a court injunction. Another paper claimed that he had bought thirty jars of gherkins which he kept in his garden shed. There have even been rumours that he has been filmed talking to trees. Henry's team are continuing to investigate all aspects of this case which are relevant to the criminal inquiry.

Gordon Dickinson was another colleague who spent some time reminiscing with Chris Dickson about the first ten years of the SFO. Dickinson, a quiet, wiry man with photochromatic glasses which can sometimes make him look slightly sinister, is currently prosecuting the Butte Mining fraud case. This case, which may last for an exhausting eight months, has been likened by some at the SFO to running a marathon. It is so complex that Dickinson himself was forced to go to Switzerland just two months before the trial began in a last-ditch effort to secure vital evidence.

Gordon Dickinson joined the SFO in 1991 and was immediately given responsibility for the remaining three of the four Guinness trials. This was a particularly tough assignment given that his first day working for the SFO was also the first day of the preparatory hearings in the second Guinness trial. However, Dickinson was fortunate in that Barbara Mills, then director of the SFO, had previously been a member of the prosecution team in the first Guinness trial: her specialist knowledge of the case allowed Dickinson to get up to speed far more quickly than would otherwise have been possible.

Dame Barbara Mills now runs the much larger Crown Prosecution Service, but she too found the time to come to Chris Dickson's leaving party. Dame Barbara was head of the SFO for only twenty months, but she is without doubt the most famous occupant of the post. There are, she believes, a number of reasons for this. 'There was a lot of interest in the Guinness case,' she says, 'and I was appointed just after the end of the first trial. I was a woman, which does seem to attract more attention, and, coinciden-tally, when I arrived, the SFO opened a press office.' But there is perhaps one other reason why Dame Barbara's period as director of the SFO attracted so much publicity.

The conviction of Ernest Saunders and the other Guinness defendants in 1990 marked the start of a honeymoon period for the

SFO which peaked in early 1992 with the sentencing of Peter Clowes and of the four County NatWest defendants (who were initially found guilty, only for those verdicts to be overturned on appeal). During this time the SFO attracted massive positive publicity, and much of it focused on the media-friendly face of the new director, then plain Mrs Barbara Mills. The public started to believe that once the SFO took on a case, it would only be a matter of time before the defendants were convicted. This meant that when the SFO swooped on high-profile targets like Asil Nadir, Roger Levitt or, just after Mrs Mills left, Kevin Maxwell, no one gave much thought to the possibility that they might be found not guilty. It wasn't so much that the SFO ever actively encouraged this rather naïve view of serious fraud prosecution as that, perhaps understandably, it certainly didn't discourage it. Unfortunately, this in turn meant that the public were not prepared for the series of blows that subsequently rained down on the SFO, and the eventual realisation that the office was no more infallible than any other body of people came as a massive shock for public and media alike.

If the wind was sown during Barbara Mills' time as director of the SFO, the whirlwind was certainly reaped by her successor, George Staple. He also took the trouble to come along and say goodbye to Chris Dickson, a man with whom he had worked closely for five difficult years. George Staple's time at the SFO had seen more downs than ups, caused primarily by the unrealistically high level of expectation that had been allowed to grow in the early 1990s but also, it should be said, by several major mistakes on the part of his staff. But Staple, who describes himself as more of a management man than an out-and-out prosecutor, had in fact addressed most of the SFO's major problems during his tenure of office. He had changed the management structure to allow for much greater supervision of individual cases by the senior management, and he had persuaded a suspicious government that the SFO was basically doing a good job. Staple's patrician manner and basic decency may have prevented him from winning the public relations war in the media, but he actually left the office in very good shape.

The most notable absentee from the gathering was the current director of the SFO, Ros Wright – and this was attributable simply to the fact that she was out of the country. Wright has worked as both a criminal prosecutor and a City regulator, and is widely regarded as being extremely capable and a good communicator as well as possessing a great sense of humour. One of her first jobs will be to sell the SFO as successfully to the country as George Staple sold it to the government. There seems little doubt that she will be successful in this task. A massive public relations offensive is now under way, masterminded by James O'Donoghue and his colleagues in the SFO's press office. O'Donoghue is convinced that Ros Wright's appointment can be trumpeted as heralding a new era in the public's perception of the SFO. Certainly, in the first nine months of her term as director, which began in April 1997, SFO conviction rates have reached an astonishing 95 per cent and most banana skins have been successfully avoided. The truth, which is freely admitted in Elm Street, is that George Staple began the process of turning around the SFO several years earlier; but it seems likely that most of the credit will eventually go to Ros Wright.

There is, however, one substantial criticism to be made of the way in which the SFO is currently taking on its critics. While conviction rates are deeply distrusted by prosecutors, it is these figures that have been fastened upon by the media as the primary criterion for judging the SFO. Over the last three years, the SFO's conviction rate has been steadily rising while the number of cases coming to trial has been steadily falling. Statistically, it is starting to look increasingly as if the SFO has decided to cherry-pick the cases it brings to court in order to drive the conviction rate ever upwards. On at least one occasion, Ros Wright has decided that a particularly complex fraud case, which would have previously been investigated by the SFO, was better left to the City regulators. While it is not yet possible to state definitively that cherry-picking is going on, it is hard to interpret the last three years' statistics in any other way. If this is the case, it would, of course, be a betrayal of the Serious Fraud Office's basic *raison d'être* – the investigation and prosecution of serious and complex fraud.

Chris Dickson's leaving party ended just after 10 p.m. The departing guests, dispersing after an extremely enjoyable evening of discussion, gossip and jokes among present and former colleagues and friends, don't see themselves as a particularly unusual group of people; and yet most had been intimately involved in some of the world's biggest fraud cases. Between them, they had investigated banks that had collapsed, public limited companies that had failed and pension schemes that had been plundered. They had interviewed and prosecuted some of Britain's most powerful and wealthy men and women. Their story is an extraordinary one. It begins back in the early 1980s.

2

Stopping the Fat Cats

The public no longer believes that the legal system in England and Wales is capable of bringing the perpetrators of serious frauds expeditiously and effectively to book. The overwhelming weight of evidence laid before us suggests that the public is right. In relation to such crimes, and to the skilful and determined criminals who commit them, the present legal system is archaic, cumbersome and unreliable. At every stage, during investigation, preparation, committal, pre-trial review and trial, the present arrangements offer an open invitation to blatant delay and abuse. While petty frauds, clumsily committed, are likely to be detected and punished, it is all too likely that the largest and most cleverly executed crimes escape unpunished.

THESE WORDS, written by David Butler, opened Lord Roskill's report on the prosecution of fraud, published in 1985. Unlike many government reports, it precisely captured what many people were thinking about white-collar criminals at the time. People were convinced that fraudsters, particularly in the City of London, were getting away with it. Everyone agreed that something had to be done, and Lord Roskill and his team were given the job of coming up with an answer.

Since the Conservative victory in the May 1979 general election, the City had come to play an increasingly important role in the lives of millions of British citizens. The new government had pledged to created 'a share-owning democracy' and had privatised many state-owned companies, often at bargain prices, encouraging people to invest on the stock market. Hundreds of thousands of new investors – the 'Sids' of the British Gas advertisements – enthusiastically subscribed for shares in formerly nationalised companies like British Telecom, British Airways and British Gas.

These privatisations were only one part of the government's strategy to popularise the financial markets. The 1986 Financial Services Act deregulated the financial services industry and laid the foundations for the personal equity plans (PEPs) and personal pensions that are taken for granted today. However, as the Roskill Committee knew all too well, these changes also meant that millions of relatively unsophisticated investors were now uniquely vulnerable to clever fraudsters.

The risks facing small investors as they began playing the markets for the first time were not the government's only concern. It was also acutely aware that if a major fraud took place in the City and was not handled properly, untold harm could be done to London's reputation internationally, ultimately perhaps undermining its position as one of the world's three top financial centres. With Frankfurt poised to take advantage of any British scandal to advance its own claim to pre-eminence in Europe, the stakes were high indeed.

On 8 November 1983, the Lord Chancellor and Home Secretary announced their intention to establish an independent committee of inquiry to examine the whole question of serious fraud. The committee's brief was 'to consider in what ways the conduct of criminal proceedings in England and Wales arising from fraud can be improved and to consider what changes in existing law and procedure would be desirable to secure the just, expeditious and economical disposal of such proceedings'. It may have been a relatively dry brief; but Lord Mayhew, then (as Sir Patrick Mayhew) Solicitor-General, says the government was very clear on what it wanted to achieve. 'There was a very strong feeling in the early eighties that fat cats were getting cleverer, were getting fatter and most of all were getting away with it. That's why we set up the committee. We wanted to find a way to stop them.'

Lord Eustace Roskill, a senior judge in the House of Lords, was the man appointed to lead the committee. Although he had little personal experience of fraud trials, he was widely regarded as being an excellent choice. He had a fine mind and a reputation for plain speaking which was reinforced by his report. According to John Wood, the first director of the Serious Fraud Office, Roskill was initially sceptical about chairing the committee that eventually made his name. 'Roskill had previously chaired another committee,' recalls Wood, 'and the government hadn't acted on any on his recommendations. So when he was asked to chair this one, he went to some lengths to check that at least some of his recommendations would be implemented.'

Lord Roskill's deputy was Lord Henry Benson, a senior partner in the accountancy firm Coopers & Lybrand. According to David Butler, one of the six other committee members, 'Roskill put together an extremely well rounded team. Besides the chairman and vice-chairman, there was another judge, a businessman, a police officer, a county councillor, a solicitor and myself, a computer expert. Everyone appeared to have reasonably open minds and no one had an obvious axe to grind.'

Butler, who had previously been chairman of Butler Cox, a computer consultancy company frequently used by the government, was originally selected because it was felt the committee might want to consider how computers could be used to speed up fraud trials. Early on in the proceedings, he remembers giving a talk to some of his colleagues on the advantages of storing evidence on computer databases, something that is now done increasingly often. Since the talk was little more than an introduction to the subject, Butler decided to keep it simple and illustrate his points with overhead slides rather than show the massively complex technology itself. Only when he finished speaking did he finally realise the scale of the task in front of him. It became quite clear to him that several members of the committee had not even seen an overhead projector before. 'Some of these legal eagles who were with me', remembers Butler, 'looked at this overhead projector as if it were magic and this, of course, was technology that had already been around for over forty years. I think if I'd shown them a good database computer system, it would probably have blown their minds.'

Despite this slightly alarming revelation, no one could really challenge the committee's intellectual prowess. Butler remembers both Roskill and Benson as enormously clever men. 'Unfortunately,' says Butler, 'they also had egos the size of planets. It got to the point that you couldn't put the two of them in the same room. It was a bit like Tyson and Holyfield. They collided every time they spoke.' It's a view confirmed by Walter Merrick, another member of the committee. He believes that Lord Benson, who had previously chaired the Royal Commission on Legal Services, resented being Roskill's vice-chairman. 'He was a domineering person,' says Merrick, 'and it was apparent that he thought he should have been the chairman of the committee. It was as simple as that.'

The tension between Roskill and Benson eventually came to a head when the committee decided to impose a strict timetable on itself, both for the gathering of evidence and for publication of the report. Benson became convinced that Roskill would miss the end date and that this would become a major embarrassment for everyone involved. The solution – to him – was clear: Roskill, he said, should resign. According to Butler, 'Lord Benson started plotting to get Roskill about three months before we were due to report. He invited me to a big dinner at the Mansion House. At first I was very flattered but, at the end of the evening, he took me to one side and told me in no uncertain terms that we were not going to complete the report on time and that Roskill should go. I told him then that I didn't agree with him and history has shown I was right.'

Lord Roskill, as Butler had perceived, had things well under control. He had realised early on, perhaps because of his background as a judge, that the report itself wouldn't take long to write. 'Roskill knew that this was going to be a relatively short report,' recalls Butler. 'It was deciding what to put in it which was going to take the time. At one point, Roskill allowed us to spend a whole day debating one single issue. I later realised that this was a key point and the time had been well spent. I don't think Benson ever really understood that.' Despite Benson's best efforts, Roskill remained chairman of the committee from start to finish.

The Roskill Committee met for the first time on 4 May 1984 and published its report less than two years later. It received written evidence from over 140 individuals and institutions and invited 24 people to make oral submissions. One government lawyer who gave evidence to the committee identified 'counsel prolixity' – the length of time counsel spent talking in court – as the major reason why fraud trials went on for so long. 'Unfortunately,' remembers Butler, 'he spent most of the morning making his point.'

Barbara Mills, a senior silk who later became head of the SFO, also gave evidence to the committee, and as a witness she impressed Butler rather more. Her view was that the prosecution often over-complicated fraud trials. This, she said, was the major reason why fraudsters were not being convicted. 'Mrs Mills was very persuasive in her arguments,' remembers Butler. 'She wanted fraud trials slimmed down, with far fewer charges being brought. She thought it was a mistake to try and throw the book at a defendant. Instead, you should try and take your best shot. She also thought that prosecuting barristers should work much harder at making the evidence easy for the jury to understand.'

While the Roskill Committee's remit allowed it to range widely over a variety of topics, it spent the majority of its time discussing the role of juries in fraud trials. Both Lord Roskill and Lord Benson believed that in serious fraud cases the jury should be replaced by a judge working with two assessors, and this proposal became the focus of the committee's work. Initially, a number of members, including John Hazan, the second judge on the committee, were against the idea of replacing the jury; but, as the evidence was gathered, five out of the six remaining members, Hazan among them, eventually found themselves in agreement with Benson and Roskill.

David Butler was one of those who slowly became convinced that it was right to dispense with juries in serious fraud cases. 'A number of us met socially during the hearings and we discussed this issue many times. I came to my view over a number of months and I think most of the others did as well. It became very clear that most people who commit serious fraud are extremely well educated and very capable people. They have to be convincing to get bank managers and accountants to go along with their plans. These sort of people don't look or sound like your everyday criminal, at least not to a normal juror. But a judge or an expert assessor would see through the charade in a second. Many jurors never do.'

Walter Merrick was the fly in the ointment as far as Lord Roskill was concerned. David Butler remembers Merrick, a lawyer himself, as being completely immovable on this point. 'He was convinced that any change to the jury system would deprive the defendant of a fundamental human right and he clearly felt this was a matter of principle. Lord Roskill was a very persuasive man and he argued with Merrick a number of times, all to no avail.'

When the rest of the Roskill Committee eventually decided to submit a majority report advocating the abolition of the jury in serious fraud trials, Walter Merrick exercised his right to record a dissenting opinion. In his note, attached to the majority report, Merrick pointed out that 'the submissions made to us by those who are closest to the existing system were overwhelmingly in favour of retaining the jury.' He added, somewhat scathingly: 'My colleagues seem to find trial by jury an anomaly. In criminal cases, it is most certainly not an anomaly. It is the basic mode of trial for all serious offences.' Today, Merrick remains convinced that he was right and the others were wrong. 'I didn't think the case for change was made then and I don't believe it has been made now. I am proud of the fact that I've helped retain the jury system for serious fraud trials. It's the best system we have.'

As it became clear that the Roskill Committee was not going to be able to present a united front on what was to have been its most radical suggestion, more and more effort was put into its second big idea: the creation of a unified organisation to investigate and prosecute serious fraud cases. 'There was a feeling that you had a whole set of separate agencies involved in detecting and investigating serious fraud, including the police, the Department of Trade and Industry, and Customs and Excise,' says Butler. 'The decision to prosecute was often more a matter of luck than judgement. There were simply too many cracks in the pavement down which fraudsters could hide.' To the Roskill Committee the solution was clear: serious fraud needed to be combated by a single organisation involving policemen, lawyers and accountants working together.

On 9 December 1985, the Roskill Fraud Trials Committee finally published its report. Its first recommendation stated: 'The need for a new unified organisation responsible for all the functions of detection, investigation and prosecution of serious fraud cases should be examined forthwith.' The report even outlined how it would work. A 'case controller' should direct both the investigation and the prosecution of serious fraud. Counsel should be brought in at an early stage, preferably during the investigation, to offer help and advice to the police officers gathering the evidence; and accountants should be used throughout the process to monitor and analyse the financial evidence. It was, without doubt, the blueprint for the Serious Fraud Office. The fact that it became so prominent in the report only because of the committee's failure to agree on the abolition of jury trials soon became little more than a curiosity of history.

David Butler believes that the multi-disciplinary approach envisaged in the Roskill Report was a major step forward in the investigation and prosecution of serious fraud. 'Police, accountants and lawyers had never been combined in this way before. It was the only way that serious fraud cases stood any chance of being successfully prosecuted.' Michael Chance, the first deputy director of the SFO, says this claim is slightly overstated. He points out that 'a multi-disciplinary approach was already being used by the Fraud Investigation Group of the DPP [Director of Public Prosecutions] when the Roskill Commission made its recommendations. It's true that Roskill wanted to take the process further, but it was simply a logical development of what had gone before.' However, while Chance is technically right to say that Roskill's ideas were less radical than some people imagined, they still represented a significant advance on anything previously attempted. The Fraud Investigation Group had been established less than a year earlier, in January 1985, and it was certainly not considered to have been a major new initiative. It was also not particularly well funded, which hampered its development, whereas the new Serious Fraud Office was to receive significant sums of money from the Treasury.

The Roskill Report was debated by the Cabinet shortly after it was published. As with the Roskill Committee itself, the government's discussions centred on the suggestion that juries should be abolished in serious fraud cases. Nigel Lawson (now Lord Lawson), then Chancellor of the Exchequer, has stated his view very clearly in his book *The View from Number Eleven*, published in 1992:

> Cabinet rejected what I regarded as the most important of Roskill's recommendations: the setting up of a special Fraud Trials Tribunal which would replace the normal trial by jury in particularly complex and serious fraud cases. Quintin Hogg, the Lord Chancellor, and I appeared to be its only supporters with the Government's law officers and the other lawyers in cabinet – apart from Quintin – particularly hostile. Subsequent events have served only to reinforce my belief in the necessity of this reform.

Sir Patrick Mayhew (now Lord Mayhew) was one of those who argued forcefully against Nigel Lawson for the retention of jury trials in serious fraud cases. Mayhew says: 'I think I was quite influential in securing the rejection of Roskill's proposal to abolish jury trials in serious fraud cases. My view was that jury trial is the last bastion of liberty in our country and if you make an exception for serious fraud, it will eventually spread to other types of crime.' As Lawson acknowledged, Mayhew's view convincingly won the day. But if the Cabinet was divided on the issue of jury trials, it was positively enthusiastic about Roskill's other suggestions. According to Mayhew, 'We adopted practically everything else in Roskill. We knew that fraud was escalating and becoming more complex with the electronic revolution and that there was this growing feeling that the old ways were too fuddy-duddy and couldn't cope. We wanted to implement Roskill and we lost no time in doing so.'

Seventeen months after Lord Roskill published his report, the 1987 Criminal Justice Act was passed into law and the Serious Fraud Office was effectively established. The legislation gave the director of the SFO the power to 'investigate any suspected offence which appears to him, on reasonable grounds, to involve serious or complex fraud'. But it also gave the director some other powers as well. Under section 2 of the Criminal Justice Act, the director can compel people whom he or she believes to have relevant information to 'answer questions' or produce 'specified documents'. Any refusal to do so is punishable by up to six months' imprisonment and a £2,000 fine. This effectively means that there is no right to silence for anybody involved in a serious fraud case. It's a draconian power that many people have said tips the scales of justice too far towards the prosecution. But others point out that these powers are actually weaker than those regularly used by the Department of Trade and Industry in Companies Act investigations. Some have even said that it's slightly foolish for the SFO to have lesser powers than the DTI. It has also become very clear over the years that the SFO's section 2 powers have actually been welcomed by many lawyers and accountants who are keen to help the SFO but in the absence of such a provision would have been prevented from doing so by the professional requirements of client confidentiality.

John Wood was the first man appointed to run the Serious Fraud Office. He had previously been head of the Fraud Investigation Group, and subsequently, as Deputy Director of Public Prosecutions, had co-ordinated much of the evidence that was given to the Roskill Committee. He also had a great deal of input into the drafting of the 1987 Criminal Justice Act. According to Tricia Howse, a long-standing friend and one of his first appointees at the SFO, the Criminal Justice Act was little more than a 'wish list' for Wood which, astonishingly, the government granted. It's a claim which seems to be confirmed in a story told by John Wood himself. According to Wood, he first knew that he had the job as director of the SFO when Sir Michael Havers, the Attorney-General, telephoned him and said simply: 'You planned it; you make it work.' It was, as Wood admits, a perfectly fair proposition. He had got his wish list, and now it was time to see if he had asked for the right things.

The man who worked most closely with John Wood in setting up the SFO was Michael Chance, its first deputy director. He and Wood started putting together the organisational structure in the summer of 1987, although they both knew that their creation wouldn't become operational until the following April. 'The first thing we had to do', recalls Chance, 'was to get the money out of the Treasury. And we did really well. The SFO was allowed to have a much bigger budget than most other outfits of comparable size.' According to the SFO's first report, it was given £6,086,000 to spend on administration and a further £2,634,000 for investigations and prosecutions.

The reason why the SFO needed a much larger budget than other similarly sized organisations lay with John Wood's determination to recruit the best people he could get. 'I was determined that the SFO would have the most capable lawyers and, because they were all on senior grades, we had to pay them big salaries. I took the cream of the Fraud Investigation Group, Customs and Excise, and the Department of Trade and Industry. I also recruited a number of senior accountants from outside the Civil Service, and some of these were partners in big accounting firms. They also cost us a huge amount of money but they brought enormous expertise and prestige to the office and so I was pleased to get them. The effect of all this was to make our staffing structure look top-heavy and over-graded; but an organisation like the SFO really does need the best people available.'

John Wood also decided very early on that the SFO would investigate only the most important fraud cases. 'I introduced a rule that all our cases had to involve at least £1 million. It was an arbitrary figure but I was very aware that we only had limited resources. We might have had very good lawyers, but we only had about twenty of them and we had even fewer accountants. It meant we couldn't investigate everything.' Wood knew that his decision would mean that some big fraud cases would inevitably be left to the remnants of the Fraud Investigation Group, which now handled only the intermediate-level cases, and even to the various police fraud squads who for the most part investigated the smaller, local frauds. But his stand was vindicated when, some time later, pressure of work forced the SFO to raise the threshold even further, this time to £5 million.

While John Wood busied himself with recruitment and policy matters, Michael Chance got on with the less glamorous although equally important job of finding a home for the new organisation.

Initially, the SFO started off with just a couple of rooms at the Treasury Solicitor's office in Broadway but, as the new recruits started to arrive, this soon became far too small. As a temporary measure, Chance moved everybody to Keysign House in Oxford Street, a building that had a great deal of space but was rather inauspiciously situated just above a Wimpy bar. Finally, in October 1988, the SFO moved to its current home at Elm Street in Holborn.

Elm House, where the SFO is based, is a rather unattractive nine-floor office block which used to be home to the *Times Educational Supplement* before News International moved to Wapping. Immediately after the SFO took it over, the whole building was refurbished; but it would take an interior designer of genius to turn its narrow corridors, small offices and overworked central lifts into a genuinely pleasant working environment. Michael Chance was acutely aware of its shortcomings even before taking on the lease. 'I'd have loved to have got us a nicer building in the City,' he says, 'but in 1988, the rents were astronomical and we had much more important things to spend our money on.'

Perhaps the biggest problem facing the SFO in its early days was its relationship with the police. The Roskill Report had identified the need for the police to work together with lawyers and account-ants, but had not really addressed the problem of how this should be done. The 1987 Criminal Justice Act also ducked this highly sensi-tive issue. The difficulty is that police officers are obliged by law to report to their chief constables. This stipulation includes any officer working with the SFO – and thus renders the director of the SFO ultimately reliant on a chief constable's goodwill for police help. According to John Wood, 'It's a problem that has never properly been resolved. Everyone has tried to make the system work, but you can't have two bosses. It just doesn't work.'

The problem created by this anomaly persists to this day, but in early 1988 it was even more acutely felt. Not surprisingly, the SFO wanted to borrow most of its police officers from the City of London force, which had the greatest expertise in investigating fraud cases. City Police officers could spend up to eight years working for the fraud squad, whereas most other forces limited the amount of time an officer could spend in a single unit to just three years. This meant that some City Police officers had become immensely experienced in combating fraudsters. But there were several difficulties in seconding these officers to the SFO, two of which in particular loomed large. The first was that the City Police was the smallest force in the country and extremely tightly stretched: sending a number of officers to Elm Street would exacerbate an already pressing problem of resources. The second was that the City Police had spent years fighting off calls for it to be merged with its big brother, the Metropolitan Police. Up to now, its best defence against merger had been its extraordinary fraud squad. If the SFO effectively removed its best officers, said some senior City Police chiefs, how long would it survive as a separate force?

Michael Chance was the man delegated to resolve this peculiarly sensitive problem. He remembers it as being a very slow process. As he discussed the issues, it became clear that there was a third difficulty hidden beneath the surface. A number of more junior police officers were deeply concerned about the reasons why the 1987 Criminal Justice Act prevented them from using the SFO's section 2 powers when interviewing witnesses. As far as they could see, it looked like an attempt to marginalise the role of the police in serious fraud investigations. After all, said one officer, 'we had all the experience in interrogating suspects and yet we were being effectively prevented from exercising our skill.' This suspicion that not everything was out in the open, that there was a hidden agenda behind the creation of this new body, made Chance's delicate job even more ticklish. 'I had a series of meetings with one senior officer in the City of London police,' recalls Chance, 'and I really thought we were starting to make progress. He then told me that he'd attended a police conference where one of the speakers had claimed that the police were being asked to be bag-carriers for a group of lawyers and accountants. The police who worked with the SFO on a regular basis knew the truth, but there was a lot of suspicion outside that very narrow band.'

Over the months, however, the City of London Police and the other forces involved slowly came on board. It gradually became clear that the formation of the SFO was not intended to lead to the destruction of the City Police and that control of any police officer working with the SFO would continue to reside with his or her chief constable. It also became obvious that the reason why section 2 powers had been withheld from the police was simply concerns over civil rights. With Michael Chance's careful wooing bearing fruit and the move to Elm Street freeing up space, co-siting became a realistic proposition, and police officers finally joined the lawyers and accountants working in Elm House in the autumn of 1988. None the less, Chance remained acutely aware that many police officers still harboured residual suspicions about the SFO, and he did all he could to allay their fears. 'I made sure that all the senior police officers attached to the SFO had exactly the same accoutrements as the senior lawyers and accountants,' he says. 'I knew that if this was going to work, we needed everybody pulling together.'

Just before the SFO finally went operational, John Wood organised a two-week training programme to bring his diverse team together. It was designed to encourage everyone to think about the new multi-disciplinary approach that they were about to pioneer and to give them a chance to hone their investigative and legal skills. The director himself ran a number of the training sessions and two DTI inspectors, specialists in inquiries relating to section 447 of the Companies Act, gave several others. Tricia Howse, who had just joined the SFO from Customs and Excise, remembers being extremely impressed by the quality of the course. 'I particularly remember the sessions run by the police,' recalls Howse. 'They were the ones – out of the three disciplines represented – who really had the investigative experience. And the lectures weren't chalk and talk theory. They showed practical ways of how you could access a series of Panamanian companies or how you could track back on money trails. The lessons were almost like Quaker meetings because if somebody could contribute anything, they simply stood up and said it. They were very useful and they were a lot of fun too.'

On 1 April 1988 the Serious Fraud Office formally opened for business. Fearing that it might take several years to establish its own caseload, John Wood had brought a number of cases with him from the DPP. Among them were the files on Guinness, Lloyd's and Johnson Matthey. In retrospect, says Wood, this was a mistake. 'I think that I brought too many cases over with me. We were a small organisation and we were stretched to the limit within weeks of starting up. Guinness took more and more of my time and I ended up being more hands-on with Guinness than was good for me or the office.' Whether or not Wood's involvement was a good idea, Guinness was to become one of the SFO's most important cases; indeed, it was on the outcome of the first Guinness trial that the SFO's initial success would be judged.

3

The City Trial of the Century

GUINNESS SHOULD NEVER really have been regarded as a Serious Fraud Office case at all. Criminal investigations into the Guinness bid for the Distillers drinks company began in December 1986, six months before the Criminal Justice Act, which set up the SFO, was passed into law. For sixteen months thereafter, all the investigative work was done exclusively by the Metropolitan Police fraud squad, liaising with the Crown Prosecution Service. While the police might have kept in close contact with the CPS, the investigation was never based on the multi-disciplinary approach which is meant to be at the heart of all genuine SFO cases.

There were a number of reasons why John Wood was so determined to take the Guinness case with him to the SFO. Besides his very real fear that the new organisation might not have enough cases, he had just lured Jeraine Olsen, the woman who was leading the Guinness prosecutions, away from the CPS. It would have been extremely difficult for Olsen simply to hand over the incredibly complex Guinness file and walk away. But perhaps most important of all, Wood knew just how high-profile the Guinness case would become. He maintains that it never occurred to him that a triumph with Guinness would get the SFO off to the best possible start, but he does acknowledge that this was a unique case. 'Guinness was a tremendously important case for a number of reasons,' says Wood. 'First, the defendants in Guinness were people in very high positions. Second, the takeover battle that led to the investigation was particularly bitterly fought and so it was extremely important that there was a good prosecution. The City needed to realise that what had been done in this case was not only shady practice but was unlawful as well.'

The Guinness affair was very much a product of its time. There was a raging bull market. Shares were going up, the economy was booming and optimism was high. For those working in the City, red braces, telephone-number salaries and Porsche cars were the order of the day. As the rewards for success grew increasingly large, so winning became the only goal. For the City players involved in the Guinness bid, some of whom really did seem to believe that they were the masters of the universe, lunch was for wimps and rules were definitely for losers.

The man who fired the first shot in the war that led to the most important City trial of all time was James Gulliver, the acquisitive boss of the Argyll supermarket group. On 2 December 1985, Gulliver dramatically announced that Argyll was willing to pay £1.9 billion, a record sum, for Distillers, a company which owned a number of the best-known brands in the drinks market including Johnnie Walker, Dewars, White Horse and Gordons. It was an astonishing bid that sent the City into a frenzy; but it was also a deeply unwelcome one to the Distillers company. Distillers was an old Scottish company and very much part of the Edinburgh establishment. It had been in the spotlight only once before, when it had marketed the thalidomide drug, Distaval, which, it transpired, if taken by women in the first three months of pregnancy, could lead to babies being born with both internal and external deformities. Distillers did not much relish being in the public eye again; and it certainly did not see itself as a division of a discount supermarket group.

One Distillers board member summed up the company's attitude to Argyll perfectly when he said: 'Mr Gulliver deals in potatoes and cans of beans. We are not selling brown water in bottles. We are selling Scotch' (*Sunday Times*, 8 March 1987). It was a foolish comment to make, particularly as it soon became clear that Distillers didn't have the strength to resist the hostile takeover bid alone. But it does explain why the Distillers board was so pleased when Ernest Saunders, the chief executive of Guinness, agreed to become their white knight and mount a counter-bid for the company. Eight weeks after Gulliver's initial assault, Saunders announced that he had reached agreement with Distillers and that Guinness was willing to pay £2.2 billion to purchase the company. The fiercest takeover battle Britain has ever seen was under way.

Ernest Saunders' bid for Distillers was the culmination of an ambitious five-year plan he had developed to turn Guinness from a sleepy family business into an international drinks conglomerate. Saunders, a marketing man all his life, had joined Guinness from the Swiss company, Nestlé, in 1981 and had already done an extra-ordinary job in developing and expanding the Guinness brands. His efforts had also revitalised the fortunes of the Iveagh clan, the Irish family who owned over 20 per cent of the Guinness stock. Saunders really did seem to have the Midas touch. One banker said at the time that 'Saunders could have walked on water. He was regarded as like his advertising. Near genius' (*Sunday Times*, 8 March 1987). But 'Deadly' Ernest, as he was known in the City because of his extremely focused approach to business, knew that Guinness needed at least one more substantial acquisition before it would have sufficient mass to become a genuinely international player. The brands that Distillers owned would complete the trans-formation process that Saunders had started five years before. The more Saunders thought about it, the more it became clear that Guinness needed to win this bid.

The Guinness and Argyll bids were structured in a remarkably similar way. Each side was offering Distillers shareholders not cash, but rather shares in their respective companies instead. Once the shareholders had voted and one side had got over 50 per cent accep-tances, they would simply swap their existing Distillers stock for shares in the victorious company. This meant that the Guinness and Argyll share prices were going to be crucial in deciding which way Distillers shareholders would vote.

What happened next was unprecedented in the annals of the City of London. The Guinness team became increasingly convinced that Argyll was persuading people to sell Guinness stock, hence forcing down the all-important share price. Oliver Roux, the Guinness finance director and Ernest Saunders' very able lieutenant, asked Tony Parnes, a stockbroker who revelled in the nickname 'the Animal', to get some people together to help support the Guinness share price. This, it was said, would help counteract the activities of the other side.

One of the first people Parnes approached was Gerald Ronson, the owner of Heron International, then Britain's second largest private company and famous for its petrol stations and property developments. Ronson initially agreed to invest £10 million in Guinness shares but, as the Distillers takeover battle became more intense, he increased this amount to £25 million. According to Ronson, 'It was, as I understood it, designed as a legitimate corrective to the tactics of the other side' (*Sunday Times*, 8 March 1987). But the deal wasn't quite as straightforward as Ronson made it appear. Ronson had only agreed to make this investment because Guinness had offered to pay him a £5 million 'success fee' if its bid for Distillers were accepted. Furthermore, Guinness had also agreed to indemnify Ronson against any loss if its share price fell while he held the shares. Ronson has always claimed that he thought that this deal was legitimate but, as one banker later remarked, 'He couldn't lose. As a straightforward banking proposition he would be entitled to a payment of, say, £50,000. What did he consider he was doing to get his £5 million?' (*Observer*, 16 February 1992). After the arrangement became public, Ronson handed back the £5 million together with a further £800,000 he had received following a fall in the Guinness share price. He also apologised to the Guinness board for ever getting involved in the first place.

Gerald Ronson wasn't the only person who tried to help the Guinness team in their war with Argyll. In the City, some merchant bankers were also doing their bit to support the Guinness share price. Roger Seelig, a stockbroker with Morgan Grenfell and another Guinness adviser, persuaded his former colleague, Lord Spens, then chairman of Henry Ansbacher, to buy £7.6 million worth of Guinness shares for his clients. Spens was initially sceptical but finally decided to go ahead when Seelig told him that he would ensure that Spens' clients were indemnified against any loss.

By late March 1986 the Guinness share support operation was in full swing. On 21 March the Guinness share price reached £2.81. Four days later it was £3.11 and the following week it rose a further 14p. Even though Argyll eventually increased its offer to £2.5

billion, the incredible soaring Guinness share price meant there was no contest. On 18 April Guinness was declared the victor and became the undisputed owner of Scotland's largest drinks company. But, unknown to the world at large, this triumph had been achieved only by Guinness spending £200 million of its own money unlawfully propping up its own share price.

It took almost eight months for details of what had really happened in the Distillers takeover battle to leak out – and even then the information didn't come from anyone in the City of London. In early November 1986 Ivan Boesky, the US arbitrageur known as the 'King of Wall Street', was accused of insider dealing and, in an attempt to keep out of gaol, agreed to tell the US authorities about the various dubious deals in which he had been involved. During his interrogation, Boesky said that he had taken part in a Guinness share support operation and had bought £40 million worth of shares in return for Guinness investing £100 million in one of his arbitrage funds. This information was passed back to the UK authorities and, on 28 November 1986, a Department of Trade and Industry inquiry into the Guinness bid was launched. Within six months, Ernest Saunders had been interviewed by the DTI no fewer than six times.

When members of the Guinness board finally discovered the truth, they were genuinely shocked. It became clear that many directors had been kept in the dark about the tactics employed by Saunders and his colleagues during the takeover battle. Saunders himself left the company in early 1987 and his replacement, Sir Norman Macfarlane, began trying to quantify the scale of the wrongdoing. In a statement to shareholders, Macfarlane said that the company's auditors had 'identified a series of invoices totalling approximately £25 million paid to third parties for advice and services believed to be in connection with the Distillers bid. As yet no satisfactory explanation has been provided for these invoices and the board is concerned that some or all of them might have involved payments by Guinness in return for buying activity in support of the Guinness bid.' These invoices included the £5.8 million paid to Gerald Ronson, a further £3.35 million paid to Tony Parnes via a mysterious Panamanian company, another £2 million paid to Sir Jack Lyons, an influential businessman who recruited members for what had become known as 'the Guinness supporters club', and a final £5.2 million to Tom Ward, a US lawyer who was later discovered to have shared a Swiss bank account with Ernest Saunders.

Perhaps unsurprisingly given the huge sums involved, the DTI inquiry soon gave way to a criminal investigation led by Detective Superintendent Richard Botwright of the Metropolitan Police fraud squad. Botwright and his seventeen-member squad focused on two potential areas of criminality. The first revolved around the possibility that the share support operation had defrauded Distillers shareholders by artificially enhancing the Guinness share price. The second was based on the fact that, since so few Guinness board members had known what was going on, it was possible that Guinness itself might have been the victim of theft and false accounting.

Botwright and his team investigated for a number of months before finally arresting Ernest Saunders on 6 May 1987. This event was followed over the next twelve months by the arrests of Ronson, Parnes, Lyons, Seelig, Spens and David Mayhew, a Cazenove stockbroker. A pattern became apparent. In each case, while the arrest itself was a relatively discreet affair, there were almost always large numbers of photographers and camera crews outside Holborn police station to record the moment when the defendants emerged from their interviews with police officers into the cold light of day. It was clear that someone was tipping off the press.

Lord Spens believes that this was a calculated decision to try to undermine the credibility of the defendants in the public mind. He says: 'I think right from the start the Serious Fraud Office decided that high-profile action was required. All the Guinness arrests were very high-profile. They were accompanied by mass media coverage and were conveniently staggered so that press interest wouldn't wane. I think they got the idea from the Americans. If you arrest people in public with a massive display of armoury, as it were, putting the handcuffs on and dragging them away, it will taint the defendants and encourage the others to behave.' While Spens may well be right about the police media strategy, it cannot be blamed on the SFO on these occasions, for the simple reason that the SFO wasn't operational at the time.

Another intriguing claim made by Lord Spens was that the decision to investigate and prosecute the Guinness case was taken primarily on political grounds. Spens says: 'In the run-up to the 1987 general election, Margaret Thatcher decided that she needed to make an example of the City. She wanted to show that she wasn't being soft on the City and there is a famous statement by one of her ministers saying, "Let's get the handcuffs on." From that, everything else followed.' It's an allegation that is often made about big SFO cases, but at that time, City fraud was a particularly big political issue. The government was keen to address the public's concern in this area, and this was one of the reasons why the SFO was set up so quickly after the Roskill Committee reported.

John Wood, who as Deputy Director of Public Prosecutions effectively took the decision to prosecute the Guinness case, dismisses Lord Spens' allegation as 'a hoary old chestnut' and says: 'As far as I was concerned there was no political dimension whatsoever. An investigation had been carried out. A set of facts had been established. As a result of that, I considered that there was ample evidence to justify proceedings being taken. There was no question of political influence whatsoever.' It seems a fairly unambiguous answer; but having given it, Wood looked up and made a very telling comment. He said: 'You don't get political interference in Britain. You get guidance as to the public interest.' It's an interesting distinction, and one that suggests that the levers of power may be subtly handled indeed.

The SFO finally took over the Guinness case on 2 April 1988, and it was transferred from Bow Street Magistrates' Court to Southwark Crown Court six months later. According to some of the more senior police officers involved, the switch from the CPS to the SFO actually made little difference to the way the case was being handled, primarily because Jeraine Olsen remained the case controller and the bulk of the investigative work had already been done. None the less, as the trial came nearer, a number of disagreements arose between the police and the SFO about the conduct of the case. By far the most serious revolved around the amount of documentation that should be handed over to the defence during the legal process. The view of the police, as well as some of the SFO lawyers, was that documents like draft witness statements were unreliable and therefore should not be passed over. But Jeraine Olsen took a very different view. She was worried that if the SFO didn't surrender virtually everything, this might be used later as grounds for appeal. Olsen eventually decided that the only way to resolve the dispute was to turn everything over to Mr (now Lord) Justice Henry, the trial judge, and let him sort it out. To the horror of the police, Henry ruled that almost everything was discoverable. It was a precedent-setting decision which meant that, from then on, the discovery process in serious fraud cases would take even longer than before. It is yet another reason why serious fraud trials became virtually unmanageable.

In September 1989 Mr Justice Henry decided that the Guinness trial was too complex for a jury to handle all at once, and split the case in two. He ruled that there would be an initial trial involving the four defendants facing the most serious charges, followed by a second trial involving the more peripheral defendants. However, the way in which the case was being divided left Ernest Saunders facing the unpleasant possibility of having to appear in both trials. In the event, he was spared this additional ordeal, but to the dismay of everyone involved, it was eventually found necessary to have four trials before the Guinness case could be finally wound up.

'The City Trial of the Century', as it was billed by the media, eventually began at Southwark Crown Court on 13 February 1990, almost four years after the takeover battle itself. In the dock were Ernest Saunders, Gerald Ronson, Tony Parnes and Sir Jack Lyons. They faced a total of twenty-four charges involving market manipulation, theft and false accounting. All four denied any wrongdoing whatsoever.

John Chadwick QC, now a High Court judge, led the prosecution for the SFO, supported by Barbara Mills QC, who was to become the SFO's second director. Chadwick provoked a lot of negative comment as lead prosecutor because he was a specialist in civil and not criminal law, and there were many sceptics who doubted that the SFO line-up would work. But, in the event, it turned out to be an inspired choice. John Steele, who reported on the trial for the *Daily Telegraph*, remembers being massively impressed by both Chadwick and Mills. 'They were a Rolls-Royce team,' he says. 'I don't think anyone who heard John Chadwick's cross-examination of Ernest Saunders will ever forget it. It was devastating.' But there was also a downside to the SFO's choice of counsel, as Steele acknowledges: 'I think Chadwick and Mills were probably the most expensive team ever used in a public prosecution.' With counsel fees of over £1.3 million for the first trial alone, he was probably right.

John Chadwick opened the case with a gripping speech that highlighted the dramatic nature of the events being tried at Southwark. 'Mr Saunders', he began, 'wanted to be the head of a major international company.' To achieve this aim, he continued, Saunders launched a clandestine support scheme with a number of leading City figures to boost the value of Guinness shares so that the company would be successful in its takeover bid for the Scottish drinks group, Distillers. 'The defendants were so carried away by greed and ambition', said Chadwick, 'that they were prepared to be dishonest and commit criminal offences. They were so greedy for money and power that they were prepared to cross the line which defines what is legal and what is dishonest.' The speech was so riveting and at the same time so damning that some people have claimed the defence never really recovered from it.

The trial itself was dominated by two people: Oliver Roux, the former finance director of Guinness, and Ernest Saunders, the company's former chief executive. Roux, to all intents and purposes, had turned Queen's evidence and was the SFO's star witness. He knew that, having blown the whistle on Saunders and the others, he could be virtually certain that he would not be prosecuted. Roux's testimony was crucial, confirming as it did the existence of the illegal share support operation and Ernest Saunders' role in controlling it. Roux also claimed that it was Saunders who had approved the secret payments to Ronson and the rest.

Ronson, Parnes and Lyons each decided not to give any evidence at the trial. While their positions varied in the detail, they all accepted that a share support scheme had been running and that indemnities and success fees had been paid by Guinness. However, all three men denied that they had individually been involved in any dishonesty. The fourth defendant, however, took a very different position.

Ernest Saunders spent eighteen days giving evidence in the witness box. He said that he knew nothing of the share support operation and little of any indemnities or success fees. He claimed that he was being made a scapegoat for the actions of others and that most of the prosecution witnesses and all the other defendants were lying. This later became known as the '*Nightmare* defence' after the title of his son's book, published in 1988, which developed the idea of Saunders as victim in some depth. While only the jury can really know what influenced their verdict, lawyers from both sides have since said that Saunders' testimony was the turning point in the trial. The *Nightmare* defence, blaming everyone but himself, was simply not credible.

The trial ended, after 113 days, on 22 August 1990 with all four defendants being found guilty. Mr Justice Henry said the fees involved were 'too big to be honest' and that greed was the driving force behind the actions of the four men. He sentenced Ernest Saunders to five years' imprisonment, although this was later reduced to two and a half years – on the grounds that the original sentence was too severe; not, as had been widely reported in the press, because Saunders was suffering from dementia. Tony Parnes received a two-and-a-half-year sentence, Gerald Ronson was imprisoned for one year and fined £5 million, and Sir Jack Lyons was fined £3 million. Lyons escaped imprisonment solely because of his age and ill health; these were not considered good enough reasons to let him keep his knighthood, of which he was later stripped.

The first Guinness trial was widely regarded as a triumph for the Serious Fraud Office. It had passed its first big test with flying colours. The fact that the SFO had not been involved for the first sixteen months of the investigation was not discussed. The view of the media was that the new organisation was a success. Even the normally staid *Financial Times* was fulsome in its praise, saying: 'The verdicts from the first Guinness case will boost the reputation and morale of the Serious Fraud Office.'

Not surprisingly, the man who insisted on taking the Guinness case from the CPS to the SFO remembers the moment very well indeed. John Wood's first telephone call after hearing the verdicts was to Sir Patrick Mayhew, the Attorney-General, to tell him the news. 'Patrick was walking in the Yorkshire Moors,' remembers Wood, 'and I knew that he was very anxious to hear the result so I called him on his mobile phone. The line was extremely bad but I told him the result and I think he was as pleased as me.' But Wood is also understandably keen to put the pleasure he felt at these convictions in a wider context. 'We did feel pretty good about it because we are human beings and because this was our most important case to date,' he says. 'But no one in the SFO thinks the conviction of the accused is the best criterion to decide success or failure. We all know that the most important thing is that the investigation has been properly done and that the prosecution has put forward a good case. After that, it's a matter for the jury.'

Yet, while the praise heaped upon the SFO gave the appearance that all was well, the case officers were acutely aware of a debate going on behind the scenes that could ultimately threaten the convictions themselves. One of the key pieces of evidence that had secured the guilty verdicts was the testimony given by the defendants to the DTI inspectors in early 1987. As noted earlier – and strange as it may seem – DTI inspectors actually have more power than SFO investigators. While both can compel answers to questions, only the DTI can routinely use these answers in court proceedings: the SFO's section 2 interviews can be introduced only if a defendant contradicts his or her previous statement in court. This means that, provided a defendant stays silent, section 2 interviews are of little evidential value.

Given this anomaly, the status of the Guinness defendants' DTI interviews was always going to be a controversial issue. The SFO argued that since they had been taken by a DTI inspector, they were admissible in court. But the defence said that this was an SFO prosecution and as the SFO equivalent, the section 2 interview, was not normally admissible it was unfair to use the DTI transcripts in this type of trial. Mr Justice Henry wrestled with this question for some time before finally ruling that the DTI transcripts could be used in the case. However, both sides knew this was not a ruling that was going to go unchallenged for long.

The primary reason why the defence objected so strongly to the use of these transcripts was that they were extremely damaging to the defendants. Gerald Ronson had told the DTI inspectors that if he had known Tony Parnes had received a £3.25 million fee for his services, he 'would have smelt that this whole thing was not right'. But Ronson's later evidence clearly demonstrated that he had known of the Parnes fee well before he finally agreed to get involved in the share support operation. The DTI transcripts had caught Ronson in a lie. John Chadwick, as prosecution counsel, also mercilessly teased Ronson over the fact that he could not answer the DTI inspector's question as to why he should be paid £5 million for something which, if lawful, Guinness could have done itself.

Tony Parnes was also in deep trouble because of the DTI transcripts. Parnes had told the DTI inspectors that he had not known about Gerald Ronson's success fee during the course of the bid. But evidence from one of the other defendants suggested that Parnes had known Ronson was going to receive a very large sum of money for his efforts. Once again, the DTI transcripts appeared to have caught someone out. The cumulative effect of these revelations was devastating.

After the trial, the judge's decision to allow the DTI transcripts to be used was referred to the European Court of Human Rights. After hearing submissions from both sides, the European Court ruled that the use of these transcripts in the trial had indeed been unfair; however, it did not award the defence all its costs, nor did it say that the Guinness case had been prejudiced. John Wood still thinks the SFO was right to use the material. 'Fraud is incredibly difficult to prosecute and every assistance is needed,' he says. 'I don't think there was anything wrong in being given this evidence or in letting the police investigate it. The only challenge that can be made is its admissibility in court and, while I can see the point the defence is making, I don't personally agree with it.'

The second Guinness trial opened in the autumn of 1991 with a new team running the case for the SFO. Both John Wood and Jeraine Olsen had left the office in the meantime and had been replaced by Barbara Mills, the former Guinness prosecutor who became the new director of the SFO, and Gordon Dickinson, who became the new Guinness case controller. Dickinson was particularly pleased with his first assignment. This was still one of the

SFO's biggest cases, and it continued to set legal precedents with startling frequency.

One of the first difficulties facing Dickinson was that Roger Seelig and Lord Spens, the two defendants in the second trial, had decided to represent themselves. Having already spent hundreds of thousands of pounds on legal fees, Seelig and Spens realised they would be bankrupt before the trial ended if they continued to retain their lawyers. Lord Spens believes they had little choice in the matter. 'I started off with a barrister and a full legal team as did Roger Seelig, who I think spent £700,000 on legal bills. But it soon became obvious that this was going to drag on and it would cost an absolute fortune. The only way we could survive financially was if we represented ourselves.'

The costs involved in a serious fraud case are always a huge problem for all but the wealthiest defendants. A case can take several years to get to court, and during this period defendants are unlikely to be able to work. One possible solution that has been mooted would be for legal aid to be offered automatically to all defendants to ensure that a proper defence could be submitted. A judge could then order the recovery of the costs if a guilty verdict were subsequently returned. This would at least allow a defendant who pleads not guilty to be certain that the case would be properly presented to the jury. The final outcome of the Seelig and Spens trial shows that the current system is deeply unsatisfactory.

For the prosecution, defendants in person – that is, representing themselves – cause particular problems. The judge, in order to be fair, is obliged to go to great lengths to ensure that each legal move is properly explained. According to one of the SFO lawyers involved in the case, 'It means that everything goes at a snail's pace, which isn't really good for anybody.' For the defendants themselves, undertaking their own defence means taking on an extremely heavy burden, as Lord Spens knows only too well. 'The legal complexities are frightening and the details are immense,' he says. 'In the second Guinness trial, there were 89,000 documents and I had to know each of them intimately. It was a huge undertaking.'

The Guinness prosecution team, its confidence enhanced by victory in the first trial, began its case well. Then, about six weeks into the trial, a massive row erupted. The defence alleged that the SFO had deliberately held back a series of documents which would show that the use of indemnities and success fees was not unusual. It was an astonishing allegation, particularly given the fact that Jeraine Olsen had apparently gone to such lengths to ensure that everything was disclosed. However, when everything eventually came out in the open, it did indeed look as if the SFO had some explaining to do.

What became known in the trial as 'the undisclosed material' related primarily to two companies, Burtons and TWH Investments. Both, like Guinness, appeared to have used indemnities and success fees during contested takeover bids. Interestingly, Gerald Ronson had been involved in the Burtons affair, while Lord Spens was a central figure in the TWH episode. The DTI, as the regulatory authority, had originally investigated Burtons following its bid for Debenhams in 1985, and had concluded that there had been a 'concert party' of Burton supporters, similar to the one seen in the Guinness bid. The DTI did not believe there was sufficient evidence to support criminal proceedings; none the less, it sent the case file over to the SFO to get a second opinion. The SFO discussed it with counsel before deciding, on 1 March 1989, that the DTI was right and that a prosecution was not warranted. But it did retain a copy of the file in case Mr Ronson ever gave evidence claiming that he was unfamiliar with City takeover practice.

It was a similar story with the TWH material. Here the Licensed Dealers' Tribunal, a trade association, had originally investigated the matter. The tribunal, chaired by Lord Grantchester, a senior City figure, established that TWH Investments had been given a series of indemnities by Lord Spens to persuade it to make a series of share purchases, including buying shares in Guinness. However, the tribunal concluded that this was perfectly acceptable City practice. The Licensed Dealers' Tribunal report has never been made public before and it makes astonishing reading.

'In our opinion,' it says, 'there is nothing intrinsically improper in the purchase and sale of shares in the market under an indemnity arrangement entered into between a dealer and a third party.' According to the report, this applies even when the shares involved

THE CITY TRIAL OF THE CENTURY 51

are from a company 'which is about to make or has made an offer for the shares in another company.' And the tribunal claims to have some powerful allies on its side. 'Our view,' it says, 'is supported by the Appeal Committee of the (Takeover) Panel.'

The Licensed Dealers' Tribunal did, however, find one thing to complain about in the way TWH had done business. It found the use of false invoices to pay for indemnity share transactions 'reprehensible'. However, even here it says that, 'After careful consideration we have come to the conclusion that such conduct was not so discreditable as would justify the revocation of the licence.'

The Licensed Dealers' Tribunal report would have been extremely useful to the hard-pressed Guinness defendants, particularly in the first trial. It has always been Tony Parnes' contention that he believed share indemnity arrangements and success fees were legitimate City practice and one of the City's most senior bodies clearly agreed with him. But, at the time of his trial, Parnes knew virtually nothing of the tribunal's findings.

The decision not to disclose either the Burtons or the TWH material to the Guinness defendants was originally taken by Jeraine Olsen. She said that, since neither case was remotely relevant, there was no need to include these files in the documents sent to Mr Justice Henry. However, Olsen's position seems strange, given the strength of the material itself, and even slightly at odds with a letter she wrote to the DTI on 13 January 1989, a document which has also not been made public before. In this letter, the point of which was to persuade the DTI not to appeal against the Licensed Dealers' Tribunal's decision on TWH, Olsen says: 'We feel that there is no purpose for the Guinness case to have this matter reconsidered on appeal. No real advantage will accrue if the appeal were successful. However, there is a real potential disadvantage if it were to fail.' If the TWH material really was irrelevant to the Guinness case, as Olsen claimed, why would a reconfirmation of the ruling adversely affect the outcome? It is hard to read this letter without concluding that the SFO thought that, in certain circumstances, the TWH papers might be of some use to the defence in the Guinness trial.

Lord Spens is convinced that the SFO took a specific decision to keep the TWH information from him. He says: 'I have no doubt that it was deliberately held back. It was obvious to any layman that this material was absolutely devastating. As soon as this got to the jury, the trial would have been stopped.' The trial judge, Mr Justice Henry, did not seem to think the material was anything like as damning as Lord Spens suggests. He certainly did not stop the trial when he saw it. However, he did rule that it should all be handed over to the defence. But at least one SFO team member thinks that the TWH incident has been blown out of all proportion. 'It's bizarre of Lord Spens to argue that he wasn't aware of the Licensed Dealers' Tribunal investigation,' says the lawyer. 'After all, he gave evidence to the tribunal and so he knew of its existence.' The SFO also says that it isn't really fair for the defence to claim that the undisclosed material suggested that indemnities and success fees were normal City practice. If this were so, there would not have been an investigation in the first place.

The SFO's failure to disclose this material until halfway through the second Guinness trial – and then only at the insistence of the judge – was eventually taken to the Court of Appeal. Like the Strasbourg court in respect of the DTI transcripts, it agreed that there had been some unfairness to the defendants, but also refused to say that the trial had been seriously prejudiced. However, the more serious charge – that the material had been deliberately suppressed by the Serious Fraud Office – has never been examined.

The strain of running his own defence had begun to tell on Roger Seelig even before the trial started. He, like Spens, had been rising at dawn and not going to bed until after midnight since the preparatory hearings began in November 1990. After five months of the trial itself, Roger Seelig suffered a complete mental breakdown. 'I was unable to go on defending myself,' he said. 'This was no spoof. I just could not take any more. The prospect of the trial going on until next March broke me. I could not cope with the sheer physical workload any more. I had four hundred files, each four inches thick. The prosecution had eight to ten people in its team with the Serious Fraud Office standing behind it' (*Observer*, 9 February 1992).

Faced with the complete collapse of one of the defendants, Mr Justice Henry decided that he had no option but to end the trial, and on 11 February 1992 he dismissed the jury. He also ruled that, under the circumstances, it would be unfair to continue with the prosecution of Lord Spens alone. The Attorney-General, Sir Patrick Mayhew, therefore exercised his considerable powers and terminated the prosecutions. However, to Spens' horror, Mr Justice Henry refused formally to acquit either himself or Seelig. Nor would he order the payment of the legal fees they had incurred earlier in the proceedings. The charges, said the judge firmly, would remain on file.

To Lord Spens, this outcome was deeply unfair. 'I was extremely irritated that the trial didn't go on to the end,' he says. 'I was unable to present my defence. Indeed, no one knows to this day what my defence is.' Spens, by now a driven man, was not prepared to let the matter rest. He doggedly went to the Divisional Court and successfully argued that he should be formally acquitted and have his legal costs reimbursed. Finally, five years after his arrest, Lord Spens was declared an innocent man.

The outcome of the trial was profoundly unsatisfactory not only to Lord Spens but also to the Serious Fraud Office. According to one of the senior SFO lawyers involved in the prosecution, 'We had put our case extremely well and I was very pleased with the way things were going. I felt very sorry for Roger Seelig and it was right that the trial was stopped. That said, I think everyone would agree that it wasn't a good way for an important trial to end.'

It was also unfortunate for the SFO that, just a few days before Seelig's breakdown, it had announced that it would not be proceeding with the third Guinness trial against David Mayhew of Cazenove, one of the City's most respected stockbroking firms. Mayhew's lawyers had provided the SFO with fresh evidence which showed that he was not aware of the arrangements behind the purchase of 10.6 million Distillers shares in April 1986. Barbara Mills did not attempt to hide the reasons behind her decision. 'The evidence in the case is no longer sufficient to give a realistic prospect of a conviction,' she said (*Observer*, 9 February 1992).

Predictably, the media lumped the SFO's failure to convict Spens and Seelig together with its decision not to proceed with the third Guinness trial against Mayhew and began to pillory the organisation. Lord Spens, who became the SFO's critic-in-chief, joined the attack, memorably asserting that the SFO was 'no better than a cowboy organisation with a gunslinger mentality'. And yet, in fact, the SFO had generally done a good job with its Guinness prosecutions. Seelig's collapse was beyond the SFO's control, and it took some courage to decide not to proceed with the David Mayhew prosecution so late in the day. There are criticisms to be made of the way the SFO handled the Guinness affair, but they were not the ones aired at the time.

Nine months after the collapse of the Seelig and Spens case, the fourth and final Guinness trial began. By now public interest in the subject had waned, and the media were distinctly unenthusiastic about reporting it. Tom Ward, one of Saunders' advisers, was charged with the theft of £5.2 million. For a variety of legal reasons, the SFO was unable to introduce all the evidence it wanted into the trial, and what it did produce clearly failed to impress the jury. The case lasted barely five weeks, at the end of which, after less than six hours of deliberation, the jury unanimously found Tom Ward not guilty.

For the vast majority of the British public, there was only one Guinness trial and it ended in triumph for the Serious Fraud Office. It was part of the SFO's honeymoon period. For the critics of the SFO, there were four Guinness trials and the SFO lost three of them. Both views are slightly naïve. The hard questions facing the SFO are not about its conviction rate. On the Guinness case, they revolve around its decision to use the DTI transcripts and not to disclose the Burtons and TWH material. On the first point, the SFO made an argument in court and Mr Justice Henry accepted it. The second point is much more difficult for the SFO to answer. There is some evidence to suggest that the SFO thought the TWH material might be of some use to the defence. If so, it should have been handed over much earlier in the proceedings. Given the litigious nature of the Guinness defendants, this failure may yet return to haunt the SFO.

4

The Only Gilt is on the Bathroom Taps

THE INVESTIGATION and prosecution of Barlow Clowes was the first really big case which the Serious Fraud Office ran from start to finish. Unlike Guinness, this was not a City crime, involving the manipulation of the stock market. It was much more of a traditional investor protection case, concerning the theft of thousands of elderly people's life savings. According to John Wood, the SFO director at the start of the Barlow Clowes investigation, 'It was a very good example of what was meant to be a typical Serious Fraud Office case. The amounts involved were very considerable and a large number of people had lost money. It was exactly the type of thing we were set up to handle.'

The combination of Guinness and Barlow Clowes as its first two high-profile cases couldn't have been better for the SFO. For one thing, they showed that it was capable of investigating and prosecuting a genuinely wide variety of fraud; for another, Wood knew that a success with Barlow Clowes would do as much for the credibility of the SFO among the general public as a success with Guinness would do for its standing among politicians. In fact, Wood now believes that the Barlow Clowes case might have been even more important for the SFO than Guinness. 'I'm not ignoring the fact that Argyll and Distillers shareholders lost money in Guinness,' he says, 'but it's not quite the same. Here we had thousands of small investors who had lost money they thought was invested in British government stock, and I think if the case had been badly handled, if it had resulted in acquittals, a large number of people would have had their faith in British justice badly dented.

Barlow Clowes really was an extraordinarily important case for us.'

The Barlow Clowes story began in Manchester where Peter Clowes was born. He left school at fifteen and went to work in his parents' hardware shop before embarking on a career selling insurance. In 1973 he met Elizabeth Barlow and together they set up the Barlow Clowes investment company. By 1978, when Elizabeth Barlow left the partnership, Barlow Clowes Gilt Managers, or BCGM as it had become known, had almost £10 million under management. The business grew steadily throughout the 1980s and eventually became so successful that Clowes decided to obtain a stock market quotation. He bought a controlling interest in a tiny plc called James Ferguson Holdings and absorbed both Barlow Clowes Gilt Managers and Barlow Clowes International, his increasingly important Gibraltar-based company, into the new business. It was a moment of real triumph for Peter Clowes, who had metamorphosed from an extremely shy and quiet young man into a flamboyant and apparently highly successful entrepreneur. His shock of white hair, tycoon lifestyle and new stock-market vehicle made him a well-known figure, not only in the Poynton area of Manchester where he lived, but increasingly across the whole of the United Kingdom as well.

Both Peter Clowes' onshore and offshore trading companies claimed to invest solely in UK government bonds, or gilts as they are more commonly known. Gilts are guaranteed by the UK government and pay a fixed rate of interest, which makes them a very attractive vehicle for cautious investors. Peter Clowes first attracted national attention in the early 1980s when his company began using a technique known as 'bond washing'. This involved buying gilts just after they had paid out their half-yearly dividend, when the price is theoretically at its lowest, and selling gilts just before the next dividend was due, when the price is supposedly at its highest. The profit to be made from this technique was by no means as certain as Clowes claimed, but it did allow him to offer a slightly better return for his investors than many of his competitors. With skilful promotion, the money flooded in, and by the beginning of 1985 Barlow Clowes had about twelve thousand investors and over £100 million under management. Then, just two months later, on 28 February, the government announced that it had decided to ban bond washing. Peter Clowes' unique selling point had been taken away and newspapers like the *Daily Telegraph*, which had always taken an extremely sceptical view of Clowes anyway, began actively recommending that its readers get rid of their investments in his company.

What the *Daily Telegraph*, like the rest of the media, didn't know was that Peter Clowes couldn't pay back his investors even if he wanted to. Bond washing had only ever given Barlow Clowes a marginal advantage over the competition, and the vast majority of investors' returns had actually been obtained by plundering new money which had just been deposited. Worse still, Peter Clowes had started to use his investors' money to finance his own millionaire lifestyle. He had purchased the *Boukephalas*, a magnificent ocean-going yacht which had formerly been owned by Christina Onassis, a huge French château and even a brace of Lear jets. For Clowes, it was unthinkable that the business could be wound up. It would show everyone that he was a crook.

Clowes had no choice but to redouble his efforts to bring new money into Barlow Clowes and to challenge those who said his business had no future. He began heavily promoting Barlow Clowes International, his Gibraltar-based company, saying that this could continue to make superior returns, all of which would be tax free – the unspoken implication, of course, being that he would continue bond washing offshore. His claim was echoed by several apparently independent financial advisers, who continued to recommend Barlow Clowes products to their clients. What was not generally known was that these advisers received 2p of every pound deposited with Clowes. Thus it was perhaps not surprising that the Barlow Clowes group continued to grow throughout 1986 and 1987, primarily through investments in BCI, its offshore arm.

What was surprising, however, was that the DTI, which had held serious doubts about the Barlow Clowes group of companies since the early eighties, had never bothered to make its reservations known to the general public. In 1983, the DTI had realised that Barlow Clowes was trading without a licence and launched an investigation. A subsequent letter sent by the DTI to Barlow

Clowes' solicitors said: 'It is apparent that the records maintained by the partnership do not come up to the standards required by statutory rules.' Yet, notwithstanding both the lack of a licence and the lax accounting records, a senior official in the DTI's Financial Services and Companies Division still felt able to write to the minister on 19 March 1985 saying: 'For what instincts are worth, mine is that Barlow Clowes is above board. I rate Mr Clowes as an addict of doing things with gilts, not a crook. But other, and very worrying possibilities, cannot yet be dismissed.' True, the civil servant quite properly flagged both possibilities, but his underlying view was clear: Barlow Clowes was an honest company. It was an error of judgement that was eventually to cost the country over £150 million.

The DTI finally granted Barlow Clowes a principal's licence on 22 October 1985, thus allowing it to keep trading. According to the DTI, this followed 'numerous assurances' from Peter Clowes that things would get better and an independent audit which failed to reveal any impropriety in the group. However, the audit had not examined both the offshore and the onshore funds at the same time, which meant, of course, that any holes in one fund could easily be covered up by transfers from the other.

The DTI's disastrous error of judgement was finally revealed just two years later when Touche Ross, now Barlow Clowes' accountants, reported that, contrary to expectations, the records remained in a mess and things hadn't improved. The Touche Ross report prompted the Deputy Governor of the Bank of England to write to the Permanent Secretary at the DTI on 28 September 1987, saying: 'We find all this rather worrying. Just as in 1985, our concern remains that the size of the Barlow Clowes operation could lead to a major "City Scandal".' It was a prophetic turn of phrase.

Extraordinarily, another eight months passed before the authorities finally moved against Barlow Clowes. On 25 May 1988 share dealing was suspended in James Ferguson plc, and two days later the Securities and Investments Board, the City's senior regulator, asked the Official Receiver to put Barlow Clowes Gilt Managers, one of the company's subsidiaries, into provisional liquidation. It was the first time the SIB had ever used these powers and the reasons given for the liquidation seemed so vague that many people were not convinced that the regulator really knew what it was doing. According to the SIB, Barlow Clowes' accounting records were still inadequate and there was some concern that there might be a shortfall of cash for its seven thousand investors. This suggestion was fiercely denied by Peter Clowes, who immediately asked the SIB for permission to repay all his clients in full. It was an aggressive counter-stroke by Clowes, who knew that the SIB was secretly worried about the possibility that he might have commingled the UK- and Gibraltar-based funds and therefore could never agree to such a proposal anyway.

Peter Clowes' offer to repay all his customers was just one part of a clever public relations strategy he had developed, aimed at suggesting to his investors that the SIB had over-reacted to some minor technical infringements of the rules. It culminated with a front-page story in the *Today* newspaper on 11 June 1988 headlined 'I'm no crook'. Clowes told the newspaper: 'My luxury has been earned through sheer hard work. As far as I'm concerned we have a properly run company. There are technical problems with accounting but there was no reason to take such draconian action.' It was persuasive stuff, and initially the media were much more sympathetic to Peter Clowes than they ought to have been; but then the crisis suddenly deepened.

The SIB lodged a number of documents in the High Court in London alleging that 'falsification has been carried out' by backdating documents. The SIB also claimed that it was not satisfied about Barlow Clowes' solvency or its ability to pay debts as they fell due. And, as if this wasn't enough for the increasingly worried Barlow Clowes investors, Peter Clowes himself then refused to reveal the whereabouts of £139 million of investments held by Barlow Clowes International in Gibraltar. When asked about this at an emergency meeting of James Ferguson plc, Clowes said: 'One third is in gilts, one third is in ninety-day paper and one third will need to be refinanced' (*Independent*, 7 June 1988). The comment sparked outrage, and several investors forcefully pointed out that the application forms they had signed clearly stated that BCI was meant to invest only in government funds. Peter Clowes, however, remained quite unrepentant, claiming that 'the purpose of Portfolio 68 [the main Gibraltar-based investment scheme] is to provide a predictable return and that is what we have done. We have got 11,000 very satisfied investors' (*Independent*, 7 June 1988).

Given all the circumstances, it was an unfortunate phrase to use. The following day, the '11,000 very satisfied investors' were told that they were not going to be able to withdraw any of the £139 million supposedly deposited in Gibraltar. BCI was going to be put in receivership and it would be months before any of them got their money back – assuming, of course, that it was there at all. It was at this point that the true scale of the problem became apparent. Many elderly BCI investors depended on the income from their investments to pay for a variety of essentials, including basic living expenses, mortgages and even nursing-home fees. The Barlow Clowes scandal was about to become very real indeed.

Leslie and Emmy Mullard were one just one couple who lost everything because of the Barlow Clowes fraud. They had just returned from their summer holiday when they heard that BCI had been put into receivership and that huge sums of money were missing from the fund – among them, their own life savings of £63,000. 'We were devastated,' says Emmy Mullard, shaking as she recalls the event, 'as were many other people who lived in this area and had invested with Clowes. We eventually had to sell our home, our lovely Pear Tree Cottage, just to make ends meet.'

It quickly became clear to the SIB that the Barlow Clowes scandal was likely to become far more than just a regulatory matter. While there was still no hard evidence of criminality, everything was starting to point that way and it was becoming increasingly obvious that the Serious Fraud Office needed to be involved. John Wood, the SFO's director at the time, remembers the moment well. 'I received a call from the Securities and Investments Board who said that they suspected there were some criminal elements in Barlow Clowes and they were going to get everyone around the table to discuss it. The only problem was, they said, that it would have to be on a Sunday.' Wood duly turned up at the SIB's very discreet offices just behind the Royal Exchange building in the City of London, only to find the front door firmly locked and bolted. On a Sunday, access for everyone, even the director of the SFO, was strictly round the back.

Once inside, Wood found himself in a unique meeting. It was the first time that the new regulatory authorities had all got together to try to resolve a problem. It seemed to Wood that the full alphabet was present, with representatives from the SIB, the DTI, the SFO and IMRO, the Investment Managers' Regulatory Organisation, which was directly responsible for supervising Barlow Clowes. Notwithstanding the potential regulatory overlaps, the meeting went extremely well. 'It was an excellent example of the regulatory system working together,' says Wood. 'A preliminary investigation had been done and a fraud had been found. Now it was a question of how best to proceed and, on this occasion, it was clear that the Serious Fraud Office had to have the lead role.'

At the end of the meeting, Wood telephoned John Tate, one of his most able assistant directors. Tate, a big, smartly dressed man with heavy glasses and a ready smile, had just joined the SFO from Customs and Excise, where he had been a senior lawyer. Tate, too, remembers the moment well. 'It was my birthday and I was sitting at home with my family eating a birthday lunch when John Wood telephoned. He said, "I've just come from a meeting at the SIB and I've got this nice little case for you. I think you're going to like it a lot." It was the beginning of four years' very hard work.'

John Tate's first move was to go and talk to the receivers and the regulators about Barlow Clowes. They left him in no doubt as to what had really been going on. 'They told me there was an enormous black hole in the company,' recalls Tate. 'If you looked at Barlow Clowes Gilt Managers in the United Kingdom and Barlow Clowes International in Gibraltar, you would see that over £150 million in total was missing. It was an enormous sum of money.'

Tate swiftly put together a multi-disciplinary team which was designed to handle all facets of the inquiry. It was to provide a template for all future SFO investigations. 'It meant that the lawyers, accountants, police officers, IT specialists and so on could all now work together in the same room on the same floor and everyone could have immediate access to whatever skill they needed,' says Tate. 'Obviously, with the Fraud Investigation Group, there had been some contact before, but now everything was that much faster. It speeded things up immeasurably.'

One of the senior police officers involved in the police part of the investigation was Detective Chief Inspector Graham Watson, a tall, quietly spoken man with a balding pate and a heavy black moustache. His opposite number leading the accountants was David Morrison, a senior SFO figure, whose forensic accounting skills were to prove crucial to the whole investigation. According to Tate, the SFO's multi-disciplinary approach was to be the key to the success of the whole case, and on this occasion it was the accountants who were most often in the driving seat. 'We really could not have functioned effectively without them spending what amounted to several years poring over bank accounts,' says Tate. 'Because of their efforts, we were eventually able to demonstrate to the jury that money passed through eight or nine bank accounts before coming out the other end where it was then used by Clowes for his luxury yacht and things like that.'

But the police also played a vital role, particularly in the initial investigation. Detective Chief Inspector Watson was the first to move, driven by a fear that Peter Clowes might try to evade the authorities and by an even more alarming newspaper story. Just a few days after the SFO had taken on the case, on 11 June 1988 *The Times* ran a front-page story headlined: 'Papers were shredded at Clowes HQ'. The paper claimed that a former Barlow Clowes employee had told it that 'documents and letters were deliberately shredded at the company's headquarters after Department of Trade & Industry inspectors moved into the crashed investment company.' Watson, a police officer for almost thirty years, soon became convinced that the *Times* story had at least some elements of truth in it. He says: 'We made enquiries in Macclesfield and Prestbury, which was where Barlow Clowes was based, and there was a definite possibility that documents were either being shredded or being taken away and so we obtained a warrant to arrest Peter Clowes for attempting to pervert the course of justice.' Watson admits that there was also a second reason why he moved so quickly on Peter Clowes. 'I was also concerned about the possibility that he would literally take off. He had access to several private jets and he had a huge amount of money. We couldn't ignore the fact that he might flee the country.' Watson's decision to arrest Clowes relatively early on in the investigation is now pointed to as an early example of the SFO's eagerness to 'get the handcuffs on'; but, like most of the other examples cited, it does appear to have been taken on purely case-related grounds.

A warrant having been obtained from a London magistrate for the arrest of Peter Clowes, Watson and a colleague began the long drive to Poynton. He told the Cheshire police what he intended to do, and asked that Clowes be put under surveillance until they arrived. 'But', remembers Watson, 'just before we got there I heard on the radio that Clowes had been spotted driving at high speed towards Prestbury, which has an airport. The local police, fearing that he might be leaving, gave chase, stopped and arrested him. It later turned out that Clowes was just going into the village to collect his newspaper.' The Cheshire police had jumped the gun.

Peter Clowes was held in custody at Macclesfield police station until Watson arrived. He was then taken back to his house which was thoroughly searched from top to bottom. A huge number of documents were found, including some that had originally come from Clowes' private office, thus justifying the original decision to raid the house. These documents were all seized and taken back to London, along with Peter Clowes himself. As Watson drove back, he remembers thinking more and more about Peter Clowes and his victims. 'I thought what Clowes had done lacked compassion,' recalls Watson. 'The people he'd defrauded were mostly pensioners who simply couldn't afford to lose this sort of money. You tend to start thinking about your own family and frankly they could have been easily taken in by a man like Clowes. It was a nasty, greedy sort of crime and I wanted to get a result because of it.'

As the investigation progressed, the international dimension of the case became more and more apparent. David Morrison and his team of accountants found themselves following money from London to Jersey to Geneva and finally to Gibraltar. John Tate, the case controller, recalls that the SFO's first visit to Gibraltar was undertaken in conditions of extreme secrecy. 'We asked the Gibraltar Attorney-General for permission to investigate in

Gibraltar and this was duly given,' says Tate. 'We then flew over to the Rock thinking that no one would know we were coming. It was on the plane that I got my first inkling of what it was going to be like on all our high-profile cases. On the front page of the *Gibraltar Times* was the headline, "SFO coming to Gibraltar". Worse still, at the end of the first day, we were having dinner in a restaurant when a waitress came up and asked me how the investigation was going. I think it was only then that I really understood just how high-profile this sort of work had become.'

The high-profile nature of the work and the intense media interest weren't the only problems confronting the SFO during the Barlow Clowes investigation. Another problem which has recurred repeatedly in major fraud investigations is the number of people with a legitimate interest in the case. If this aspect isn't properly handled, no one is able to do their job properly. It was a problem that John Tate was determined to avoid. 'By mid-July,' he remembers, 'it became clear to me that a log-jam was developing. So I called a meeting of everyone involved including ourselves, the regulators, the DTI and the receivers for both Barlow Clowes Gilt Managers and Barlow Clowes International. Initially, it didn't go well but, after the lunch-time sandwiches and a glass of wine, everyone started to talk more openly and began to share information. Finally, you felt the log-jam beginning to break and that meant we could all move ahead.'

It was as a result of this meeting that John Tate and his team got their single most valuable piece of information. Ernst & Young, the receivers of BCI, had produced a flow chart showing where all of the money invested in the company had actually gone. As everyone suspected, precious little of it had been invested in gilts as it was meant to have been. The majority had gone to fund Clowes' champagne lifestyle, his executive toys and some extremely poor financial investments including the purchase of a brewery and a loss-making chain of jewellers.

When questioned about this by the SFO, Peter Clowes argued that his companies had never actually guaranteed to invest exclusively in British government stocks. He pointed out that the application form sent to all potential investors authorised Barlow Clowes to buy and sell British government stock 'on a fully discretionary basis and to place any uninvested funds with any bank, local authority corporation or any other body on such terms and conditions as you [Barlow Clowes] see fit whether bearing interest or not'. The reason, he said, why he bought things like yachts and Lear jets was not for personal gratification but as business investments. These could be hired out, said Clowes, and were part of a diversification strategy which was intended to allow Barlow Clowes to continue to pay the high rates of return which its investors wanted. It was not an argument which impressed the SFO investigators, and Peter Clowes was charged along with three colleagues, Dr Peter John Naylor, Guy von Cramer and Christopher Frank Newman. Together they faced a twenty-count indictment involving offences against the Prevention of Fraud (Investments) Act 1958 and the Theft Act 1968.

One of John Tate's abiding memories of the Barlow Clowes case was his visit to Peter Clowes' yacht which was moored off Gibraltar. It was 101 feet long and Clowes had paid over $2.5 million for it. It was the classic floating gin palace; but it didn't impress Tate one bit. 'It was a sleek boat, it could cruise at thirty-five knots, but frankly it made me sick to look at it,' he says. 'I knew where the money had come from to pay for it and so I knew what its cost really was. I couldn't look at it in any other way.'

While Peter Clowes and his colleagues always remained the primary focus of the SFO investigation, the media's attention switched for a while back to the role of the Department of Trade and Industry. The DTI had harboured concerns about Barlow Clowes for many years; yet not only had it failed to act on those concerns, it had even legitimised the company by granting it a licence. The Barlow Clowes Investors Group, which represented most of the company's victims, claimed that the DTI's failure was so great that it amounted to negligence and that the government should compensate everyone who had lost money. They backed up their claim with some extremely skilful public relations, including filling the Manchester Free Trade Hall with Barlow Clowes victims, many of whom were willing to tell their stories of real hardship to anyone who would listen in the hope of embarrassing the government into compensating them for their losses.

Initially, the government seemed prepared to tough out the barrage of negative publicity, but its position became unsustainable with the publication of the Parliamentary Ombudsman's report on the matter. Sir Anthony Barrowclough concluded that the DTI had indeed been guilty of significant maladministration in its handling of Barlow Clowes. While the DTI never formally accepted these findings, it did decide to make a £150 million *ex gratia* payment to the eighteen thousand investors caught in the collapse. The payment was unprecedented and, above all, reflected the degree of real suffering that was caused by the Barlow Clowes affair.

The trial of Peter Clowes and his three former colleagues finally opened at Chichester Rents in Chancery Lane on 2 July 1991. At this point it was the largest fraud case ever to have come before the English courts. Alan Suckling QC represented the SFO, while Anthony Hacking QC appeared for Peter Clowes. Just before the trial opened, a mysterious sign suddenly appeared on Anthony Hacking's door. Peter Clowes had got fed up with walking past Alan Suckling's door with its portentous sign saying, 'Serious Fraud Office' and so had commissioned a new sign for Anthony Hacking saying 'Serious Defence Office', which he then ceremoniously fixed to his defence counsel's door. Given the weight of evidence against Clowes, it seemed an extremely optimistic thing to do.

John Tate and Alan Suckling's first task was to simplify what would otherwise have been an extremely complex case to make it more easily intelligible for the jury. 'The first thing we did', recalls Tate, 'was to experiment with computer graphics to show the movement of monies. Our early attempts looked more like cats' cradles than anything else, but by the time we got to court, they were very simple and very clear and the jury could easily see how the money had been used.' The cost of all the computer equipment installed in the courtroom at Chichester Rents came to £63,687, but Tate believed it had been money well spent. His second attempt at simplification was by no means as expensive but every bit as effective. 'We produced a seventy-six-page bundle of papers called the "Statement of Agreed Facts",' says Tate, 'which told the story of what had happened in as much as it was agreed with the defence. It meant that when counsel questioned witnesses, they could simply refer to the relevant page in the bundle, which helped the jury and speeded things up a lot.'

Overall, John Tate was pleased with the way the SFO case was presented. Alan Suckling's opening assertion that 'the taps on Christina Onassis's yacht were the only gilt-edged objects ever bought by the Barlow Clowes offshore funds' went down extremely well with the jury, and the prosecution witnesses generally came up to proof. 'There were no real surprises,' says Tate; 'and when you get something that actually mirrors your initial plans, it's quite an achievement.' Tate does, however, admit to one moment of pure panic. Early on in the trial he had gone to the exhibits store at Elm House where he stumbled across a document he had never seen before. It was a spreadsheet which seemed to suggest that Peter Clowes had actually bought £600 million worth of British government gilts. 'I couldn't believe it,' recalls Tate. 'Our whole case was based on the fact that there were virtually no gilts in Barlow Clowes. I went at the speed of light from Elm Street to the court, but closer examination by our accountants showed that there was only about £2 million worth of actual gilts on the sheet. Everything else had been made up by Peter Clowes on his computer. Nonetheless, it was quite a shock at the time.'

Peter Clowes' team, led by the very able Anthony Hacking, did what they could do for their client, but it was not an easy case to defend. The public interest was extremely high and the thousands of victims were very vocal. 'Our biggest difficulty', recalls one member of the defence team, 'was that our client was so obviously guilty.' Another abiding memory was when the judge adjourned the trial because a juror had been bitten by a mosquito and so had become unwell. As soon as the court rose, Peter Clowes immediately dashed out of the building. Asked why he was leaving in such a hurry, he replied: "I'm going back to Manchester. To breed mosquitoes."'

The Barlow Clowes trial lasted for just over one hundred days before finally concluding on 10 February 1992. Peter Clowes, the principal defendant, was convicted of ten theft and eight fraud charges. His second-in-command, Peter Naylor, was convicted of one theft charge, bizarrely involving a crime against Clowes himself. Both Guy von Cramer and Christopher Newman were acquitted on all counts. Before passing sentence, Mr Justice Phillips told Clowes: 'I don't believe any judge has been called upon to sentence a worse case than yours. Anyone who deliberately carries out this kind of massive fraud must face the fact that if he is caught he must go to prison for a very long time.' It was, he added, a 'breathtaking financial scandal'. He then sentenced Peter Clowes to ten years' imprisonment, although he was actually released after serving just four years.

Graham Watson, the Detective Chief Inspector who had been on the case virtually from the start, felt the outcome was a complete vindication of all his efforts. 'I was delighted, as were my colleagues,' he recalls. 'Peter Clowes received one of the longest sentences ever imposed for this type of crime, and I think the sentence was absolutely right. A lot of elderly people had suffered a great deal because of Mr Clowes and some of them had died because of the stress. Even the families of victims had suffered. I thought justice had been done regarding Mr Clowes.' It was a sentiment shared by the whole team. Even John Tate, the case controller, while anxious to point out that professional prosecutors do not judge their work by convictions alone, acknowledges that 'it was a job well done, and after the sentence we went out and bought an awful lot of champagne.'

Despite Tate's understandable reservations about triumphalism, the Barlow Clowes trial was clearly another major success for the SFO. It had now made its mark on the City with the first Guinness case and also shown that it could be equally effective with a massive investor protection case. For Barbara Mills, the Guinness prosecutor who, in August 1990, replaced John Wood as director of the SFO, it was clear evidence that the new organisation was living up to expectations. 'I think morale was very high in the spring of 1992,' says Mills. 'The office had only recently been set up and it had done well with some very difficult cases. These were cases which no one else would have been able to take on and it was rather encouraging to be able to break into new territory like that. It was doing what it was set up to do.'

But the SFO was to climb even higher in the public's estimation before plummeting into the nightmare on Elm Street. Another case had been developing in parallel with Barlow Clowes, and it was, if anything, even more significant for the office. The initial convictions in the Blue Arrow case were seen by many as proof that the SFO was an organisation that could no wrong. The subsequent acquittals at the Court of Appeal and the realisation that the case had cost almost £40 million changed that view radically and marked the end of the SFO's honeymoon period. But the Blue Arrow case would also drastically alter the way all future serious fraud cases would be handled. Blue Arrow is arguably the most important SFO case of all.

5

The Minnow that Swallowed a Whale

'THE SERIOUS FRAUD OFFICE never got nearer to taking on the City establishment than with Blue Arrow.' That's the view of one of the lawyers most closely connected with the SFO's prosecution of the Blue Arrow case. Unlike Guinness, where some of the key players were entrepreneurs, Blue Arrow revolved exclusively around some of the most senior figures and reputable companies in the City of London. The fact that the SFO managed to bring the case to trial at all was a triumph for the office, particularly given that many of the City's most influential people did all they could to stop it ever coming to court. But the way in which the case was prosecuted was, with retrospect, something of a disaster. It allowed those in the City who wanted to sweep everything under the carpet to snatch victory from the jaws of defeat. The consequences of the Blue Arrow case are still being felt today; some of the SFO's most senior people believe that Blue Arrow undermined its confidence to such an extent that it has still not fully recovered.

The Blue Arrow affair started back in the summer of 1987, at the height of the bull market. It was a time when City financiers believed that almost anything was possible, a vision shared by many of Britain's most entrepreneurial businessmen. One such man was Tony Berry, the boss of Blue Arrow, then the fastest-growing recruitment agency in the world. Berry, a flamboyant and charismatic man whose receding hairline often makes him look older than he is, was a typical eighties deal-maker. He was liked by the press, had extraordinary drive and vision, and believed that buying rather than growing businesses was the quickest route to success.

Back in the early 1980s, Berry spotted that the recruiment business was fragmented and ripe for rationalisation on a grand scale. In 1984 he floated Blue Arrow, his rapidly expanding employment agency, on the Unlisted Securities Market, valuing it at just over £3 million. Three years later, when the company had acquired its two major rivals, the Brook Street Bureau and Reliance, as well as the corporate head-hunters Hoggett Bowers, Blue Arrow's market capitalisation had risen to a staggering £400 million. It was a phenomenal achievement; but Tony Berry had still bigger plans. He wanted to play on the international stage and, as he confided to County NatWest, Blue Arrow's merchant bankers, his 'dream' target was the US-based company Manpower, the biggest recruitment agency in the world.

Tony Berry believed not only that he could successfully launch a hostile takeover bid for Manpower – which was much larger than Blue Arrow – but also that he could run it more profitably than the existing management. Berry justified his view by pointing to Manpower's poor investor relations and open share register, with no one holding a controlling interest: these factors, he said, would make a takeover bid a relatively simple process. He also argued that, because Manpower provided only temporary staff, it wasn't maximising its profit potential. By providing permanent staff as well, claimed Berry, he could significantly increase profits.

At almost any other time in its history, County NatWest would have walked away from such a high-risk deal. County, although a subsidiary of the giant National Westminster Bank group, was not a major City player and, if anything, was generally considered slightly conservative in its approach. While Tony Berry talked a good game and had already proved himself a very able businessman, the fact remained that Blue Arrow was a minnow trying to swallow a whale. But these were not normal times for either County NatWest or the City of London. Since the Big Bang of 1986 had introduced a new competitiveness into the City, old-established reputations counted for nothing and there was a growing consensus that only the most powerful merchant banks would survive. County knew that if Berry's audacious raid was successful, it offered his banker a real chance of leaping into the big league. It was simply too good an opportunity to miss.

Jonathan Cohen was County NatWest's chief executive at the time. He hasn't worked in the City since the Blue Arrow débâcle, but he still looks every inch the highly successful merchant banker that he used to be. Cohen agrees that to understand the Manpower bid, it is important to recognise what was going on in the City at the time. 'There was a roaring bull market,' he says, before adding resignedly, 'which, had we but known, was about to come to an abrupt end. The City was completely frenetic with takeover bids. Blue Arrow was going to be one of the largest deals ever seen and its success was incredibly important for both County NatWest and the National Westminster Bank.'

The mechanics of the Manpower bid were surprisingly simple: it was the numbers that were truly frightening. County NatWest had arranged for its parent company, the National Westminster Bank, to give Blue Arrow a £767 million short-term bridging loan so that it could bid for Manpower. If this bid was successful, Blue Arrow would then go to its shareholders and raise £837 million by selling additional shares through what is known as a rights issue. This would allow the bridging loan to be repaid, and the remaining money could be used to settle the hefty fees charged by County NatWest and Blue Arrow's other corporate advisers.

Blue Arrow finally launched its bid for Manpower on 4 August 1987. Initially it was aggressively opposed by the Manpower board, but an increase in the price offered from $75 per share to $82.50 per share persuaded the US company to recommend acceptance to its shareholders. On 7 September the bid was declared 'unconditional' and Tony Berry's extraordinary dream had, it seemed, come true. All that remained was for Blue Arrow's shareholders to back the rights issue and buy more shares in the enlarged company so that its huge debts could be settled. As is common with these deals, any shares that were not purchased by Blue Arrow shareholders would be bought either by County NatWest, which was acting as both lender and chief underwriter, or by the sub-underwriters (other institutions who, for a fee, had agreed to help out).

In theory, any rights issue which is fully underwritten in this way cannot fail; but in practice, if large numbers of unwanted shares fall to the underwriters, the share price inevitably falls too. Everyone in the City soon finds out that the rights issue has fallen flat and that the underwriters have huge quantities of shares which they will have to dump on the market sooner or later, depressing the price. A failed rights issue can destroy a company's reputation and its share price in a matter of hours.

County NatWest always claimed in public that the success of the Blue Arrow rights issue was a virtual certainty. Nicholas Wells, the aggressive young turk who led the County team responsible for the whole Blue Arrow deal, was reported in the press as saying: 'We are getting lots of support from institutions and other shareholders.' The rights issue, he added confidently, 'is looking pretty good'. But despite this public optimism, there was increasing private concern. According to the DTI's later report into the affair, Wells approached a number of friendly institutions and asked if they would be willing to hold Blue Arrow shares in exchange for an indemnity against any losses they might incur. Wells told Dillon, Read, Blue Arrow's US adviser, that County could only swallow 5 per cent of Blue Arrow's shares before it would be obliged to tell the market about its share stake. Such an announcement, said Wells, would 'act as a depressant on the share price of Blue Arrow'. Unfortunately for County, Dillon, Read's lawyers said that it wasn't able to hold any additional Blue Arrow shares in this way as it would breach US 'anti-warehousing rules' and might even infringe UK disclosure requirements. However, it did agree to help County out by underwriting a small parcel of Blue Arrow shares.

As the possibility grew that the Blue Arrow rights issue might not be quite as successful as everyone hoped, a contingency meeting was held at County NatWest's prestigious offices in London's Drapers Gardens to consider what might be done if it was not fully subscribed. Forty-eight hours later, however, Wells still felt sufficiently confident to tell an early morning meeting of salesmen and analysts that he expected the take-up level to be as high as 70 per cent and that the remaining shares would probably all be sold at a premium.

The Blue Arrow rights issue finally closed at 3 p.m. on 28 September 1987 and everyone gathered expectantly at County

NatWest's headquarters to hear the news. Among those present were Tony Berry, Nick Wells and his boss, David Reed, plus Christopher Stainforth and Philip Gibbs from Blue Arrow's stock-brokers, Phillips & Drew. Predictions varied around the table but everyone remained upbeat. Tony Berry was still convinced that the take-up would be about 70 per cent, the County NatWest people thought it might be just a little lower, while the Phillips & Drew representatives suggested an altogether more modest 50 per cent. But no one even got close to the true figure. A bombshell was about to hit Drapers Gardens.

At 6.30 p.m. the registrars, whose job it was to count the number of acceptances, finally telephoned through with the first realistic estimates. To the horror of everyone in the room, they announced that the take-up figure was a paltry 35 per cent. Even though, as the evening wore on, this slowly crept up to 38 per cent, the result meant, as everyone instantly recognised, that County NatWest was going to be left with a huge quantity of Blue Arrow shares on its books. It seemed inevitable that, when the City found out, the Blue Arrow share price would collapse and County would be left nursing huge losses. Moreover, because everyone at the table had an interest in at least some of the shares, no one was going to be immune from the impending disaster.

David Reed, the head of County's corporate finance division, quickly did some sums on the back on an envelope. Because of its underwriting commitments, County NatWest was committed to buying 80 million Blue Arrow shares at a cost of £133 million. Phillips & Drew would have to take 17 million shares at a cost of £28 million. Dillon, Read would end up spending £9 million to purchase 6 million shares. Taking this many shares in these circumstances would clearly be extremely costly to all concerned. David Reed later told the DTI that 'the view emanating from the brokers, with which I did not disagree, was that one was talking about a 20 to 30p fall in the share price on the announcement of the result of the issue. I can recall calculating that meant a loss to us of between £16 million and £24 million.' If nothing was done, the Blue Arrow fiasco threatened to wipe out County's entire profits for the year.

There was, however, one way in which the situation could still be retrieved. If the remaining Blue Arrow shares could be placed with third parties, they would not fall to the underwriters and the subsequent collapse in the share price could be avoided. In the days running up to the disaster, Phillips & Drew had sounded out various institutions about just this possibility, and some companies had indeed expressed an interest in buying Blue Arrow shares. The problem was that no one had anticipated being left with anything like this many shares. Even if all of Phillips & Drew's contacts took the shares as planned, there would still be 132 million shares remaining with a face value of £219 million and representing 26 per cent of the entire issue. It still looked unavoidable that the underwriters would have to be involved.

It was at this point that Tony Berry and a number of others left the meeting to have a sombre meal together, leaving the hard-core City professionals to wrestle with what appeared to be a virtually insoluble problem. But they had not reckoned on Nick Wells' and David Reed's absolute determination to save the issue. Over the next few hours an extraordinary plan slowly began to emerge. Phillips & Drew contacted all the institutions who had originally expressed interest in Blue Arrow shares and confirmed that they were still prepared to honour their commitments, but only if 50 per cent of the rights issue was taken up. What, said Wells and Reed, if County NatWest, Phillips & Drew, and Dillon, Read secretly boosted the actual 38 per cent take-up figure by buying a further 12 per cent of the rights issue? Then the magic 50 per cent figure would be achieved, the remaining shares could be placed as planned and the share price would not fall. The additional shares bought by the Blue Arrow advisers could then be sold into the stock market whenever was deemed appropriate.

It was an ingenious plan, but there were some obvious problems with it. First, it meant that County NatWest, Phillips & Drew, and Dillon, Read would all end up with more Blue Arrow shares than would be the case if the rights issue went directly to the underwriters. In other words, to save the issue, they would all have to increase their risk. Secondly, the rights issue had technically closed, and it was not clear if it could legally be opened up again. Finally,

County NatWest would obviously end up with far more than 5 per cent of the Blue Arrow share issue and some way would have to be found to get around the law obliging it to declare any stake over 5 per cent. If the City ever discovered that County was sitting on such a large number of Blue Arrow shares, the stock price would collapse anyway.

David Reed, the most senior County NatWest man present at the meeting, decided it was time to telephone his chief executive, Jonathan Cohen, and get his approval for the tentative plan. 'I went to the chairman's office,' Reed later told the DTI, 'and phoned Cohen. I said, look, we have a problem. The level of acceptance is far lower than we thought. We have two choices. We could let the issue drop on the underwriters. I believe that would cost us between £15 million and £24 million against fees in the order of £15 million. Alternatively, we can try and save the issue. But it will mean that we will have to increase our exposure. What is your reaction? I think his words to me were, "I don't think we have any choice, David."'

This telephone call and the plan that was taking shape in Drapers Gardens would eventually come to be at the heart of one of the longest fraud trials in history, but Jonathan Cohen himself has little recollection of it. 'Sadly, I don't remember it terribly well,' Cohen told me. 'I remember Reed phoning me and putting a number of points and my feeling content that what he was doing was appropriate in the circumstances he described. I went to bed and slept soundly that night. I was not aware of having sanctioned anything which was later to be labelled a conspiracy and dishonest behaviour.'

When Reed returned to the meeting, he was ebullient. Philip Gibbs of Phillips & Drew told the DTI that he remembered Reed saying: 'I have been speaking upstairs. We have got some more money. We can do it.' Flushed with enthusiasm, the stockbrokers then turned their attention to the mechanics of how to increase the number of acceptances from the current 38 per cent to the 50 per cent needed for Phillips & Drew to be able to place the bulk of the remaining shares. After some haggling, County agreed to buy 34.6 million extra Blue Arrow shares while Phillips & Drew and Dillon, Read agreed to take 10 million each. In total, 54.6 million shares

were 'added in' to the rights issue, some six hours after it had been
formally closed.

The question of the legality of subscribing to the Blue Arrow
issue at such a late stage was raised by several people during the
meeting. Philip Gibbs claims that Nick Wells said it would be
'perfectly all right', although no legal advice was actually taken at
the time. None the less, the registrar did allow the extra acceptances
to be registered, though he later admitted to the DTI that he
thought they had all been received by County before the 3.00 p.m.
deadline. If the registrar had been aware of the real situation, he
would never have agreed to add in the extra shares and so the whole
rescue plan would have failed.

Once the rights issue acceptances had reached 50 per cent, the
second half of the operation swung into action. As agreed, most of
the residual shares went to the institutional investors identified by
Phillips & Drew; but a huge quantity remained. This meant that
both County and Phillips & Drew were forced to purchase yet
further amounts of Blue Arrow shares. By the end of the evening,
County held 94,801,743 Blue Arrow shares, representing some 13.4
per cent of the company's entire stock, while Phillips & Drew held a
further 34 million shares. It was an unprecedented situation.

At 10.51 the following morning, an announcement flashed on to
the screens of stockbrokers and dealers all over the City of London.
It was headed 'Blue Arrow plc: results of rights issue' and said
jubilantly: 'County NatWest announces that, in connection with
the rights issue of 504.4 million new ordinary shares by Blue Arrow
plc, acceptances have been received in respect of 246.5 million
shares, representing 48.9 per cent of the issue.' No mention was
made of the fact that this had been achieved by adding in an extra 54
million shares secretly purchased by Blue Arrow's corporate
advisers. When Nick Wells, who authorised the press release, was
later asked by the DTI why this information had been left out, he
replied that 'it would have made the placing very much more difficult.' It was something of an understatement.

But placing the remaining shares was not County NatWest's only
problem. It now had to disguise the sheer size of its own holding.
The first thing it did was to split the share stake into three tranches

of just under 5 per cent each. It kept one tranche for itself and gave a second tranche to County NatWest Securities, its market-making arm. Market makers are not required to declare stakes of less than 5 per cent and County claimed that the two positions didn't need to be added together. None the less, it must have been extremely difficult for County NatWest Securities to convince itself that this was a normal market-making position. Mark Potashnick, the senior market maker at CNW Securities, later told the DTI that 'a holding of up to 5 per cent of Blue Arrow greatly exceeded anything CNW Securities had previously held. I was running the whole firm's position of twelve hundred stocks on less than the capital required to buy this size of holding.'

The final tranche of County NatWest's Blue Arrow shares was eventually handed over to the Union Bank of Switzerland, Phillips & Drew's parent company, which placed them in one of its nominee accounts. County had offered UBS an indemnity against loss to persuade it to do the deal, but even this didn't fully allay the Swiss bank's fears. It remained concerned that, since its subsidiary already held a 5 per cent stake in Blue Arrow, these additional shares might force it to declare the holding itself. Philip Gibbs therefore obtained legal advice from the law firm Allen & Overy, which reflected on it for a while before saying that, since the shares didn't technically belong to UBS, it wasn't necessary to declare them. Allen & Overy did, however, admit to the DTI that 'the point involved is finely balanced.'

The fact that UBS bothered to obtain legal advice on this point puts it in a very different position from that of County NatWest. According to the DTI, neither Reed nor Wells took the trouble to get similar advice, and the National Westminster Bank itself later concluded that the use of the so-called 'market maker's exemption' to support the Blue Arrow rights issue was unacceptable.

For several weeks it looked as if the Blue Arrow rescue plan was going to work. The media, which had no idea what had really happened, were so full of praise for County NatWest's audacious coup that Phillips & Drew became quite envious. By 2 October 1987 it had decided it could take no more, and placed a full-page advertisement in the *Financial Times*. The advert proudly announced that 'Phillips & Drew are brokers to Blue Arrow and have successfully placed at a premium the 258 million shares not taken up by the existing shareholders.' It failed to mention certain key points, such as the fact that County NatWest and Phillips & Drew had together been forced to buy 78 million shares on top of those they had already purchased to take the rights issue up to the 50 per cent level, in order to ensure a full placing.

But even if this advert, like the earlier press release, did mislead people, it soon ceased to matter. Just seventeen days later, on 19 October 1987, stock markets around the world crashed and the Blue Arrow share price collapsed. A few days before Black Monday, Blue Arrow shares were trading at 167p. By the end of the month they were down to just 80p. County NatWest, Phillips & Drew, and Dillon, Read, who between them now owned tens of millions of Blue Arrow shares purchased at 166p each, had lost a fortune.

In these circumstances, it was inevitable that everything would eventually come out into the open. Both the National Westminster Bank and the Professional Standards Panel of the Stock Exchange immediately launched investigations into the Blue Arrow affair. But it was the DTI's report which was to have by far the greatest impact and eventually involve the SFO.

On 19 December 1988 Nicholas Ridley, the Secretary of State for Trade and Industry, asked Michael Crystal QC and David Spence, a chartered accountant, to investigate the whole Blue Arrow affair under section 432 of the 1985 Companies Act. Crystal and Spence heard evidence from 102 witnesses and examined a huge amount of written material. Yet, despite the complexity of the issues involved and the fact that the vast majority of the people questioned were legally represented, they still managed to submit their report on 12 July 1989, just seven months later. It was, by any standard, an astonishingly quick piece of work.

The report itself ran to 221 pages, including twelve appendices. It chronicled the whole Blue Arrow débâcle in some detail, giving, at the end of each section, a view as to the behaviour of the key players. The first significant criticism came at the end of their examination as to how the rights issue acceptances were increased from 38 per cent to almost 50 per cent. Here the report's authors said:

We regard Messrs Reed, Wells, Gibbs and Stainforth as responsible for the decision to add in 54,625,000 shares. Each of them knew that this was to enable public statements to be made to prospective placees and to the market that the rights take-up level was of the order of 50 per cent. We regard the conduct of Messrs Reed, Wells, Gibbs and Stainforth as falling far below that to be expected from responsible executives of County NatWest and Phillips & Drew.

It was a damning indictment of the four named individuals; but Crystal and Spence's criticisms didn't end there.

The report then went on to examine the County NatWest press release put out the day after the rights issue was closed. The DTI inspectors considered each of the justifications given by Blue Arrow's advisers for the press release: that it was literally true, that it protected the share price and that Blue Arrow authorised it. But, having heard them all, Crystal and Spence concluded: 'We regard Messrs Reed, Wells, Gibbs and Stainforth as responsible for the misleading of the market. We regard their conduct as falling well below that to be expected from responsible members of County NatWest and Phillips & Drew.'

The report also criticised the Phillips & Drew advertisement placed in the *Financial Times* a few days later. Once again the authors pulled no punches, saying: 'We regard Messrs Gibbs and Stainforth as responsible for this misleading advert. We regard their conduct as falling well below that to be expected of responsible executives of Phillips & Drew.'

But the most important part of the report is unquestionably its examination of County NatWest's decision to conceal its enormous 14 per cent stake in Blue Arrow. As with the press release, all the arguments in support of County's behaviour were carefully studied before being comprehensively rejected. And this time the report pointed the finger squarely at one man. 'We regard Mr Wells', it says, 'as responsible for the failure of County NatWest to fulfil its relevant statutory duties. We regard his conduct as falling well below that to be expected from a responsible executive of County NatWest.'

Crystal and Spence's report was dynamite, and was reported in the press accordingly. Never before had a DTI report been published which so aggressively attacked so respectable a group of individuals and companies. The national broadsheets devoted literally hundreds of column inches to the Blue Arrow story. The *Guardian* even splashed one quote across an entire page. It seemed to sum up everything in just a single line. 'The market was misled,' it said. 'There was no justification for what happened.' The obvious question for the authorities was what to do next.

John Wood, the director of the SFO at the time, remembers reading the DTI report in the Attorney-General's garden. 'It was a beautiful day,' he recalls, 'and we spent the whole of it discussing whether this was a serious fraud and whether the SFO should investigate it. I think we agreed about both questions. It seemed to us the report showed serious wrongdoing.' It was a view shared by most of his senior colleagues at the SFO. One very experienced lawyer summed it up very clearly indeed: 'The DTI report was compiled with the help of criminal counsel and it made clear that what had happened was criminal. It was our job to take it on. It was as simple as that.'

James Kellock was the man appointed by John Wood as case controller for Blue Arrow. Kellock, who had worked for Customs and Excise before joining the SFO, is a quiet, understated man who seems to adopt a low-key approach to life. In many ways, it made him the ideal choice to run the Blue Arrow investigation, which was obviously going to be an extremely high-profile case. But the QC chosen by Kellock to lead the SFO prosecution had a very different attitude. Nicholas Purnell is regarded as an extremely bright barrister with a more assertive personality than Kellock. As he looked into the Blue Arrow affair, he came to a very controversial view. Purnell became convinced that there had been a conspiracy to deceive the market on a huge scale. He and Kellock eventually decided that the SFO should prosecute not only the four people originally criticised in the DTI report, but seven other individuals and three institutions as well.

Nor was this their only decision which was to prove controversial. Kellock and Purnell also decided to use the DTI report as the template for their investigation. In itself, this made perfect sense. As one man close to the case says, it would have been foolish to do anything else. 'The DTI report into County NatWest was a quite exceptional document. It was very thorough, well written and well argued. Had we not used it, the investigation could have taken us three to four years to complete.' But Kellock and Purnell also came to the rather more surprising view that, because the DTI report was so thorough, nobody interviewed in the process of its construction needed to be seen again. This was an astonishing departure from normal procedure and eventually led to the arrest of a number of people who were not even aware that they were suspected of serious criminal wrongdoing.

Jonathan Cohen was one of those who were not questioned by the SFO before being arrested: an event which was the more bizarre given that he had not been personally criticised in the DTI report, although he had resigned from his position as chief executive of County NatWest shortly after the details of the episode became public. The first Cohen knew of his involvement in an SFO inquiry was when he was suddenly woken early one morning. 'There was this very insistent ringing of the doorbell,' he recalls. 'I went to the door to be confronted by two plain-clothes officers who read out a charge in relation to Blue Arrow and arrested me. It was like a bolt from the blue. I wasn't handcuffed but I was led away in front of my wife and small child. It was one of the most shattering experiences of my life.'

Cohen was taken to Bishopsgate police station, where he met a number of his former colleagues who had also been arrested in a series of similar dawn raids. According to Cohen, 'Myself and my other alleged co-conspirators were ushered into a very large cell. I hadn't even met some of them before which I thought made the whole idea of a conspiracy laughable. We were told by one of the police officers that there wouldn't be any publicity, at least not from them. But when I came out of the police station, I was met with a battery of cameras.'

Cohen claims that the police themselves were never convinced that he and his co-defendants were really criminals at all. 'I remember one occasion', he says, 'when I and a couple of my former colleagues were taken to another floor to watch the Barlow

Clowes case. The police officer who took us said "This is where the real villains are." It was slightly amusing at the time but, in reality, it was cold comfort.'

Jonathan Cohen has always accepted that the Blue Arrow affair was 'a monumental cock-up' and concedes that 'the County NatWest press release which went out was misleading to the market.' He even agrees, under pressure, that some people involved in the case behaved so recklessly that their behaviour could be classed as criminal. 'If the case had been presented as one of recklessness,' he says, 'it would have been very short and there might been some convictions, although I doubt it.' However, Cohen insists forcefully that this was primarily 'a market operation which went wrong'. He says: 'I don't believe that there was a fraud or that there was any clear evidence of dishonest intent. There were misjudgements. That's all.'

Cohen believes his treatment by the SFO was grossly unfair, particularly given the fact that he was never allowed to put his side of the story directly to the investigators. 'I can't imagine any other set of circumstances', he says angrily, 'where charges have been brought on this sort of scale without the defendants at least being given a chance to explain answers which were originally given in the course of a DTI inquiry. An inquiry, it's worth saying, that decided not to criticise me in any way.'

But the SFO rejects Cohen's criticisms out of hand. 'It's ridiculous for the defendants to claim that they were somehow prejudiced by our decision not to take statements from them,' says one man who was intimately involved with the Blue Arrow investigation. 'The DTI inspectors had already covered the ground in detail. The defendants were shown their statements and given a chance to add to them. Finally, they were given a chance to comment on the DTI report itself. I don't think that they can claim their views weren't fully represented or that we didn't understand their true position.' He also points out that any of the defendants could have given a voluntary statement immediately after his arrest.

John Wood had left the SFO by the time all this was happening. But he, for one, doesn't seem completely comfortable with

Kellock's and Purnell's decision not to question the defendants before charging them. 'I think you should always go and interview people,' he says. 'Although it's not very often that you've got the DTI handing over a completed report of a criminal offence, which may alter things slightly.'

If the SFO was making it difficult for defendants, the City was making it difficult for the SFO. James Kellock became increasingly exasperated by the fact that he could not persuade any City experts to explain to the court that what had happened in the Blue Arrow affair was not normal City practice. Both the Stock Exchange and the Securities Association initially suggested a whole host of people who could normally be relied on to testify; but when Kellock contacted them, no one was willing to give evidence. In the words of one senior SFO insider, 'It soon became clear to us that the City establishment simply did not want this prosecution to succeed.'

Eventually Kellock did convince one non-executive director of a well-known City firm to give a statement. He seemed genuinely to want to help the SFO and was appalled at what had gone on in the Blue Arrow affair. However, shortly after agreeing to testify, he telephoned back and told Kellock that his company was absolutely adamant that he shouldn't get involved. He wasn't being given a choice, he said.

Despite the immense difficulties put in its way by the City, the SFO slowly managed to assemble its case. In contrast to the DTI report, which concentrated primarily on the events of 28 September, the SFO claimed that there had been a conspiracy which stretched from the end of the rights issue to almost the end of the year. According to the SFO, as more and more people became aware of what had really happened with Blue Arrow, so they too became tainted by it. The conspiracy was a ripple emanating from a central point which eventually involved almost a dozen people in serious criminal activity.

The argument developed by James Kellock and Nicholas Purnell had some intellectual merit, but it was always going to be a daunting case to put to a jury. Because of the period spanned by the alleged conspiracy and the number of people charged, it was clearly going to take a huge amount of time to hear, a fact upon which the defence lawyers seized almost from the start. Alun Jones, one of the UK's most senior barristers and a defence QC in the case, describes the SFO's strategy as 'ridiculous'. Jones admits that 'at the heart of the Blue Arrow case was a prima facie case of fraud, involving the fact that the market had been told there was a 49 per cent take-up of the rights issue whereas, in fact, it was only 38 per cent. But it was an absurd act of executive arrogance to prosecute fourteen defendants for events that had taken place over so many months.'

Even Mr Justice McKinnon, the trial judge, expressed serious doubts about the wisdom of prosecuting a case of this size. However, the SFO was determined that its case would be put in full and steadfastly refused to make any significant concessions. It was, argued Nicholas Purnell, 'an indivisible unity' and should be treated as such. None the less, he did finally agree that the trial could be split in two. At the time, some saw the SFO's determination to present so massive a case on such a complex issue as an act of considerable courage; with hindsight, it looks more like *folie de grandeur*. Eventually, as both the defence and the trial judge had warned, the case would collapse under its own weight.

The first to appear in the dock at Chichester Rents were those charged with the more serious offences. They were Nicholas Wells, David Reed, Philip Gibbs, Christopher Stainforth, Jonathan Cohen, Alan Keat and Stephen Clark, plus the three corporate defendants, NatWest Investment Bank Ltd, County NatWest Ltd and UBS Phillips & Drew Securities Ltd. Those who were charged with more peripheral activities – Charles Villiers, Paul Smallwood, Timothy Brown and Elizabeth Brimelow – would face trial later. All pleaded not guilty.

The Blue Arrow trial finally began on 11 February 1991. Nicholas Purnell opened the proceedings by sketching out the overarching allegations of dishonesty. There was, he said, 'an agreement to rig the market', and this amounted to a conspiracy to defraud those who traded in Blue Arrow shares. Purnell then began the slow and difficult task of explaining to the jury how, in the view of the SFO, more and more people had been drawn into the fraud and how each person in the dock had ended up playing a vital part in it. But, as Mr Justice

McKinnon had always feared, it took the SFO prosecutor over five months to present his case in full. It wasn't that Purnell was being particularly slow or that his witnesses were long-winded; it was simply that the allegations were so complex that this was the amount of time needed for the case to be properly explained to the jury.

Shortly after Purnell finally sat down, the first major cracks in the SFO's case began to appear. Mr Justice McKinnon immediately ruled that both Stephen Clark and Alan Keat had no case to answer and were therefore not guilty. For two defendants to walk away without even being called upon to give an explanation of their actions was a major humiliation for the Serious Fraud Office. Even Sir Nicholas Lyell, the Attorney-General at the time and a strong supporter of the SFO, concedes that this was something of an embarrassment. 'I think, with hindsight,' he says as diplomatically as he can, 'the case wasn't quite as tightly focused as it should have been.'

Yet even after the acquittals of Clark and Keat, the Blue Arrow case still ran for another seven months. There were eight defendants left and each was represented by a QC funded by the National Westminster Bank. There have been some suggestions that it was part of the defence strategy to delay the progress of the case, so as to make a mis-trial more likely. But as it was the defence who had continually asked the SFO to simplify matters, this allegation simply doesn't stand up to scrutiny. Indeed, Mr Justice McKinnon acknowledged at the end of the trial that 'neither the defence nor their legal advisers have engaged in time-wasting tactics during the trial. The defences have, in my estimation, been conducted skilfully and professionally throughout.'

When the final speeches had finished, the judge also ruled that the three corporate co-defendants had no case to answer and were therefore not guilty. But five defendants still remained and, as the judge considered his summation, he gradually realised that he was in a virtually impossible position. The trial had gone on for 184 days and had become the second longest criminal case in English history. It had been over six months since Nicholas Purnell had finished the presentation of the prosecution case, and the likelihood of the jury's being able to reflect accurately on the key points of the case seemed remote indeed. Mr Justice McKinnon therefore decided that he had only one course of action left open to him. He unilaterally removed a whole series of charges from the charge sheet and told the jury that he intended to sum up on just one part of the evidence. They should concentrate on this one single issue.

It was a final attempt by the judge to salvage something from a trial that had got completely out of control. Even at this late stage, Nicholas Purnell was reluctant to concede that his strategy had failed. He urged the judge still to sum up on all the evidence, albeit selectively. But Mr Justice McKinnon was not persuaded. 'I would not', he said, 'embark upon such a summing up for this jury or any other jury.' It would defeat the purpose of a summation.

The defence lawyers, who had been urging the SFO to adopt a more pragmatic agenda from the preliminary hearings onwards, were ecstatic to hear that they were finally to be vindicated. One turned to Mr Justice McKinnon and triumphantly said: 'I think that even Mr Purnell is, at long last, prepared to concede that the case is now unmanageable. I will not add that this is what we have being saying since last year, be that as it may.' The judge himself couldn't resist joining in the general teasing of Purnell, saying: 'I think the defence, perhaps each counsel, is entitled to at least one "I told you so."'

The judge may have made a considerable effort at the end of the case to resolve the problems; nevertheless, he must also accept some of the responsibility for allowing them to be created in the first place. However difficult it may be, it is still the job of the trial judge to manage the case effectively, and Mr Justice McKinnon seems to have done too little, too late. It was exactly one year since the trial began when the jury finally retired to consider its verdicts. As the judge said at the time, 'What is beyond all doubt is that each of us involved in this case have had to endure what no one in our courts should be called upon to cope with. That includes the defendants, their families, the jury and me. There must be some other way.'

The jury finally acquitted Christopher Stainforth but found Nicholas Wells, David Reed, Philip Gibbs and Jonathan Cohen all guilty as charged. Reed, Wells and Cohen were each sentenced to eighteen months' imprisonment, suspended for two years, while

Philip Gibbs received a twelve-month sentence, suspended for two years. Cohen was so shocked by the result that he broke down in the court and wept. 'It was one of the worst days of my life,' he says. 'I simply did not believe it would happen. I always thought that you could tell an honest man at a hundred yards.'

The public, unaware of the massive problems that surrounded the Blue Arrow case, initially saw it as a further triumph for the SFO. It had apparently taken on the City establishment and won. But those who knew what had really happened at Chichester Rents always expected the convictions to be overturned. Less than five months after the sentences were passed, the Court of Appeal ruled that the verdicts should be quashed. According to Lord Justice Mann, 'The weight, length and complexity of the case was such that a fair trial was not possible and therefore the verdicts were unsafe and unsatisfactory. The trial will rightly be regarded by the public as having been a costly disaster.' For Cohen, relief at the appeal court's verdict was tinged with regret at the length of time the whole process had taken. 'I felt elated that this burden had been removed from me,' he says; 'but I also felt an overwhelming sense of sadness that it had ever happened. It's taken me a long time to get over it.'

It has also taken the SFO a long time to get over the Blue Arrow affair. At the centre of it was real wrongdoing, spelt out in the DTI report. But, in trying to go so much further than the DTI, the SFO over-reached itself, with the result that no one has been punished. As news of the débâcle reached the press and the realisation dawned that the trial had may have cost anything up to £40 million, an extraordinary backlash against the SFO began.

The media, convinced that the City had 'got away with it', suddenly turned on the SFO with real ferocity. The Blue Arrow disaster, the collapse of the second Guinness prosecution and the scrapping of the third Guinness trial were all pulled together to create the illusion that the SFO was in deep crisis. By August 1992 the aura of invincibility that had surrounded the SFO only months earlier was a distant memory. Worse still, questions were now being raised about the delays in prosecuting the Polly Peck, BCCI and Maxwell cases. The SFO's honeymoon was over. The nightmare on Elm Street had begun.

Part II

Nightmare on Elm Street

6

'Cock-up and Cover-up'

O F ALL THE CRITICISMS advanced against the Serious Fraud Office, the most aggressive and probably the most valid have been those concerning its handling of the Roger Levitt prosecution. George Staple, the director of the SFO during the latter part of the Levitt affair, remembers the time he spent being cross-examined about the case by the Treasury and Civil Service Select Committee as the most difficult period of his professional life. Asil Nadir, George Walker and Kevin Maxwell were all part of the nightmare on Elm Street, but the SFO's biggest bogeyman was undoubtedly Roger Levitt.

Frederick Forsyth, the man who wrote the *The Day of the Jackal* and who lost over £2 million as a result of Roger Levitt's activities, describes the SFO's prosecution of Levitt as 'blitheringly incompetent from start to finish'. But his criticisms don't stop there. Forsyth says: 'It was cock-up followed by cover-up. The SFO let an open and shut case slip through their fingers and then did all they could to prevent the truth from coming out.'

It's an extraordinary allegation to make; but the Levitt case is an extraordinary story. Essentially, Forsyth claims that the SFO made three major errors of judgement during the prosecution of Roger Levitt, which led to charges involving £57 million being plea-bargained down to one single count of lying to a regulator. Because of the technical nature of this charge, Levitt was eventually sentenced to just 180 hours' community service. And when it became clear that the media were determined to find out why a major fraudster had been given such a derisory sentence, the SFO focused on the alleged failings of the defence counsel and the judgment rather than its own shortcomings. When the truth did finally emerge, the Attorney-General ended up having to return to the despatch box and clarify his earlier answers to Parliament. Echoes from the Levitt affair resonate to this day.

Roger Levitt was the highly visible founder of The Levitt Group, supposedly a one-stop financial services shop for the rich and famous. It offered advice on pensions, mortgages, personal and business investments, commercial property and even sports management. As well as Frederick Forsyth, Levitt's client list included such luminaries as film director Michael Winner, championship boxer Lennox Lewis and singer Adam Faith.

The Levitt Group grew at a phenomenal rate throughout the middle and late eighties. Levitt used his friendship with his celebrity clients to lever himself into the big time. As he met more and more wealthy individuals, he saw huge business opportunities opening up. The Levitt Group bought an executive box at Arsenal Football Club to entertain potential customers and began providing lavish hospitality at some of the country's top racecourses, including Epsom, the home of the Derby, to guarantee regular contacts with its blue-chip client list. In an effort to ensure that maximum use was always made of the business opportunities created at these events, Roger Levitt recruited some of the most aggressive financial salesmen in the country, promising them fat salaries, big bonuses and even bigger cars if they could successfully close the deals he set up. Even Levitt's corporate advertising was cleverly pointed, with its strapline saying 'Knowing where you want to go isn't the same as knowing how to get there'.

The whole package was a heady mix of flash and cash, and by 1988 Roger Levitt's distinctive moustache, large Havana cigar and colourful bow tie were attracting a huge following. Roger Levitt became one of the two hundred wealthiest men in Britain, and The Levitt Group, according to its annual accounts, trebled its sales and increased its profits from £600,000 to a staggering £8 million. Levitt himself tried to capitalise on this fantastic success by selling one third of his company to the US futures and options giant LIT for £16.5 million, only to buy it back again twelve months later following a disagreement after an LIT board reshuffle.

The LIT setback was little more than a blip for Roger Levitt, the archetypal eighties super-salesman. In 1989 he sold 4.9 per cent of the company to Legal & General for £4.7 million, valuing it at £96 million, almost double the LIT figure. And Legal & General's view of The Levitt Group was endorsed by the mighty Chase Manhattan Bank, which even prepared a report confirming the group's value. Chase then backed its own judgement by taking a 4.9 per cent stake in the company, although not quite at the same price as that Legal & General had paid. Unknown to almost everyone else in the City, Chase Manhattan had bought its shares at a preferential rate. Chase said that the shares were worth almost £5 million, but it had paid just £2.75 million for them.

Chase Manhattan's involvement in The Levitt Group was enough to persuade both General Accident and Commercial Union to get on the bandwagon, and they too bought 4.9 per cent share tranches in the company, each paying £7.35 million. Two months later Fininvest, the private vehicle of Italian media tycoon Silvio Berlusconi, joined the party, again paying £7.35 million for a 4.9 per cent stake. By the end of October 1990 Roger Levitt, the north London businessman who had opened his first insurance brokerage just fourteen years earlier, was personally worth £85 million, while The Levitt Group was valued at an astonishing £150 million. Even members of Levitt's defence team were astonished at how many apparently prudent financial institutions had been persuaded to invest. One of them memorably said: 'There's really been nothing like it since the South Sea Bubble.' But not everyone was taken in by Roger Levitt's extraordinary sales patter. One mystified financial services company chief told *Business Magazine* in December 1990: 'I just couldn't understand how The Levitt Group could jump in value by so much in such a short space of time.'

Looking back, the anonymous chief executive's scepticism was entirely justified. The Levitt's Group's profits were almost completely illusory. Unknown to anyone else, Levitt had transferred much of his personal fortune, including all of the money Berlusconi had paid him, back into The Levitt Group in a last-ditch effort to keep the company afloat. Far from being the money-making machine Levitt claimed, The Levitt Group was bankrupt. It had been making huge losses for several years. The whole Levitt facade was an illusion.

The truth started to leak out just weeks after the Berlusconi purchase. In early October 1990 Roger Levitt gave the City regulator FIMBRA (the Financial Intermediaries, Managers and Brokers Regulatory Organisation) a series of false documents purporting to show that the company had received millions of pounds in consultancy fees. In reality, this was the money that Levitt had received for the sale of his shares to the various City institutions. This one single act of wrongdoing is the only thing of which Roger Levitt has ever been convicted in a court of law.

As FIMBRA investigated further, it became clear that The Levitt Group had not been profitable for at least a year, if at all. On 13 November 1990, Roger Levitt resigned as a director of The Levitt Group, and three weeks later the outside shareholders, including Legal & General, Chase Manhattan, General Accident and Commercial Union, convened an emergency meeting to discuss the situation. They concluded that they had paid tens of millions of pounds for a company that had been insolvent all the time. There was nothing for it but to pull the plug, and the company was put into administration.

If the shareholders had been conned, so too had the personal investors. Many of them lost every penny they put into The Levitt Group. Frederick Forsyth perhaps suffered more than anyone else. Not only did he lose over £2 million personally, he was also betrayed by a man he regarded as a friend. Forsyth and Levitt had known each other for thirteen years and their families had grown close. They dined together and their children attended the same school. In 1990 Forsyth had been guest of honour at Levitt's youngest son's barmitzvah. It was a very elaborate affair, and it was only later that Forsyth realised he had probably paid for it himself. 'I'd just given Levitt a £200,000 cheque to invest in stocks and bonds,' he says bitterly. 'I see now that he probably spent it all on his son's party.'

When Forsyth first heard about the collapse of The Levitt Group he was, appropriately enough, writing his book *The Deceivers*. His first reaction was one of sympathy towards Levitt. 'I thought "poor chap" and assumed that Levitt must have suffered a heart attack or something. Then my wife told me that the police were involved and I began to fear the worst.' When Forsyth finally realised that he stood to lose millions, he went down to The Levitt Group's headquarters in Great Portland Street in the heart of London's West End and was amazed by what he saw. 'Men in overalls were literally taking away everything. It turned out the coffee machines, the desks and the staplers were all leased. Even the toilet bowl was taken away. The company had no assets at all. The receivers were left sitting on orange crates.'

The Levitt Group was a natural case for the Serious Fraud Office to take on, and it launched an investigation almost immediately. It was clear from the start that most of the personal investors' money had simply been frittered away and that the financial institutions had been tricked into investing in the group to cover up these losses. The SFO put the total amount of money at risk as £58 million. On the face of it, it should have been an easy case to prosecute. But the nightmare on Elm Street was about to begin.

Fred Coford was the man assigned to lead the case for the SFO. He was an experienced fraud investigator who had worked for the Fraud Investigation Group of the DPP before joining the SFO in 1988. Coford too believed that the case was going to be quite straightforward. Levitt was a dishonest businessman who had used investors' money to support his millionaire lifestyle. When it was all gone, he began taking funds from the banks in a desperate attempt to keep going. It really did seem an open and shut case.

Coford's investigation didn't need to take long. Roger Levitt was arrested on 12 December 1990 and charged just three months later on sixty-two counts of fraud.

Frederick Forsyth was initially impressed by the SFO. 'The police who were conducting the investigation were quite brilliant,' he says. 'They took statements from me and many other people, including a number of former employees. They put all the pieces together and by the time they finished, the entire jigsaw was clear for anyone to see.'

The SFO decided to split the prosecution into three sections: deceiving the personal investors, deceiving the financial institutions and deceiving FIMBRA. At first, there seemed ample evidence to justify all three charges. But, despite the seriousness of the case against him, no one at the SFO really thought that Roger Levitt was in the top tier of criminality. 'I didn't believe Levitt's excuses for a minute,' said one senior lawyer involved in the case, 'but I didn't think he was the world's most evil man either.' This was always expected to be a fairly run-of-the-mill case.

David Cocks was the QC asked by the SFO to run the prosecution. He was the head of his chambers and a well-respected barrister. Roger Levitt, for his part, hired a man of a very different ilk. He brought in Jonathan Goldberg, a much more aggressive QC, whose forceful style stood in stark contrast to Cocks' studied patrician manner. Goldberg had, until recently, been in Cocks' chambers but had left to become the new head of his own chambers at 3 Temple Gardens. While the cards were clearly stacked against Goldberg, the very different styles of the two leading silks promised to make it an intriguing courtroom fight.

One of the SFO's first moves was to offer Alan Johnson, The Levitt Group's investment manager, a deal. In exchange for giving evidence, it was agreed that he would not be prosecuted. Johnson accepted the offer with alacrity and informed the SFO that Levitt had a list of personal investors whom he had cheated on a regular basis. This was known inside the company as 'the Dibble List'– a play on the word 'diddle'. People on the Dibble (or Diddle) List were told that their money had been deposited in insurance bonds and other blue-chip investments and were sent regular statements showing how well their money was doing. In fact, the money had been spent maintaining Levitt's lavish lifestyle and later propping up his ailing company. Both the investments and the dividends were entirely fictitious.

Johnson's first-hand evidence, combined with the testimony of men like Forsyth and the mass of documentary material available to the prosecution, appeared to make the personal investor charges against Levitt almost unanswerable. According to Jonathan Goldberg, Levitt's QC, it was the part of the prosecution case that

Levitt feared most. 'Johnson's evidence', he wrote in a letter to the Treasury and Civil Service Select Committee on 3 July 1995, 'was overwhelmingly strong against Mr Levitt and his co-defendants and it was corroborated in many material particulars by other witnesses, not least the losers themselves. Straightforward charges of the kind alleged here in relation to the personal investors would have been easy for a jury to comprehend.'

But then the SFO made its first major mistake. Urged by Mr Justice Laws, the trial judge, to reduce the number of charges to avoid a Blue-Arrow-style situation developing and the trial running on indefinitely, it decided to drop the entire personal investor side of the case. It seemed an astonishing decision, although the SFO claims it had no real option.

The SFO says that it was faced with two major problems which it feared would prove insurmountable in court. The first was that, while it was clear that money had been misappropriated, it was not clear beyond reasonable doubt that Levitt had done it; after all, as Levitt would undoubtedly point out, the money was actually handled by the accounts staff. The SFO's second problem was rather more technical in nature and involved a recent judgment in an obscure case called Gomez. It had been successfully argued in the Gomez case that if property passes from one person to another on a consensual basis – even if that consent has been obtained as a result of deception – it is not theft. Everyone knew that this was a strange judgment which was unlikely to stand, but it was the law of the land until it was overturned by the House of Lords. It meant, said the SFO, that its hands were tied on the personal investor side.

Levitt's defence team couldn't believe their luck. They thought the SFO's decision was 'legally illiterate' and lost no time in telling a jubilant Roger Levitt that 'now, we just might have a chance.' They weren't the only ones amazed by the SFO's decision. Frederick Forsyth was outraged by this extraordinary turn of events. A £400,000 investment he had made in The Levitt Group figured in the original charges, and he had given the SFO a number of witness statements as well as a host of supporting documents, complete with signatures, to corroborate his testimony. Forsyth was even looking forward to going to court and giving evidence against his former friend. According to Forsyth, 'The personal investor charges were clear and simple. Levitt nicked the money off his mates. A jury would understand that. Nicking your mates' money is the ultimate Cockney sin. It's a moral crime. A jury would convict him.' Michael Winner was equally perplexed by the SFO's decision not to press ahead with the personal investor charges. 'The worst thing about Levitt was that he screwed his best friends. Not to give Forsyth a chance to testify was ridiculous.'

This wasn't the only bizarre decision made by the SFO during the run-up to the trial. Still under pressure from the judge, who had now received a formal statement from the Court of Appeal on the Blue Arrow case, it was asked to reduce the number of charges further. After much consideration, it decided to proceed with just one count of fraudulent trading. According to an SFO lawyer closely involved with the case, 'The decision to go for one over-arching fraud charge was taken by our counsel, David Cocks, but it was one which everyone supported. Despite the reduction in the number of charges, we thought we could produce about 80 per cent of our evidence, which wasn't bad.' George Staple also believes that this was the right decision, in the circumstances. 'The view of the prosecution team was that this was a case of fraudulent trading. We had to reduce the number of charges to ensure it was a manageable trial but, in our view, this charge embraced most, if not all, of the criminality involved.'

Despite the SFO's public unanimity on this point, a number of people at the office have said privately that the decision to proceed with just one charge of fraudulent trading was a mistake. Unlike conspiracy to defraud, which carries a maximum sentence of life imprisonment, fraudulent trading carries a maximum penalty of only seven years, and in Levitt's case this would inevitably be reduced given the defendant's previous good character. Fraudulent trading is also considered an extremely technical charge for a jury to understand, and is therefore very hard to prove.

The likely reduction in sentence wasn't the only problem that this decision caused for the SFO. Part of the case against Roger Levitt was that he had personally deceived the financial institutions when he sold them millions of pounds' worth of shares in The Levitt

Group. However, as Jonathan Goldberg pointed out with some relish in the May 1993 preparatory hearings, section 458 of the Companies Act makes it clear that fraudulent trading applies only to a company. In other words, an individual cannot personally be guilty of fraudulent trading. Therefore, said Goldberg, this part of the charge against Roger Levitt must fall. Whether it is criminal or not is irrelevant. It isn't fraudulent trading.

The SFO was completely wrong-footed by this argument. After an increasingly ill-tempered spat in court, Mr Justice Laws announced that Goldberg was right and that the part of the case relating to the institutions would have to be dropped. It was a second massive blow for the SFO: first they had lost the personal investor theft charges; now they had lost the chance to prove that Levitt had personally defrauded the financial institutions. Almost everyone on the SFO team regarded this ruling as something of a disaster. 'Our strongest point', said one case officer, 'was that Levitt had defrauded a number of financial institutions in order to raise over £20 million with which to keep the company going. Now we couldn't use this at the trial. It was a major blow.'

But perhaps most extraordinary of all is the fact that the SFO had known of Goldberg's intended line of attack for over three months and yet had apparently done nothing about it. In February 1993, earlier in the preparatory hearings, Goldberg had sketched out his whole skeleton argument in a short, four-page document. As is always the case, this was made available to the prosecution. On the third page, headed 'Allegedly Injecting Funds (Drip Feeding)', Goldberg clearly stated: 'How Levitt obtained these funds is irrelevant, we say, to the main issue of fraudulent trading by The Levitt Group.' To an untrained eye, it may seem opaque; but for the SFO's highly experienced team, it should have jumped off the page. Goldberg had spotted that personal dishonesty is no part of a fraudulent trading case and that this was therefore an inappropriate charge to bring.

The SFO accepts that this issue was flagged by Goldberg before it took the final decision to go ahead with the fraudulent trading charge, but says it is only with hindsight that it is possible to see the full power of the defence barrister's argument. One of the senior

officers involved in the case concedes that Goldberg had identified
this line of attack in his skeleton defence, but says: 'We decided –
obviously wrongly – that our argument was superior. In retrospect,
this was a mistake and we decided not to appeal the decision
because it became pretty clear that we wouldn't win.' There are a
number of technical reasons why the SFO wouldn't have won an
appeal on this point, but the first is relatively simply to understand.
Section 458 of the Companies Act is headed 'Fraudulent Trading
by a Company' (my italics); and even a cursory reading of this
section shows that it relates more to the actions of a company than
to those of an individual.

By now, the tide was running strongly against the SFO. It had
already made two major errors of judgement, and the tensions
within the prosecution team were beginning to show. One SFO
lawyer involved in the case recalls: 'Our counsel was becoming
increasingly worried about what was happening on the Levitt case.
At one point he sent us all out of the room for over an hour and said
he simply had to think. I don't think I've ever seen a senior silk do
that before.' But despite the mounting concerns, the office still
believed that Levitt was a winnable case and it continued to prepare
for the trial. As the focus was narrowed, it became clear that the
overarching fraudulent trading charge on which everything rested
still had three central elements to it: fraudulently producing
accounts, fraudulently injecting funds into The Levitt Group and
fraudulently misleading FIMBRA; and there remained strong
evidence to support all three allegations.

The case of Roger Joseph Levitt and others finally began at
Chichester Rents on Thursday 11 November 1993. David Cocks'
opening speech took over two days to hear, concluding the following
Monday lunchtime. Then Jonathan Goldberg began his response. It
took only forty-five minutes to deliver, and it provoked absolute
uproar in the court. At the heart of Goldberg's speech was what he
had always believed was his 'best point': namely, that Roger Levitt,
far from taking money out of The Levitt Group, had actually ended
up putting millions of pounds of his own money into the company.

'If Roger Levitt had intended to defraud creditors of the
company,' argued Goldberg to the jury, 'he would have siphoned

money out. He would never – this is an agreed fact in the case – have punched vast sums of his own money in, all of which he lost in the collapse. If Levitt had believed his group was on the point of collapse, would he have signed every penny of his own and his wife's money into it with nothing to show at the end of the day but worthless paper shares? He lost every penny in the collapse of the company . . . The Crown are rubbishing him, are they not? Rubbishing him because he injected about £22.5 million of his own personal money into the company in order to keep it off the rocks.'

The prosecution team couldn't believe what it was hearing. It was true that Roger Levitt had indeed put a great deal of money into The Levitt Group in a last desperate attempt to stave off financial ruin; but not all of it could be described as 'his money' in any meaningful sense. Much of it had came from the sale of his shares to financial institutions like Chase Manhattan, General Accident and Commercial Union; and the evidence suggested that Levitt had tricked them to get it. Goldberg might have forced the prosecution to drop this part of their case by spotting a legal loophole; but as far as the SFO was concerned, some of this was tainted money and yet now it was being treated as if it had been honestly earned. David Cocks, in particular, was absolutely infuriated by Goldberg's speech. He lost no time in telling Mr Justice Laws that the jury had been prejudiced beyond help and that a retrial was the only viable solution. The judge, very much aware that things were already starting to spin out of control, went away to think about it all.

On Friday 19 November Mr Justice Laws returned to court. His view was unambiguous. 'Mr Goldberg says', ruled the judge, 'that he has gone no further than to indicate the amounts of money obtained and their sources. In my judgement this gravely misrepresents the true effect. To suggest that this was no more than a neutral description of the facts is, to put it bluntly, forensic myopia of a high order.' However, Justice Laws concluded by saying: 'The unfair prejudice created by Mr Goldberg's opening is not irreparable and I will not abort the trial.' Three years later, following a long and bitter struggle, the Bar Council privately admitted that Mr Justice Laws' criticisms of Goldberg's speech were mistaken.

Jonathan Goldberg, unaware of all that was to come, began working on a retraction for Monday morning which, while not vastly generous, did alter the offending phrase from 'his own money' to the less contentious 'monies available to him'. But this retraction was never going to be heard by the jury. On Saturday 20 November the financial pages of the national press were dominated by one story: the suspended sentence handed out to Terry Ramsden, the former City high flier who had just been convicted on four counts of fraudulently inducing people to invest in his company, Glen International. Once again, the SFO was behind the prosecution, and it contained many echoes of the Levitt case – a fact that Roger Levitt spotted immediately.

Levitt telephoned Goldberg and told him that he would be willing to plead guilty to certain charges provided that he, like Terry Ramsden, also received a non-custodial sentence. Since the prosecution had already made several attempts to do a deal, Levitt knew that they were keen to avoid a contested trial. But, as Goldberg immediately pointed out, the prosecution had up to now always insisted that Levitt plead guilty to at least some offences which carried the virtual certainty of a prison sentence, and so it was unlikely that such a deal could be struck. None the less, Goldberg agreed that it would be foolish not to try, and so he contacted his junior counsel, Sasha Wass, outlined Levitt's proposal and asked her to get a response from the prosecution as soon as possible.

It took twenty-four hours for Wass finally to track down Jonathan Fisher, her opposite number on the prosecution team, and tell him about Levitt's offer. According to her letter to Jonathan Goldberg of 8 January 1994, Wass told Fisher that Levitt was 'up in arms' about the Ramsden sentence and would be 'interested in doing a similar deal with the prosecution' as long as he would not lose his liberty. However, he was 'only prepared to offer a plea to the FIMBRA count'. The reason for this was that Levitt knew that misleading FIMBRA was the only part of the charge which might not automatically attract a prison sentence on conviction. Jonathan Fisher, for his part, was non-committal and said he would take instructions and get back to Wass as soon as possible.

The following morning a meeting was held at the SFO rooms at Chichester Rents at which David Cocks, Jonathan Goldberg, Sasha Wass, Jonathan Fisher and Jane Bewsey, another member of the prosecution team, assembled to discuss the proposed deal. It was a particularly frosty affair, as relations between Cocks and Goldberg had reached an all-time low, and Goldberg ended up laboriously writing out the entire proposal by hand and sending it round to Cocks. The note reads as follows:

Dear David,
1. We have been instructed by Mr Levitt to ask of you whether you will accept a guilty plea from him to Count One on the basis of an admission to FIMBRA solely – and that all other and outstanding charges and indictments whatsoever will not be proceeded with thereafter.
2. If you are instructed to accept such an plea, I am then instructed to seek an indication from the learned judge on sentence – and Mr Levitt will then decide what to do.

It was signed Jonathan Goldberg and dated 22 November.

The SFO was now in an extremely difficult position. The judge had accepted its claim that Goldberg had prejudiced the jury, but was not prepared to grant a mis-trial. The easy solution would be to accept the plea bargain that was being offered. But the SFO also knew that Roger Levitt would be perceived as having been treated extremely leniently if he were to be convicted only of misleading FIMBRA.

It fell to George Staple, as the director of the Serious Fraud Office, to make the final decision on what to do. The more Staple thought about it, the more convinced he became that misleading a City regulator was a serious offence in itself. After all, the government had spent some considerable time putting in place a system of self-regulation that relied on honesty for its success. Deceiving the regulator was not a matter that should be treated lightly, and Staple believed that when Mr Justice Laws had fully considered the matter he would share this view. The offence did, after all, carry a maximum sentence of seven years' imprisonment. 'Levitt had pleaded guilty to a very serious charge,' says Staple. 'I judged that it was right and in the public interest to accept his plea.'

Having been told that the SFO would accept the deal, Jonathan Goldberg and David Cocks went to see Mr Justice Laws in his chambers to get an indication as to the likely sentence. The phrase 'an indication from the judge' is a term of art in the legal profession and is more restrictive than it sounds. Judges will not discuss length of sentence, but they are prepared to offer guidance as to the likelihood or not of a custodial sentence being handed down. Roger Levitt wanted his counsel to find out whether or not he would go to prison before finally deciding whether he would plead guilty to misleading FIMBRA.

Goldberg began the meeting by outlining to Mr Justice Laws the terms of the deal that had been agreed between Levitt and the SFO. He then launched into a comprehensive plea for mitigation on behalf of his client. He pointed out that Levitt had lost everything and that FIMBRA had only actually been misled for two months. Then Goldberg suddenly introduced another extraordinary legal point. He told the judge that, while it was true that the overarching fraudulent trading charge carried a maximum sentence of seven years, there was a more specific offence of misleading the regulators in section 200 of the 1986 Financial Services Act and that this only carried a two-year penalty. This was the maximum, Goldberg contended, that Parliament intended to impose for this type of offence. He then went on to suggest that Roger Levitt's offences were at the bottom end of even this much reduced tariff.

Mr Justice Laws was initially taken aback by Goldberg's argument, but it clearly had some intellectual merit. The judge acknowledged that he would need to hear from David Cocks for the prosecution before taking a final view, but said that 'if the plea is made simply and solely on the basis of misleading FIMBRA, which of itself would fall square within section 200, it would be hard to see how it would be right to impose a higher sentence.' Mr Justice Laws was obviously minded to accept Goldberg's point.

David Cocks was now in a difficult position. He didn't feel it was appropriate to debate the sentence in this particular forum, and although this was clearly a view not shared by the judge, he decided it was best to stick to his guns, telling the judge: 'It would be quite wrong for me to make any submissions here in chambers.' But Mr Justice Laws was not prepared to let matters rest. He wanted to hear as many arguments as possible before finally making up his mind about whether or nor to give Levitt a non-custodial sentence. He therefore turned to Cocks again and said: 'Would you take the same view if I were to ask you to say anything as to the propriety of the plea, given the rest of your case?' But Cocks was determined not to be drawn. 'What we have indicated', he said, 'is that this is a plea which we would accept in the circumstances. That is a matter for us. We have taken instruction on it with the Director of the Serious Fraud Office and we have come to that conclusion.'

Thus rebuffed by the prosecution, Mr Justice Laws retired to consider the matter, having been told that two years was the maximum sentence available and with Goldberg's pleas for mitigation still ringing in his ears. He returned an hour later and finally gave Goldberg the indication he was seeking. 'I am able to indicate that on the basis of the prospective plea outlined to me – namely that there will be an admission of the deception of FIMBRA but no admission to any other part of the case – that I would not pass an immediate prison sentence.' The defence was elated. The prosecution was stunned. Levitt was not going to gaol.

Sir Nicholas Lyell, the Attorney-General at the time, is still amazed by the judge's view, although protocol prevents him from being as frank as he would like. 'It's not for any Attorney-General, past or present, to criticise an individual sentence,' he says. 'But there is no doubt that the fact that this was a non-custodial sentence caused a great deal of public disquiet, and Parliament did change the law so that this type of case can be referred by the Attorney-General to the Court of Appeal in appropriate cases.'

Three days after Mr Justice Laws' ruling, Roger Levitt, a man who had cheated his friends out of millions of pounds and who had conned a number of financial institutions out of millions more, was sentenced to just 180 hours' community service. The media went apoplectic with rage. Headlines like 'A rotten deal' and 'Levitt, the basking shark' accompanied pictures of him sunbathing and drinking champagne. It was, without doubt, one of the biggest humiliations ever suffered by the SFO; and the office soon realised that if nothing were done, it would get the blame for what appeared to be a poor prosecution and an even poorer piece of plea bargaining. As soon as the trial was over, therefore, it discreetly began drawing attention to the judge's sentencing policy. At the final hearing, David Cocks aggressively challenged the contention that two years was the maximum possible sentence for misleading the regulator and instead insisted that Parliament intended seven years to be the statutory maximum. He even told the judge that 'the prosecution only accepted the plea upon that basis.' It was a line immediately echoed by the SFO's press office, which had drawn up a press briefing statement which had, as its first point, the fact that Roger Levitt pleaded guilty to 'an offence punishable by seven years' imprisonment'. But if the prosecution really felt that seven years was the appropriate maximum sentence, surely it would have been better to have made this point to Mr Justice Laws in his chambers when he asked to hear it, not later, when the decision had already effectively been taken?

What happened next is probably unprecedented in the history of the Serious Fraud Office. It had made three major mistakes during the prosecution of Roger Levitt. It had dropped the investor protection charges; it had allowed itself to be stopped from taking action over Levitt's personal defrauding of a number of financial institutions; and it had made a mess of the plea bargaining. Against this, the SFO believed that Levitt's counsel had prejudiced the jury and that the judge had taken a overly lenient view of Levitt's misleading of FIMBRA. The more the SFO thought about it, the more it became clear that if these points could somehow be brought to the fore, it might be possible to divert the media onslaught away from the office and on to the judge and the defence.

The SFO's attempt to shift the blame for the Levitt fiasco on to the shoulders of Mr Justice Laws and Jonathan Goldberg began in earnest on Monday 29 November, when David Cocks complained to the Bar Council's Professional Conduct Committee about Goldberg's opening remarks in the Levitt case. Eight days later Cocks returned to the fray again, this time writing an article in *The Times* headlined 'Judges miss the mark' in which he baldly stated that 'many judges are not up to trying serious fraud.' Finally, Cocks appeared on the BBC's *Business Breakfast* programme, where he told the interviewer that 'the charge of fraudulent trading covered the nub of the Levitt case. It's punishable by seven years' imprisonment. The restricted basis on which the plea was tendered, in my view, would have merited a prison sentence of about two and half years to three years.'

The attempt to divert attention from the shortcomings of the SFO's prosecution of Roger Levitt wasn't over yet. On 9 December John Marshall, the MP for Hendon South, intrigued by the growing row, asked the Attorney-General, Sir Nicholas Lyell, a series of very pertinent questions about the Levitt affair in Parliament. The Attorney-General's replies were, to say the least, controversial.

John Marshall's first question concerned the date at which the SFO had 'first suggested to counsel that Mr Roger Levitt plead guilty to only some of the charges'. Sir Nicholas replied that 'no such suggestion of that nature was made by or on behalf of the Serious Fraud Office. The offer by Roger Levitt to plead guilty to fraudulent trading on the basis upon which he in fact pleaded was first made on Monday, 22 November by his leading counsel.'

The Attorney-General must have felt reasonably confident of his reply at the time. It had, after all, been drafted by the Solicitor-General, who had previously been a barrister in David Cocks' chambers, and had been carefully checked with Mr Cocks himself. But in retrospect the reply looks unsatisfactory, to say no more. The reality was that, over the course of the prosecution, the SFO had discussed Roger Levitt's pleading guilty to just some of the charges on a number of occasions, the last time being as late as 9 November. While this last offer would have included Levitt serving some time in gaol, it bore more than a passing similarity to the one which was finally agreed on 22 November.

But the question of why the Attorney-General's answer to Parliament was so much less than frank does not lie at the door of David Cocks alone. Both Fred Coford, the case controller, and George Staple, the SFO director, also knew that there had been discussions between counsel on this point; and yet they too allowed the Attorney-General's answer to go ahead unchallenged. Indeed, the exact question of what George Staple knew eventually became the focus of a Treasury and Civil Service Select Committee hearing.

In June 1995, George Staple was giving evidence to the select committee about the regulation of financial services in the UK when Michael O'Brien, the MP for North Warwickshire, suddenly introduced the subject of Roger Levitt into the discussion. He asked George Staple to read out the December 1993 exchanges between John Marshall and Sir Nicholas Lyell and then invited him to comment on them. Initially, Staple followed the Attorney-General's line to the letter, saying: 'I did not give any instruction either to make an offer or to accept an offer. That did not happen until November 22nd.'

At this point, O'Brien introduced a startling piece of new evidence. It was a letter from Geoffrey Goldkorn, Levitt's solicitor, to Roger Levitt, dated 5 November 1993. The letter said:

On Monday and Tuesday of this week informal overtures have been received from different members of the prosecuting team concerning limited pleas that might be acceptable to the prosecution in order to avoid a contested trial. In particular, it has been conveyed that the minimum plea which would be acceptable in your case was an admission of the FIMBRA matter, but combined with an admission which would include you admitting knowledge of the false valuations sent to personal investors in The Levitt Group.

The letter went on: 'Mr Cocks has telephoned Mr Goldberg to say that he has taken instructions from a high source (unspecified) and this does indeed represent the best and final offer of the prosecution.'

Michael O'Brien then turned to George Staple, the director of the Serious Fraud Office, and asked him outright: 'Were you the high source?'

George Staple's reply was equally direct. 'No, I was not. I certainly did not give any instructions and no offers were made with my instructions or on my authority.' It seemed to be an end to the affair; but less than a month later, George Staple was back in front of the select committee, this time with a very different story to tell.

'On the last occasion,' began Staple at the second hearing, 'I failed to remember a meeting which had taken place on the morning of November 5th 1993. I have now got my 1993 diary from storage and there was indeed an entry showing that I had a meeting with Mr Cocks and his juniors and the case controller. I have discussed this with counsel and we did gradually recall that there was a meeting at which they reported to me on the discussions that had taken place.'

In fairness to George Staple, it should be said that it was he who requested the second meeting with the select committee to set the record straight. He also pointed out that he had held 'over eight hundred' meetings since November 1993 and he couldn't be expected to remember them all, particularly with no warning. However, the select committee, by now convinced that a cover-up of some sort had taken place and that the Attorney-General had misled the House of Commons, was not prepared to let the matter rest there.

Michael O'Brien, sensing blood, led the attack, using the *Oxford English Dictionary* as his weapon of choice. 'Suggestion', he said, checking his dictionary, 'means the action of promoting one to a particular course of action . . . the putting into one mind of an idea, a hint or an inkling. Mr Staple, I will put it to you quite clearly, that the answer given by the Attorney-General that "No suggestion was made by or on behalf of the Serious Fraud Office" was simply untrue.'

George Staple was by now extremely uncomfortable with his predicament. None the less he continued to deny that any suggestion had been made by the SFO that Levitt should plead guilty to only some of the charges; and he even tried to turn the Goldkorn letter to his advantage. 'At the top of the second page,' Staple told the committee, 'Mr Goldkorn says to his client: "You will appreciate that", talking about these discussions between counsel, "it is a private matter which in no way binds them or you." I think Mr Goldkorn is showing there an understanding of counsel to counsel discussions which I have been trying to convey to this committee.' It was a good effort, and it diverted attention away from the key word that Michael O'Brien had so effectively homed in on. However, taken in the round, Goldkorn's letter makes it quite clear that a deal was being offered and that it had been sanctioned by 'a high source' at the SFO. George Staple's sophistry might have muddied the water, but it didn't stem the flow.

George Staple, a deeply decent man, now regards that second meeting with the Treasury Select Committee as the most difficult of his professional life. His recollection of it is simple and straightforward: 'It was very, very unpleasant.' Staple is at pains to say that he hasn't changed his view of these events since leaving the SFO. None the less, when he thinks about the episode now, he seems to choose his words with even greater care than usual. 'The statement by the Attorney-General was drafted by David Cocks, who was Crown counsel and who knows the case best. As far as I know,' he says, 'it represents the truth.'

But the Attorney-General's answer on the plea bargain question wasn't the only statement that he gave on 9 December 1993 which later attracted criticism. John Marshall also asked him 'whether the Serious Fraud Office knew when it accepted the guilty plea by Roger Levitt that the judge would impose a non-custodial sentence'. Again, Sir Nicholas Lyell answered in the negative, saying: 'The SFO was not aware that the judge would impose a non-custodial sentence when it informed the defence that the proposed plea of guilty by Roger Levitt was acceptable.'

This answer, like the first, is nowhere near as full as it might have been. Levitt's defence team is certain that the prosecution knew that he would do a deal only if he was assured of a non-custodial sentence. They point to Sasha Wass's conversation with Jonathan Fisher on Sunday 21 November, when, she says, she made this clear, and to their repeated use of the phrase 'to seek an indication from the judge', which, they claim, specifically relates to their interest in a non-custodial sentence.

Yet this is an accusation that the prosecution team stoutly deny. Jonathan Fisher says that Sasha Wass told him that Levitt would keep all his options open, ruling nothing in and nothing out until he had heard from the judge. They also point to the contents of the handwritten note from Jonathan Goldberg, which ends by saying that 'Mr Levitt will then decide what to do', indicating that he had not yet decided on any specific course of action. George Staple, too, is immovable on this point. He has made it clear on a number of occasions that he never knew that Roger Levitt would plead guilty only if he were offered a non-custodial sentence. Indeed, he has privately argued that no one in Levitt's position would ever rule out everything but a non-custodial sentence in advance. After all, says Staple, some custodial sentences can be extremely short.

On the evidence so far, then, the balance seems to be firmly in the prosecution's favour. Goldberg's note does give credence to the suggestion that Levitt was reserving his position, and Staple's view seems eminently reasonable. But the evidence from the other counsel in the case seems to tilt the balance in favour of the defence version of events.

There were three other counsel involved in the case, each representing one of Levitt's co-accused. Desmond de Silva QC was one of them. He is unambiguous in his recollection. He told the select committee that 'everybody who went into the chambers of Mr Justice Laws on 22 November knew that Levitt was willing to offer pleas of guilty if, and only if, his counsel could secure an assurance of a non-custodial sentence from the judge.'

Brian Lett QC also unambiguously supports the defence position. In his letter to the select committee of 27 June 1995 he wrote:

The gossip in the robing room was that the Ramsden case had made a major impression upon Levitt. What proceeded forward was that Levitt might plead to the FIMBRA particular of Count 1 if: (a) the prosecution dropped all other charges and (b) the learned judge gave an indication that he would not sentence Levitt to a term of immediate imprisonment. I confess it is my belief that the prosecution knew that Levitt wanted both (a) and (b).

But perhaps most damaging of all for the prosecution, and particularly harmful to David Cocks personally, is the letter sent from Howard Godfrey QC to Jonathan Goldberg shortly after the row began. While the letter does not engage in the detail of the debate, it does lend powerful support to the theory that the prosecution was engaged in a damage limitation exercise to conceal a botched prosecution. On 19 December 1993, Godfrey wrote to Goldberg saying: 'You had steadily and obviously out pointed Cocks in important preparatory hearings.' He then went on to say: 'To suggest that the prosecution had to accept Levitt's offer of a FIMBRA only plea because of the contents of your opening speech and the judge's refusal to grant a retrial is nonsense.' Finally, Godfrey concluded:

I fear that this Cocks induced rumpus has been designed to cover his own lack of preparation or enthusiasm for the trial. I regard his attack upon you and Justice Laws as unfair and unjustified. I much regret having to write this letter, if only because I have always enjoyed the warmest of professional relations with David Cocks. But, in the circumstances of his complaint against you, it would be wrong to stand by and do nothing.

It is now probably impossible to establish conclusively which side is right; but, given the testimony of the other QCs involved, the mostly likely scenario does seem to be that the prosecution was told that Levitt would do a deal only if he were offered a non-custodial sentence. Certainly the Attorney-General, while not changing his view, decided it would be wise to clarify his position. On Wednesday 28 June 1995, Sir Nicholas Lyell told the House of Commons that 'there were differences of view between the prosecution and defence about the case.' He also acknowledged that he had received copies of correspondence written by all the counsel in the case which 'confirmed the degree of the difference'. However, he concluded by saying that 'he was assured by prosecuting counsel and representatives of the Serious Fraud Office that the answers given on 9th December 1993 were accurate and not misleading.' With four QCs saying virtually the exact opposite, it seems a rather strange position for the country's leading law officer to have taken.

The Roger Levitt case has now become a *cause célèbre* for critics of the Serious Fraud Office. The prosecution, they say, made a number of very serious mistakes. The dropping of the personal investor theft charges was a major error. The decision to run with the fraudulent trading charges, which led directly to the dropping of the charges relating to the financial institutions, was a second mistake. Even the plea bargain itself was extremely poorly handled. But, in the SFO's defence, all these mistakes were made in response to external events and are capable of some explanation. Where the criticism sticks is in respect of the attempt to try to divert attention away from these failings. Was it really fair to launch an attack on the judge and the defence and allow less than full answers to be given to Parliament without at least acknowledging the SFO's own short-comings in this affair?

Jonathan Goldberg eventually lodged a counter-claim against David Cocks with the Professional Conduct Committee of the Bar Council. Both hearings were held behind closed doors and both complaints were rejected. The one public statement to emerge was a letter from Jonathan Goldberg published in *Counsel*, the bar house magazine, in which he says: 'I was totally cleared and awarded my costs against the Bar Council, on a submission of no case to answer.' Perhaps more significantly, Goldberg then goes on to say that 'leading Counsel for the Bar conceded that the public criticisms of my opening speech by Justice Laws were misconceived and wrong.' Apparently, in law, as Goldberg always claimed, it was perfectly acceptable to talk about Roger Levitt's 'own money', even when he got some of it by defrauding others.

As for Roger Levitt himself, he served his 180 hours' community service making toys for toddlers at a probation service workshop. His duties included making toy train sets and dolls' houses. Since paying his debt to society, Levitt has gone overseas and, at the time of writing, has just successfully promoted a fight in New York between Larry Holmes, a former world heavyweight boxing champion, and Maurice Harris. It was described by one unkind commentator as 'a kid fighting a whale', but it was a commercial success. Levitt has apparently kept faith with his moustache, bow tie and Havana cigar; but now he has a new trademark. He's started calling himself 'Lord' Levitt. Of Elm Street, perhaps?

7

The Bird that Flew

IF THE LEVITT GROUP was a comet in the eighties firmament, Polly Peck was a supernova. It was one of the star stocks of the decade. Once an almost bankrupt clothing manufacturer, Polly Peck grew to be a FTSE 100 company. Every City broker knew the story: if you had purchased £1,000 worth of Polly Peck shares in 1979, you could have sold them ten years later for over £1 million. Polly Peck was the example always quoted by the supporters of penny shares to prove their point, and by the late eighties thousands of small investors had climbed on the bandwagon.

The man who transformed Polly Peck from a loss-making rag trade company into a £2 billion conglomerate which, at its height, reported annual profits of over £161 million was Asil Nadir. Born in the village of Lefke in Northern Cyprus on 1 May 1941, at the age of five he was encouraged to go out and earn pocket money, selling newspapers and razor blades in the port area of Famagusta, then one of the most exciting cities in the Mediterranean. After studying economics at Istanbul University, he joined his father in London running a factory manufacturing ladies' clothing. But it was the Turkish invasion of Northern Cyprus in 1974 that gave Nadir the chance to transform himself from just another successful businessman into a genuinely international tycoon. Nadir set up Unipac, a company devoted to commercialising the Northern Cyprus citrus fruit industry. He introduced new packaging and distribution techniques and, within a few years, turned a cottage industry into a major international business.

Then, on 14 March 1980, Asil Nadir acquired a controlling interest in Polly Peck, which was to be his master company for the next ten years. He immediately set the tone for the future by going straight to the stock market and raising £1.5 million so that the publicly quoted Polly Peck could buy Unipac from its upwardly mobile chairman. Two years later, Nadir began diversifying the Polly Peck group and launched Vestel, an electronics company based in Turkey, which began by making televisions and videos. Polly Peck's profits soared from a mundane £2.1 million in 1981 to a sensational £61 million in 1985 and the share price took off.

By the late 1980s Asil Nadir had become one of the City's golden boys. His obvious success, coupled with his charismatic person- ality, dark good looks and a shark's-teeth smile, convinced the city that he had the Midas touch. Nobody was concerned about the huge debts being taken on by his company, nor the fact that the vast majority of its businesses were in the eastern Mediterranean and not open to easy scrutiny. Even the stock market crash of 1987 didn't seem to slow down Asil Nadir. In 1988 Polly Peck struck a ten-year deal with the US giant, Pepsico, to open Pizza Huts in Turkey. Then, a year later, Polly Peck pulled off its biggest coup yet. It bought the Del Monte fresh food business from RJR Nabisco, the US food and tobacco group, for £560 million. Finally, in early 1990, it took a majority shareholding in the Japanese company Sansui Electric. This was to be the high-water mark for both Asil Nadir and Polly Peck.

When the tide finally turned, it did so with a ferocity rarely seen in the UK. Within the space of two months, Polly Peck the eighties success story became Polly Peck the nineties disaster. For the public, it began with a *Sunday Times* article, published on 12 August 1990, which said that Asil Nadir's personal finances were being investigated by the Inland Revenue. It was quite a coup for the newspaper but, as is so often the case with hugely complex financial stories, the journalists had only managed to report the tip of the iceberg.

The Inland Revenue's Special Office 2, responsible for cases where large-scale tax evasion is suspected, had actually been inves- tigating Asil Nadir's offshore share dealings for over eight months.

Michael Allcock and Richard Cooke, the officers in charge of the case, wanted to know about a series of deals made by Jason Davies, a young stockbroker, on behalf of a number of Swiss nominee companies. These companies had been buying large amounts of Polly Peck shares and the Revenue suspected that Asil Nadir might have been behind the purchases and not declared the income.

Cooke asked the surveillance division of the London Stock Exchange for help with the investigation and he was duly provided with a huge quantity of material relating to the Swiss share deals. The names of the companies involved were already well known to the Stock Exchange, who had been monitoring their activities for some considerable time. Yet, despite widespread suspicions in the City, no conclusive evidence had been found that anything improper was taking place, and so no action had been taken.

But the Inland Revenue investigators, using very different methods, did manage to make some progress. Cooke and Allcock established that Jason Davies worked closely with Elizabeth Forsyth, the woman who ran South Audley Management, Nadir's key private company. And, more importantly, they began to suspect that the recent purchases were part of an orchestrated campaign to keep the Polly Peck share price high. This information was communicated back to the Stock Exchange, which later passed it on to the Serious Fraud Office.

It was with all this going on in the background that the *Sunday Times* finally published its first story on 12 August. To the amazement of the journalists involved, Asil Nadir called a board meeting on the day of publication and, instead of issuing a comprehensive denial, suddenly announced that he intended to buy the entire company. Nadir subsequently claimed, in his August 1990 statement to the Stock Exchange Quotations Panel, that he had been 'contemplating the possibility of taking the company private for at least two years', but he appears not to have mentioned it to anyone else until the day before the *Sunday Times* article.

On Saturday 11 August, Asil Nadir held three informal discussions with his advisers about the proposed buy-out. George Magan, the most experienced of those consulted by Nadir, urged him not to mention his plan to the board, saying that a great deal of work would need to be done before it would be possible to decide if it was realistic or not. For example, Nadir would need to obtain acceptances from at least 90 per cent of the non-family share-holders for the buy-out to go ahead; and, even if this were successfully accomplished, he would still need to find well over £1 billion to finance the purchase.

Despite Magan's entreaties, Asil Nadir stuck rigidly to his game plan. At the board meeting the following day, Nadir tabled a letter drafted by his lawyers, S. J. Berwin & Co., which said: 'Subject to the availability of finance, an offer would be made to acquire all of the shares not presently owned or controlled by family interests.' The letter, which did not mention price, went on to claim that the offer 'would be at a level which fairly reflects the value of the company'. Nadir later told the Stock Exchange that he anticipated paying 'a conventional premium in the region of some 20 to 30 per cent above the company's then share price'. This would value Polly Peck at about £1.5 billion. Finally, Nadir explained to the board that he had decided to tell them about his plans at this early stage so that 'the creation of a false market in the company's securities might be avoided'.

The Polly Peck directors were stunned by what they heard. But, faced with an apparently serious offer, they had no choice but to make the contents of the letter public. Initially the company's share price soared but soon, as early as the Monday afternoon, doubts began to surface and the shares slipped back to 417p, a gain of just 24p on the day. One senior executive at Hoare Govett, a City stock-broker, quoted in the following weekend's *Sunday Times*, summed up what the whole financial community was thinking: 'The buy-out plan seemed to me driven by negative press publicity,' he said, 'although I cannot believe this is the whole story. The difficult thing is to see how on earth it can be funded.' By Thursday, scepticism about the buy-out was virtually universal and the share price had retreated to 405p, just 12p above the price when it was announced. The City simply didn't believe Nadir could pull it off. And it was right.

Just six days after announcing his offer to a shocked board, Asil Nadir finally bowed to the reality of the situation and informed the

Polly Peck directors that his bid would not be going ahead. He claimed that money was not the issue and said, in a statement: 'Since the time of my letter to the board, I have received approaches from both significant institutional and individual shareholders who have indicated that they would not wish to see Polly Peck becoming a private company. Therefore I have decided to discontinue my approach made last Sunday and do not intend to proceed with my possible offer.' Without the support of the vast majority of the non-family shareholders, Nadir knew that his bid was dead in the water anyway.

Interestingly, the Stock Exchange didn't seem to believe that this was the real reason for Nadir's pulling out of the deal. In a statement issued some weeks later, the Stock Exchange said: 'Prior to the announcement of Mr Nadir's withdrawal on August 17th, no shareholder in the company had approached either the brokers of the company or otherwise made public their intention not to accept any offer made by Mr Nadir.' In his defence, Asil Nadir did eventually come up with the names of three shareholders who, he claimed, had contacted him about the bid and were willing to discuss the matter with the Stock Exchange.

It had been a bizarre week, even for a company as unusual as Polly Peck. Elizabeth Forsyth, one of Asil Nadir's most loyal supporters, says: 'The proposed buy-back was a disastrous error of judgement that shook both his own and his company's credibility to its foundations.' It was a view shared by many others.

The Stock Exchange Quotations Panel, which is responsible for regulating bid activity, immediately launched an investigation into the Polly Peck affair. Its report was highly critical of Asil Nadir. Bid offers are not meant to be made lightly, and this one seemed to have been launched almost on a whim. Without explicitly citing it as the reason behind Asil Nadir's extraordinary behaviour, the panel's report did seem to dwell on one particular aspect of these events. 'Given one of the main reasons for having the board meeting and tabling the proposal was Mr Nadir's concern to avoid the creation of a false market,' it said, 'the absence of the company's brokers was particularly significant.' It then went on to say that this 'may have put undue pressure on the Board to make an immediate public announcement, notwithstanding the fact that Mr Nadir's proposals were actually at a very preliminary stage'. The suggestion, coded though it is, seems clear enough. The Stock Exchange Quotations Panel thought that Asil Nadir's buy-back plan had helped support the Polly Peck share price when it would otherwise have been under considerable downward pressure. The damning report then ended with a further twist of the dagger. It said: 'The Stock Exchange has conveyed these findings and the supporting papers on which they are based to the relevant authorities.' In other words, the Stock Exchange had passed on its suspicions to the Department of Trade and Industry and the Serious Fraud Office.

With so many allegations flying around, the SFO decided that it needed to take a long, hard look at Asil Nadir and Polly Peck. Concerns about a possible share support operation were no longer just being privately discussed by the Stock Exchange and the Inland Revenue; they were also starting to surface in Fleet Street. The SFO began its inquiry on 20 August 1990 by calling a meeting with the DTI and the Metropolitan Police. A representative of the Inland Revenue was also invited to attend but declined, saying the Revenue's own investigations were 'proceeding satisfactorily towards a monetary settlement'. Worryingly for the Serious Fraud Office, the Inland Revenue man (quoted in a note by Asil Nadir's lawyer, Peter Knight of Vizards, of 21 September 1990) also added that he thought the SFO was going on 'a fishing expedition led on by the newspaper articles and that they were unlikely to find anything'.

By now, Polly Peck was starting to unravel fast. Asil Nadir's cavalier attempt to take the company private had backfired on the group and his personal credibility had been severely dented. The City was starting to focus much less on the chairman's personal charisma and much more on the company's huge debts. The press, sensing that Polly Peck was in play, was putting more and more resources into investigating Asil Nadir's labyrinthine offshore companies. The SFO was spending a great deal of time talking to Timothy Wood, a man who had formerly worked for both Polly Peck and South Audley Management. And Wood was telling the SFO that he thought Jason Davies really was buying shares for Asil Nadir through the Swiss companies.

On 17 September 1990 Lorna Harris, the SFO case controller assigned to the Polly Peck investigation, obtained a section 2 warrant to search the offices of South Audley Management. Harris's affidavit says that the SFO investigation was focusing on two Swiss-based companies, Blade Explorations and Newbridge Investments. Both had bought shares in Polly Peck shortly before Asil Nadir announced his intention of taking the company private and sold them just before the bid was discontinued. Harris's affidavit concluded by saying that 'it is suspected that Asil Nadir controls or owns the companies involved which thereby profited from the price rise.' The suggestion of insider dealing seems unambiguous.

On the morning of Wednesday 19 September 1990, two days after obtaining the warrant, the SFO raided the offices of South Audley Management, the company which looked after all of Asil Nadir's personal business affairs. The following day the Polly Peck share price plummeted from 243p to 108p and the Stock Exchange suspended dealing in the shares. Elizabeth Forsyth, the head of South Audley Management, is adamant that it was the SFO raid that caused the crash. 'I think the SFO is responsible for the collapse in the Polly Peck share price,' she says angrily. 'A £1.5 billion company was virtually wiped out in twenty-four hours.' The charge is vigorously denied by Robert Wardle, the SFO assistant director who later took over the running of the case from Lorna Harris. Wardle is adamant that 'the collapse of the Polly Peck share price was a direct result of the state of the company and had nothing whatsoever to do with the investigation by the Serious Fraud Office.' He adds: 'News of the search did not get into the public arena until the share price had already began to collapse.'

Wardle is quite right in that the Polly Peck share price had been moving steadily downwards ever since Asil Nadir aborted his plan to take the company private almost a month earlier. Coincidentally, because of this inexorable drop in value, a number of financial institutions had executed large sell orders the day after the raid. Even more sadly for Asil Nadir, the vast majority of the shares sold that day were actually owned by him but had been pledged to the banks as collateral for loans. When the value of these shares fell below the value of the loans, the banks simply cut their losses and sold the stock. This heavy selling sent the Polly Peck share price into virtual free fall. By the time the news of the SFO raid finally leaked out later that morning, the damage was already done. While Forsyth is certainly right to suggest that the SFO raid on South Audley Management didn't help Polly Peck, it was the banks' selling rather than the raid itself which finally led to the share price collapse.

The Stock Exchange's decision on the Thursday afternoon to suspend share dealing in Polly Peck marked the beginning of the end for the company. Asil Nadir, having already been heavily censured by the Quotations Panel, was now facing a major SFO investigation, and the company directors had no answers to the difficult questions that were being posed by creditors, shareholders and journalists alike. The best they could come up with was a short statement saying: 'The board of Polly Peck International met this afternoon and intends to make a more detailed statement early next week. It wished to emphasise that it deplores the recent attacks on its chairman.'

There was, however, one small crumb of comfort for Asil Nadir. His lawyer, Peter Knight of Vizards, had met Michael Allcock and Richard Cooke, the Inland Revenue investigators, on Friday 21 September, and they confirmed that the Revenue investigation was indeed coming to an end. And, according to Knight's file note of the meeting, they didn't think much of the SFO's actions. 'As far as they could see,' wrote Knight,

the whole of yesterday's operation and Wednesday's was a monumental disaster caused by the Serious Fraud Office. They could see no purpose whatsoever in the warrant having been executed at the premises of South Audley Management, knowing that it would have such a disastrous effect and also knowing, as they do, that there would be nothing of any consequence or evidential value that would be obtained in such a raid. As far as they were concerned, they regarded the SFO as having acted very badly and that the SFO would succeed whichever way, and that either they would find something or they have destroyed the company.

If this was really the view of the Inland Revenue, which had already spent nine months investigating Nadir, things certainly didn't look good for the Serious Fraud Office. But Michael Allcock, one of the most colourful of all Inland Revenue inspectors, couldn't always be relied upon to tell the truth. Indeed, he was later charged with dishonestly running a number of Inland Revenue investigations and subsequently imprisoned. It's still not clear whether Allcock really was accurately reporting the Inland Revenue's view of the SFO investigation to the Nadir camp or whether he simply didn't want to threaten the financial settlement he had made with Nadir by suggesting that he was sympathetic to the SFO's actions.

It took ten days for the Polly Peck board to issue the statement that it had originally promised would be out 'early next week'. It began by saying that it was not seeking the reinstatement of the Polly Peck share quote on the London Stock Exchange, and then acknowledged what many people had started to suspect. The company had massive liquidity problems. In the current circumstances, it couldn't change its short-term borrowings into longer-term loans. Polly Peck was now fighting for its corporate life.

Asil Nadir seized this opportunity to put out a personal statement of his own. He confirmed that he had been questioned by the Serious Fraud Office and that he had 'answered the questions put to the best of my information'. Additionally, he said that he had agreed to the SFO's request that its investigating accountants move into Polly Peck's palatial head offices in London's Berkeley Square to continue their forensic work.

But despite Nadir's apparently co operative stance, he had certainly not convinced the SFO of his innocence; if anything, the office was redoubling its efforts to get to the bottom of the Polly Peck share deals. At the same time, the company's bankers were beginning to crawl over the Polly Peck accounts with a magnifying glass. It was becoming alarmingly clear that Polly Peck, a company that had only ever reported profits, actually had a gaping £200 million hole in its finances. This discovery was fatal. With no end in sight to the share suspension and the chairman effectively *hors de combat*, on 25 October 1990 the Polly Peck directors resigned themselves to the inevitable and put Polly Peck, a FTSE 100 company, into administration.

Five days later, just before 8 a.m. on 30 October, Robert Wardle, then second-in-command of the SFO investigation, accompanied by five Metropolitan Police officers, arrived at Polly Peck's Berkeley Square headquarters armed with another search warrant. Wardle recalls the moment well. 'There were a lot of us involved,' he says. 'Police officers, accountants and lawyers. We started the search quite early in the morning and it went on until well after midnight. It was very quiet when we first went into the building. No press were outside that I could see, although they certainly turned up later in the day. I think what struck me most when we first went into the building was its sheer size and the opulence of the furnishings. But frankly we had a job to do and so we just got on and did it.' To some, it may have seemed odd that the SFO, who had already had account- ants working inside the building for almost three weeks, should execute a search warrant, but Wardle's reasoning is irresistible. 'Asil Nadir was continuing to effectively run the company,' he says, 'and we wanted to ensure that we had access to all the key files.'

This determined approach is typical of Robert Wardle. He, like many of the SFO's more senior officers, has been at Elm Street since the very beginning in 1988. His resolute approach is tempered by a pleasant, humorous manner and a genuine warmth towards those who know him well. In many ways, he is the exact opposite of Asil Nadir, whose easy-going outward charm conceals an altogether more ruthless streak inside. By the end of 1990, the two adversaries were becoming well acquainted with each other's strengths and weaknesses.

It was just before Christmas when the SFO made its next move. Asil Nadir was returning from Istanbul aboard his Jet Star aeroplane when the SFO decided the time had come to arrest him. The plane was scheduled to land at Stansted airport in Essex, but at the last minute was diverted to Heathrow. It has since been claimed that the destination was changed so that armed police could be involved in the arrest. In fact, Stansted was fog-bound at the time and the diversion caused even more of a problem for the arresting officers than for Asil Nadir.

As soon as the Jet Star touched down, Asil Nadir was removed from the plane, cautioned and driven at high speed to Holborn police station. By the time he arrived and the formalities had been completed, it was too late for the SFO officers to begin questioning him, and so he was forced to spend an uncomfortable night in the cells. The following day was no more pleasant for Nadir, as he spent the entire time answering the SFO's questions. Significantly, the investigators made very few enquiries about illicit share dealing in Switzerland. Now all they wanted to know about was the transfer of money from Polly Peck in London to Unipac in Northern Cyprus. Finally, after thirteen hours' interrogation, at 11 p.m. on Sunday 16 December, Asil Nadir was charged with eighteen counts of theft and false accounting involving sums of almost £25 million.

Nadir's immediate response was to request bail, a move bitterly contested by the SFO, which was always convinced that Nadir would be a flight risk. After all, he had access to a great deal of money and held a passport issued by the Turkish Republic of Northern Cyprus, a country with which Britain did not have an extradition treaty. Against this, the SFO knew that a trial was at least a year away and that imprisonment on remand for the entire period would be punitive. Perhaps unsurprisingly, the judge decided the balance of the argument lay in Nadir's favour and granted bail. He did, however, set the bail bond at a record £3.5 million and insist that Nadir surrender all his passports.

As the SFO investigation progressed, its team got larger and larger. Eventually it took over the whole of the third floor of Elm Street. Meanwhile SFO accountants, seconded from KPMG Peat Marwick McLintock, continued to beaver away at Polly Peck's Berkeley Square offices. They became convinced that Asil Nadir had bled huge sums of money out of Polly Peck and transferred them through Jersey to Northern Cyprus, where they finally disappeared from view. But the SFO's biggest difficulty was evidencing the money trail. The Foreign and Commonwealth Office refused to send an official letter to the Northern Cypriot authorities asking for help as Britain, along with all other western countries except Turkey, did not recognise the Turkish Republic of Northern Cyprus. Consequently, progress was extremely slow.

Asil Nadir didn't deny that this money had left the United Kingdom, but he was adamant that it hadn't gone into his own pocket. According to him, there wasn't a black hole in the company and all the monies which had been transferred to Northern Cyprus had been used to build various leisure projects on the island. Proof of this, said Nadir, could be found by examining the accounts of Polly Peck's Northern Cyprus subsidiaries. And, to prove his claims, Nadir instructed independent accountants from BDO Binder Hamlyn to go to the island and see for themselves.

The Binder Hamlyn accountants' report concentrated almost exclusively on the whereabouts of the £25 million mentioned in the SFO's eighteen theft and false accounting charges. According to Binder Hamlyn, while it was true that payments had left the UK, it was also true that matching amounts had been received elsewhere. In other words, there might not be a fraud at all. Anthony Scrivener, Nadir's QC and a former chairman of the Bar Council, found the report extremely convincing. 'It was a very impressive piece of evidence. So impressive, in fact, that I took the view we should present it to the prosecution and invite them to drop the charges.' On 26 June 1991 the report, along with its supporting documents and extracts from various company bank accounts, was sent to the SFO's Elm Street headquarters. It was accompanied by a letter inviting the SFO to come to Northern Cyprus and examine the Unipac accounts for itself.

The Binder Hamlyn report put the SFO on the back foot for the first time during the entire Polly Peck investigation. Lorna Harris, the case controller, was initially minded to accept the offer and go to the island. On 19 July 1991 she wrote to Nadir's lawyers confirming the date of the visit and saying that her 'initial team will comprise four members of staff'. But, just days later, she was forced to change her mind. The Turkish Republic of Northern Cyprus, seeing a political opportunity developing, insisted that a *commission rogatoire*, effectively a letter of request, be sent from the Foreign Office to the appropriate TRNC authorities before the SFO visit could go ahead. Since this would mean de facto recognition of an outlaw state, the UK government refused, and the visit was off.

The first Guinness trial –
Ernest Saunders outside Southwark Crown Court, August 1990.

The Barlow Clowes trial – Peter Clowes and Peter Naylor (glasses) are led away after their conviction, February 1992.

Nick Leeson arrives in Singapore, 23 November 1995.

Roger Levitt, sentenced to 180 hours' community service.

Asil Nadir arrives at Bow Street Magistrates' Court, 1 August 1991.

Abbas Gokal – Britain's biggest fraudster.

George Walker, acquitted of fraud after eighteen days in the witness box.

Kevin Maxwell leaves Snow Hill police station
following his arrest, 18 June 1992.

SFO officers removing documents relating to the Maxwell inquiry, 18 June 1992.

Kevin and Ian Maxwell, acquitted on all charges.

The Serious Fraud Office team, June 1997:
back row, left to right: James Kellock, Paul Rayner,
Fred Coford, Philip Henry, Robert Wardle, Chris Dickson;
front row: David Morrison, Ros Wright, Gordon Dickinson.

While the SFO couldn't ignore the Foreign Office, it certainly wasn't willing to let matters rest there. Initially, it tried to gather evidence through the back door. According to David Madden, the British High Commissioner in Cyprus, 'between 1991 and 1993, the High Commission has made informal requests on nine occasions for TRNC co-operation in allowing officers of the SFO to investigate this case in Northern Cyprus.' All of these requests were rebuffed. When the SFO finally realised that both formal and informal channels were closed, it did some lateral thinking. It asked the Polly Peck administrators, who were spending a great deal of time in Northern Cyprus, to help. The administrators, faced with the SFO's section 2 powers of compulsion and not bound by diplomatic protocol, came up with some fascinating information.

According to a court transcript dated 15 December 1992, Mr Howell of the accountancy firm Coopers & Lybrand told the SFO that he had travelled to Northern Cyprus the previous February. Here he met Kemal Birgen, a former manager of the Kirbris Industrie Bank, the bank which Asil Nadir claims to have used to repay the money taken from Unipac. Mr Howell says in his affadavit:

We discussed the cash deposits set out in the Binder Hamlyn report. Mr Birgen said that the deposit slips I had been shown were forgeries for two reasons. Firstly, no such large amounts of cash were ever received by the bank during his time as manager. Secondly, the deposit slips all had the word 'ALINDI' stamped on them, which is the equivalent of 'RECEIVED'. In fact, the bank continued to use the stamp with the English word 'RECEIVED' for deposit slips until after the date of most of the purported deposits.

Court documents also show that Mr Birgen had another meeting, this time with Mr Downing of Touche Ross. Downing claims that Birgen said to him: 'All the back-up documents included in the BDO report had been put together after his departure from IBK. Old-style bank forms had been printed especially and the information on these forms was false.' It was damning testimony which, if true, both gave an indication of Asil Nadir's power and influence on the island and showed the lengths to which he was prepared to go to avoid conviction.

The SFO was by now convinced that the Binder Hamlyn team had been misled by Asil Nadir, a possibility that the accountants themselves had never discounted. None the less, the fact remains that the SFO had never actually seen the Unipac books and, moreover, apparently decided it no longer needed to. In mid-1993, Robert Wardle and Lorna Harris finally got permission to visit Northern Cyprus but, despite being there for several days, they never went to see the Unipac books. Wardle justifies his action by saying: 'We wanted to look at all the books, not just the ones Nadir wants to show us.' Even so, it is a curious stance to take. Investigators normally want to see all the evidence, however tainted it might turn out to be.

The Binder Hamlyn saga, which had begun in June 1991, wasn't the only problem facing the SFO investigators at that time. The search of Polly Peck's London headquarters carried out on 30 October of the previous year had uncovered a number of documents which Peter Knight, Asil Nadir's lawyer, said were legally privileged and therefore confidential. It is normal practice for documents of this type to be placed in sealed bags until the matter at issue has been decided in court. On 14 November 1990 the SFO wrote to Peter Knight saying that the police had opened both of these sealed bags, but that this had been done solely for the purpose of preparing an inventory. While Knight wasn't pleased with this departure from routine, there was little he could do. He finally inspected the documents himself on 5 December and confirmed to the SFO that he regarded them all as legally privileged. The SFO then gave him a formal undertaking that the documents would not be touched again until after the matter had been properly resolved.

Unfortunately, the SFO's letter of 14 November didn't tell anything like the whole story. Just over three years later, George Staple, the director of the SFO, wrote to Knight saying he had discovered that, while preparing the inventory, the police had 'copied documents with a view to circulating them to members of the prosecution team, including counsel'. According to Staple's letter, dated 2 December 1993, copies of these privileged documents had also been sent to Coopers & Lybrand and Touche Ross, two of Polly Peck's administrators.

This was a major embarrassment for the SFO, but it wasn't the only breach of privilege to occur during the Polly Peck investigation. Some additional documents had also been seized during Asil Nadir's arrest on 15 December 1990. Once again, Peter Knight stated that these documents were legally privileged; but the SFO rejected this claim out of hand, saying that the letters were not communications between a solicitor and client for the purpose of obtaining or giving legal advice. The disputed material was then circulated to all the SFO's Polly Peck team members. However, nine months later, an independent lawyer adjudicating on the claim ruled that the source of the documents was indeed legally privileged and that the prosecution team should remove all copied material from their document sets. Unfortunately, said an apologetic George Staple to an apoplectic Peter Knight, 'we cannot be completely certain that all privileged documents were removed.' Apparently, a lack of page numbers coupled with poor descriptions of the documents themselves made them extremely hard to trace.

Anthony Scrivener, Nadir's counsel at the time, found the SFO's behaviour regarding the privileged legal documents both arrogant and incompetent. 'I was amazed at what had happened. The SFO seized a huge number of documents which should have been immediately logged, sealed in bags and then submitted to an independent QC to decide what, if anything, was relevant. Instead these bags were not only opened but some of the documents were circulated, not only to other members of the prosecution team but to outsiders as well. It was an extremely serious breach of Mr Nadir's legal rights.'

The Serious Fraud Office's mistakes were then further compounded when the Attorney-General, Sir Nicholas Lyell, acting on information provided by the SFO, misled Parliament. On 30 June 1993 he told the House of Commons: 'It is correct that two bags containing some privileged documents were opened in error by some police officers but the privileged documents were not copied.' Five months later, on 3 December 1993, he was back at the despatch box, this time to apologise for his earlier remarks. 'My statement was incomplete on the issue of privileged papers and therefore misleading,' he said. 'I am taking the earliest opportunity to correct it. It now appears that copies of privileged documents were circulated to the prosecution on two occasions. I regret that the fact that copies of privileged documents had been circulated was not acknowledged by the then case controller to Mr Nadir's solicitors.'

The story of Asil Nadir's legal documents does not reflect well on the Serious Fraud Office, but the significance of the SFO's actions should not be over-emphasised. According to Robert Wardle, 'The way some of these documents were handled was unfortunate, but nothing was done that actually undermined the defence in any way.' However, it was one of the factors which eventually led to George Staple's complete restructuring of the SFO to ensure, among other things, that there were better checking procedures and more supervision at all levels of the office.

Nor does the saga of Asil Nadir's privileged documents end with the SFO. A claim for £378 million was lodged against Asil Nadir personally by Polly Peck's administrators and he was subsequently made bankrupt in 1992. Neil Cooper, of accountancy firm Robson Rhodes, was appointed as his trustee in bankruptcy and soon set about trying to force Nadir to disgorge all his personal assets. While serving a warrant, Cooper's team removed yet more documents that Nadir claimed were legally privileged. While this claim was never fully established in court, the seizure further contributed to Nadir's growing distrust of the British legal system.

Asil Nadir was finally charged, on 22 October 1991, with seventy-six counts of theft and false accounting. The total sum involved amounted to a staggering £155 million. No charges were bought concerning the original share support allegations, although Wardle doesn't see this as a problem. 'I believe we were right to investigate,' he says, 'and we've found evidence of serious wrongdoing. The fact that the original suspicions don't figure in the charges is neither here nor there.' Then, on 8 June 1992, Mr Justice Tucker, the trial judge, suddenly dismissed forty-six of the SFO's charges. The reason, as with Levitt, was the success of the Gomez case in the Court of Appeal. The court had ruled that any money transfers done with the consent of both sides could not be theft, even if the victim had been defrauded into giving consent. It was a purely technical point, and Mr Justice Tucker made it clear that if the House of Lords reversed the decision, as it was likely to do, he would immediately allow the reinstatement of the charges. None the less, at this point it was seen as another humiliation for the SFO. On 9 June the *Independent* carried a major article headlined 'Nadir wins dismissal of charges' and Peter Lakin, Nadir's new solicitor, was quoted as saying: 'This is one of the best Monday mornings we've had for a long time. We are obviously very pleased with the outcome.' In fact, all forty-six charges were reinstated the following year.

It was with high hopes that Asil Nadir moved on to his next court battle with the SFO. He believed that Mr Justice Tucker's latest ruling suggested the judge was becoming more sympathetic towards him, and he wanted to get his passport back and have his bail terms varied so that he could visit Northern Cyprus. On 2 October 1992, Asil Nadir and Anthony Scrivener turned up at the Old Bailey hoping that the bail application would be approved. But, to their astonishment, there was no judge. According to Anthony Scrivener, 'it was amazing. I knew that he was in the building because I had spoken to him on the telephone. But he wouldn't come to court. And no one would say why. Eventually we were offered another judge, but the case was so complex that I turned that down. We all wanted to know what had happened to Justice Tucker.'

What had happened was actually the start of one of the most extraordinary stories in British legal history. The previous day, George Staple had been contacted by Acting Commander McStravick of New Scotland Yard, who said that one of his senior officers needed to see the SFO director as a matter of urgency. Detective Superintendent Jim Davies then came round to Elm Street and had a long conversation with George Staple in his large private office on the ninth floor of Elm House. According to Staple, 'Davies told me that they had been informed that a plot existed to bribe Mr Juctice Tucker and, although there was no evidence to support this, there was an assertion from the informant that the judge himself was involved.'

It was, by any standard, a shocking allegation and George Staple was taken aback, to say the least. 'I was absolutely astonished,' he says. 'It was simply unbelievable that a judge of the High Court could in any way be involved in anything of that kind and I certainly didn't believe that aspect of it. But, when a senior police officer comes and tells you that there is evidence of some kind of plot, it can't be ignored and it has to be investigated.'

The bribery allegation had been made by Michael Francis, also known as David Kent, a long-time police informer and a man with a conviction for attempted murder. Francis had first told his story to the police back in July 1992 when he was being held at Crawley police station. Since he was facing a number of drugs charges at the time, the police were initially sceptical. But Francis then showed them a typed and photocopied document which appeared to support his story. It said: 'We, Safiye Nadir and Bilge Nadir, irrevocably guarantee payment of £3,500,000 to David Kent within seven days of my departure from the United Kingdom. We declare this document to be legally binding and irrevocable.' Added to it was a handwritten note saying: 'We, the above named persons, sign on and for Mr Asil Nadir.' Safiye Nadir and Bilge Nadir are, respectively, Asil Nadir's mother and youngest sister. Francis then told the police that he had already received £500,000 from the Nadir family for his part in the plot. Later, in October, Wendy Welsher, a friend of Francis, came forward and claimed that he was indeed telling the truth.

While the evidence was far from convincing, George Staple knew that Mr Justice Tucker was due to hear Nadir's bail application and that he would have to move fast. 'I personally informed the senior judicial authorities of what was taking place the following morning,' says Staple. As a result of his intervention, Mr Justice Tucker was persuaded not to sit that day and the hearing was postponed. But it was several weeks before even those most intimately connected with the case were allowed to know the real reason why.

On 5 November, the day before Mr Justice Tucker was due to hear Nadir's rescheduled bail application, the SFO finally faxed a statement about the Michael Francis allegation to the judge's chambers. The document, which was marked 'confidential', was also sent to the Lord Chief Justice, the Attorney-General and Nadir's QC, Anthony Scrivener. It began by sketching out the details of the Francis story before continuing:

> Urgent investigations were made into the allegation and the origins of the document and further information was obtained. This information was to the effect that a) Nadir had personally been involved in an arrangement to pay money to influence the course of his bail application and b) Nadir had personally been involved in the disposal of assets, the property of either the administrators of PPI or of the trustee in bankruptcy. Investigations into both these areas continue urgently.

It was an astonishing message and, not surprisingly, it dominated the following day's court hearing. Robert Owen, the SFO's QC, then added fuel to the fire by telling Mr Justice Tucker that 'those responsible for the investigation instruct those instructing me that there is a probability that officers involved in the investigation would wish to interview your Lordship.' George Staple is adamant that the SFO was right to bring the matter to the attention of the trial judge. 'I think it was important to be candid with Justice Tucker,' he says, 'even though no one actually believed the allegations. If we hadn't done what we did, the entire Nadir case could have foundered.' It was not a view shared by Anthony Scrivener, who thinks that 'the whole bribery allegation was handled extremely poorly. The police should never have given it the weight they did and the SFO should never have raised it openly in court.'

Despite the fact that it was the SFO that sent the fax and told Mr Justice Tucker that he would probably be interviewed by the police, the SFO has always maintained that it had nothing to do with the investigation of the bribery allegation. The Attorney-General actually went to some lengths to spell out the position to Anthony Scrivener in a letter dated 13 November 1992. 'The nature of the allegation involving conspiracy to pervert the course of justice is quite distinct from those areas that are the province of the SFO and made it appropriate for these fresh allegations to be investigated by the Metropolitan Police as a separate issue,' wrote Sir Nicholas Lyell. 'This is what is happening at the moment with the Police seeking advice from the Director of Public Prosecutions as appropriate.'

But some of Asil Nadir's closest supporters remain convinced that the SFO was controlling the investigation in an attempt to get rid of Mr Justice Tucker following his decision to drop the forty-six theft charges. As well as the SFO's early involvement in circulating the Francis bribery allegation, they point to the contents of a search warrant drawn up by the Metropolitan Police while pursuing enquiries. According to testimony given by Chief Superintendent Thomas Glendenning, one of Scotland Yard's most senior officers and the man heading the bribery investigation, the warrant was executed 'on behalf of the SFO'. Nadir's supporters also believe that several of the police officers involved in the search had previously worked for the SFO and that one had even reported back to Elm Street on the success of the operation. Finally, they highlight the stark contrast between the SFO QC's claim that police officers would probably want to interview the judge and Glendenning's later statement in court that 'I never had evidence that would justify such a course of action.' Why, say the Nadir camp, should the SFO become so closely associated with this allegation unless it was trying to intimidate the judge?

That charge is comprehensively denied by the SFO. According to George Staple, the situation was unprecedented and it was important to keep the judge fully informed to ensure the trial was not jeopardised in any way. That, he says, is why the fax was sent setting out the situation and why Robert Owen made the statement that he did. Staple also points out that if Owen's statement is examined carefully, the phrase 'those responsible for the investigation instruct those instructing me' clearly implies that someone else – presumably the DPP – was responsible for suggesting that the police intended to question the judge. As to the warrant itself and the officers used in the search, that, says Staple, was a matter for the Metropolitan Police and not the Serious Fraud Office.

It's a strong defence, and it's almost certainly true. The one point that undermines it is the fact that the SFO – contrary to its claim – was not completely candid with Mr Justice Tucker. This deficiency was finally revealed in court on 8 March 1993. The DPP at last instructed its own QC and Alun Jones was given the unenviable job of telling Mr Justice Tucker the real extent of the Michael Francis allegations. It has to be said that had the DPP instructed its own QC rather earlier in the day, some of the confusion over the SFO's role in this affair might never have come about.

Alun Jones vividly remembers going to the Attorney-General to receive instructions and his astonishment on learning what he was being asked to do. According to Jones, 'The judge had to be told what the investigation was, whether well or ill founded. He had to be told because he didn't know the true nature of the allegation and otherwise it could have been said that there had been a cover-up. I knew it was going to be one of the most daunting moments of my professional life.'

When the time came, Jones rose to his feet and began. 'My Lord,' he said, 'there is a factual matter that should be cleared up. Although I am instructed, I feel it professionally right to tell your Lordship that the allegation that is being investigated is that the parties to the allegation of corruption are Mr Nadir, your Lordship . . .' There was a pause as Mr Justice Tucker realised what he was being told. 'Me?' he exclaimed. 'Your Lordship,' Jones repeated and then added, for good measure, 'Mr Scrivener and Assistant Commissioner Wyn Jones.' Mr Justice Tucker's face went puce with anger. He looked at Jones and said, in a voice full of disbelief: 'Is there anyone else you are going to include?' Jones, having finally outlined the extraordinary allegation in full, relaxed just a little. 'My Lord,' he said, 'that is the allegation which the police are investigating.'

It was a moment of pure theatre. Never before had a leading QC claimed that a High Court judge, the former chairman of the Bar Council and the Assistant Commissioner of the Metropolitan Police might have conspired together with an international tycoon to pervert the course of justice. But Jones wasn't done yet. 'My Lord,' he said, 'the police and I know more about the details of the allegations than I can disclose in court. My Lord, it is right to say that the police are pursuing enquiries and that the police have got to the stage from which it is reasonable to conclude that the allegation is not a hoax or a prank.'

Mr Justice Tucker was by now almost apoplectic with rage. 'Would you mind telling me what is the alleged connection between Mr Nadir, me, Mr Scrivener and Assistant Commissioner Wyn Jones?' he hissed. Alun Jones, perhaps now beginning to enjoy himself just a little, replied firmly: 'I cannot tell your Lordship that. It is an operational matter. The identity of the informants is an important consideration I have in mind.'

Not surprisingly, Jones still recalls the moment clearly. 'I can still remember the judge's expression,' he says with just the hint of a grin. 'He was flabbergasted by it. But it was the right thing to do because the judge could then make fully informed decisions about disclosure of documents and the like. And I'm pleased to say that I've appeared in front of Mr Justice Tucker on several occasions since and he always gives me a nice smile. I don't think he holds it against me.'

Michael Francis' allegations were investigated by the Metropolitan Police for almost twelve months. Francis told the police that the original of the photocopied document was in Switzerland. He also said that he had tapes which would corroborate his testimony and details of bank accounts which would show the money transfers. His close friend, Wendy Welsher, told the police that she had actually heard Asil Nadir bragging of his involvement in the plot and that she and a close relative of Nadir's had taken £300,000 to Switzerland in September 1991. Because of this, both Asil Nadir and his sister were arrested. However Francis, despite being taken to Switzerland by the police, never managed to produce either the original documentation or the bank statements. Welsher's testimony was also ultimately discredited.

On 30 June 1993 the Crown Prosecution Service finally announced to the relief of all concerned that there was 'no credible evidence' to substantiate any of the Francis allegations. This was immediately changed by a still furious Mr Justice Tucker to 'no evidence at all'. The judge went on: 'I have known from the start that all this is outrageous nonsense as far as I am concerned. I was very offended and very hurt when I heard these allegations made in open court. However I am gratified to hear you now say, as I of course know, that there was absolutely no vestige of truth in these allegations. I am surprised that anyone thought for any time that there could have been.'

Four years later, Michael Francis and Wendy Welsher appeared with Asil Nadir on Central Television's *Cook Report*, this time with a very different story to tell. In the programme transmitted on 13 May 1997 they claimed that the SFO and New Scotland Yard had forced them to make these allegations in an attempt to have the judge removed following his dismissal of the forty-six theft charges. Even putting aside Francis and Welsher's lack of credibility and the fact that they now live in Northern Cyprus as guests of Asil Nadir, their story still bears no scrutiny.

In an early statement made in support of this new fiction, Michael Francis said: 'Between January and February 1991, I was approached by a Detective Superintendent attached to the Serious Fraud Office. He asked me to contact Asil Nadir with the proposition that if Mr Nadir were to pay £3.5 million he could have the immediate return of his passport. The idea was to present the monies as part of a bribery plot designed by Asil Nadir to pervert the course of justice.' Wendy Welsher again echoed Francis, saying that she too was approached by a senior police officer before February 1991. The problem with their latest story is, of course, that Mr Justice Tucker had not thrown out any charges by February 1991. Indeed, he was not even the trial judge at the time.

Michael Francis' fantasies have actually helped no one. It seems most likely that he first made up the story simply to get himself off a drugs charge. He and Wendy Welsher might even have been trying to defraud Mr Nadir and his family. The police, in retrospect, gave their allegations far too much credence and should have dismissed the story more quickly than was actually the case. It undoubtedly led to Asil Nadir and his sister suffering a grave injustice. But Nadir's subsequent willingness to use Francis and Welsher for his own ends is equally unpalatable. He must know that they are liars, and the fact that he was prepared to appear in a television programme with them ultimately undermines his own claims to honesty.

The Francis and Welsher allegations reached their height in March 1993 when Alun Jones told the court that there were grounds to believe that the bribery story 'was not a hoax or a prank'. Asil Nadir's faith in British justice, already dented by the repeated removal of his legally privileged documents, was effectively shattered. But it wasn't the police and the SFO that finally convinced him it was time to flee from Britain to the relative safety of Northern Cyprus; it was the activities of his trustee in bankruptcy, Neil Cooper of Robson Rhodes.

Cooper's search for Nadir's assets had been frustrated for almost two years. Initially, Cooper had taken a low-key approach, trying to work with Nadir to identify and liquidate his assets in an orderly fashion to pay off his creditors. But Nadir was having none of it and did all he could to be as obstructive as possible. The tension between the two men came to a head in the spring of 1993 when Asil Nadir's Eaton Square flat was raided and all the furniture confiscated. As the Robson Rhodes men finished the job, one turned to Nadir and insisted he remove his wristwatch. According to Nadir, speaking on the *Cook Report*, 'The person that was conducting the raid saw a watch on my wrist, an inexpensive watch and, as he was leaving, he came back and said, I will take that watch off your wrist now.' At this point, it became clear that nothing more would be accomplished by agreement and so Cooper obtained a series of court warrants which meant that if Nadir did not surrender all his assets, he would ultimately be put in gaol. It was the last straw.

On 4 May 1993 Nadir was driven by Peter Dimond, a pilot and a family friend, to Compton Abbas airfield in Dorset, where he and Dimond took off for France in a small plane. From there Nadir flew to Turkey and then to Northern Cyprus. He told British newspapers immediately after his flight that he had been carrying a gun and would have been prepared to shoot anyone who tried to stop him. Nadir now joined Elizabeth Forsyth, the former head of South Audley Management, who had also taken refuge in Northern Cyprus.

Since Nadir's escape, it has been alleged that the SFO knew that he was going to flee. This claim is based on a letter that Ramadan Gurney, the man who had put up most of Nadir's £3.5 million bail money, sent to the Central Criminal Court on 29 April 1993. Gurney said that he wanted to ask the court to withdraw his surety as a matter of urgency. However, what is rather less well known is that just twenty-four hours later a second letter was received from Gurney saying that no further action need be taken and that the original request was based on a misunderstanding between himself and Asil Nadir. In retrospect, perhaps it should have set alarm bells ringing; but, as Robert Wardle says, it is difficult to see what more the SFO could have done. 'We were in an impossible position,' he says. 'The SFO had always objected to bail, but when the court decided to grant it, there was very little more that we could do. The SFO simply doesn't have the resources to keep a man under surveillance for twenty-four hours a day, seven days a week for a period of two or three years and neither should it have to. It's for the court to evaluate the risk and it had decided it was safe for Nadir to remain at large. After that, it's out of our hands.'

Nadir's return to Northern Cyprus wasn't the end of the affair. One of Nadir's greatest allies in Britain was Michael Mates, then Northern Ireland minister. Mates first met Nadir in the autumn of 1991 and soon became convinced that the authorities had treated him very badly indeed. While never commenting on Nadir's guilt or innocence, Mates had expressed his concerns in Parliament several times. But it wasn't until after Nadir had fled the country that the media discovered that Michael Mates, a government minister, had bought Asil Nadir, a fugitive from justice, a new watch to replace the one that had been so unceremoniously removed. On the back of the watch was the inscription: 'Don't let the buggers get you down'. Unsurprisingly, this discovery caused a massive parliamentary row. Then, a few days later, it emerged that one of Nadir's associates had briefly given Michael Mates' wife free use of a car and the row boiled over again. Finally, a letter that Mates had written to the Attorney-General, expressing grave doubts about the way the Nadir case was being handled, was leaked to the press. The media went into a complete frenzy and Mates resigned from the government. But he still had one shot left.

At 3.32 p.m. on 29 June 1993, Michael Mates began one of the most powerful resignation speeches of recent years. He started by criticising the raids on South Audley Management and Polly Peck, claiming that the searches were done in the full glare of publicity. 'A trial by media had begun,' he announced, 'aided and encouraged by the Serious Fraud Office.' It's a claim that has been made by many people, but the fact is that no press were present at the start of either of the SFO raids.

Mates then went on to chastise the SFO for not following up the Binder Hamlyn report. He said the SFO had maintained that it is impossible to go to Northern Cyprus because it is not a recognised country. 'But', said Mates, 'it is well known that the police have on occasion visited Northern Cyprus to make enquiries in connection with criminal proceedings in this country. I simply do not know why they could not follow up the usual practice.' However, Mates made no reference to the nine informal approaches which were rebuffed by the TRNC, or to Kemal Birgen's evidence that the report itself was based on forged documents. While Mates is right to suggest that it would have been better for the SFO to have physically examined the documentation, he should also have mentioned that it seems extremely unlikely that the source material on which the report was based was genuine in the first place.

Undoubtedly Michael Mates' most telling point concerned the SFO's handling of Asil Nadir's privileged legal documents. 'It was admitted', he told Parliament, 'that two bags were opened, but it was claimed this was a misunderstanding. In fact, more than two bags were opened. This is another unsatisfactory part of the story that needs to be investigated.' Unlike his previous two points, this criticism was well founded and George Staple later took action to correct the situation.

Mates finished what was unquestionably an electrifying resignation speech by retelling the story of the Francis bribery allegation. He claimed that 'the SFO misled the judge about the intentions of the police.' But, as has already been shown, Robert Owen, the SFO's QC, was simply reporting what the DPP believed to be the position at the time. Indeed, the DPP went much further four months later when Alun Jones told the judge about the real nature of the conspiracy allegations.

Mates' speech shocked the country Few people then understood all the intricacies of the Nadir case, and not everything is clear even now. But Robert Wardle remains convinced that the criticisms of the SFO were blown out of all proportion. He says: 'Mates' resignation speech was extraordinary. I watched it on television open-mouthed. I kept thinking, does he mean us? So much of it was unfair. Eventually things got so bad that George Staple had to go on television and try to put things in context.'

George Staple, too, watched the broadcast in amazement. 'I remember it very well,' he says. 'It was a much heralded parliamentary occasion and nobody who watched could have been disappointed. In some respects, it was a tour de force. Unfortunately, I thought much of its contents were quite unjustified and very unfair to the Serious Fraud Office. I knew straight away that these points would need to be answered by the House of Commons, and so we spent all evening briefing the Attorney-General to enable him to get up in the House the following day and deal with the complaints.'

Despite Mates' intervention, Asil Nadir has stayed in Northern Cyprus since May 1993; but his loyal lieutenant, Elizabeth Forsyth, returned to Britain on 19 September 1994. She was memorably described by the *Guardian* as 'Britain's most wanted grandmother' and, even less flatteringly, by a senior SFO officer as 'Asil Nadir's stalking mare'. When Forsyth arrived back, she was taken directly to Holborn police station and later charged with two counts of knowingly handling £400,000 of stolen money. According to Robert Wardle, 'we interviewed her at length and recorded over thirty tapes in the process. I was primarily concerned about the jurisdictional problems, that is to say where the crime had been committed. But, as we interviewed her, it became increasingly clear that a UK trial was appropriate and so we decided to prosecute.'

Elizabeth Forsyth's case was transferred to the Crown Court in February 1995 and began just twelve months later with Mr Justice Tucker presiding. Both sides were soon confronted by major problems. Forsyth was horrified to learn that the judge was not prepared to allow Asil Nadir to testify via satellite link from Northern Cyprus. And the SFO was distraught to find out that two of its key prosecution witnesses, both based in Switzerland, were unwilling to give evidence. None the less, the SFO remained determined to proceed. It knew it had a lot of high-quality paper evidence and it was confident it could still mount a strong case. Interestingly, it decided to reveal everything it knew about the Francis/Welsher allegations, and yet this never became an issue in the trial. This seems to suggest that the defence may have come to the view that there is ultimately little or nothing to be gained from it for either Elizabeth Forsyth or Asil Nadir.

The five-week trial was described by one journalist who attended every day as 'bitty'. Another reporter summed up the proceedings unflatteringly for both sides by saying that 'the Serious Fraud Office's case seemed surprisingly weak – until Forsyth gave evidence. She virtually convicted herself.' It took the jury, consisting of seven women and five men, almost twelve hours to reach an eleven to one guilty verdict on each of the charges. Finally, on 22 March 1996, Elizabeth Forsyth was convicted of two counts of handling stolen money and sentenced to five years' imprisonment. To most onlookers it seemed an overly harsh sentence, almost as if Forsyth were being punished as a proxy for Asil Nadir. But the conviction itself only stood for ten months: the Court of Appeal ruled that it had to be considered unsafe on a number of grounds, primarily because the judge's summation was technically flawed.

Elizabeth Forsyth's release was seized upon as yet another stick with which to beat the Serious Fraud Office. The SFO's very vocal critics now pointed to six separate areas where, they said, the Polly Peck case was handled poorly: the original raids; the SFO's unwillingness to go to Northern Cyprus to examine the Binder Hamlyn documents; the removal of Asil Nadir's legal papers; the SFO's involvement in the corruption investigation; Nadir's flight; and Forsyth's release. There is no doubt that, in the public's mind, the Polly Peck saga was very much part of the nightmare on Elm Street. Yet, when each of these criticisms is examined in the cold light of day, only one seems to stand serious scrutiny, namely the handling of Nadir's legal papers; and even that has been blown out of all proportion. Robert Wardle is convinced that the SFO's handling of the Polly Peck case will eventually be fully vindicated. 'The SFO has assembled a very large body of evidence against Asil Nadir,' he says. 'If he ever does come back to Britain, we will certainly prosecute the case and a jury will have to decide his honesty or dishonesty with regard to Polly Peck.'

8

Down but not Out

ASIL NADIR'S DECISION to flee the country rather than stand trial stands in stark contrast to that taken by another equally high-profile defendant. George Walker, the former chief executive of Brent Walker, also faced a series of theft and false accounting charges brought by the Serious Fraud Office. But Walker, once a successful boxer, never considered running away. Instead, he was determined to have his day in court and give evidence in the witness box. Still angry over his treatment by both his former company and the SFO, he says: 'I insisted on going in the box. I'd done nothing wrong. I'd stolen nothing. I knew that if I wasn't prepared to stand up and be counted, the jury would think I was guilty.'

George Walker's pugnacious stance is typical of the man who literally fought his way to the top. Walker, an East End boy, left school at fourteen with no qualifications and began working as a porter at Billingsgate fish market. It was his boxing ability that first marked him out. Fans of the sport still recall Walker's utter determination to win, and in 1951 he became a British champion. However, it was some years later, as boxing manager to his younger brother Billy, nicknamed the 'blond bomber', that George Walker finally discovered his true vocation. He used Billy's prodigious earning power to set up a series of businesses, including a fast food chain called Billy's Baked Potatoes and the Uppercut night club in London's Forest Gate. By the early sixties, Walker's ability to see what would appeal to the average punter had turned him into a highly successful businessman. He began specialising in buying under-performing property assets like swimming pools and cinemas and transforming them into successful modern leisure facilities. In 1967, Walker took his company public and then doubled its size again by merging with Hackney and Hendon greyhound stadiums. His reputation was finally made by his gutsy decision in the mid-1970s to back the construction of the Brent Cross shopping complex in north London, then one of the largest shopping malls in Europe.

Yet despite these early successes, George Walker's relationship with the City was never a particularly happy one. In 1982 he took Brent Walker private, only to refloat the company three years later. But even this period away from the limelight did not allay the City's fears and, although Brent Walker continued to produce above-average profits throughout the mid-eighties, its shares always traded at a discount to the market. Surprise acquisitions, like the 1985 purchase of the Brighton Marina, and the company's apparent inability to stick to a coherent management strategy made many institutions wary of what looked suspiciously like a one-man band.

For all its reservations, though, the City could not ignore the fact that Brent Walker continued to grow at a frenetic pace and, by 1988, had become a very successful diversified leisure company. Although financed primarily through borrowings, Brent Walker's asset sheet looked impressive and included 386 pubs, a number of casinos, the Trocadero shopping complex in London's Piccadilly and Goldcrest, the British film production company. Even the company's share price seemed to have firmed up and a rights issue was planned to fund further investments. But it was at this moment that things started to go very badly wrong for George Walker.

On 8 August 1988, the *Independent* published the results of a secret three-month investigation into Brent Walker. Headlined 'Brent Walker's paranormal profits', it raised serious doubts about the film division's apparent profitability. Using leaked internal documents, the *Independent* had come to the conclusion that a large proportion of Brent Walker's profits growth had come from the fictitious sale of film rights.

The leaked papers showed that Brent Walker had told its auditors that a 1986 drama series on the paranormal, called *Worlds Beyond* and starring Denholm Elliott, had been sold in the United States for £3.2 million. The following year, according to the company, the same series had brought in a further £4 million. But, said the *Independent*, these figures were as fantastic as the series itself. Such large returns would have made it one of the best-selling series of all time, whereas entertainment industry experts believed *Worlds Beyond* had actually netted only about $400,000.

The *Independent* then asked the question: who would have paid such ridiculously large sums of money for such a run-of-the-mill series? The answer, it said, was an obscure Isle of Man nominee company called Universal Talent Management. The one person the paper could find who had ever heard of UTM was Sallie Yong Murphy, a French woman living in Virginia. According to UTM's company records, Sallie Murphy was a director of the company, although she was apparently not aware of this fact until the newspaper told her.

Ms Murphy told the *Independent* that, in 1979 or 1980, she had been approached by an Englishman who wanted to set up a discreet private company. 'I had to act as a witness, or something of that sort,' she said. 'I didn't realise that they had listed me as a director.' The man who had asked her for help almost a decade earlier was John Quested, now the managing director of Brent Walker's film division. The implication was clear: Brent Walker had artificially boosted its profits by pretending to sell film rights to a company with which it had a connection.

It was a first-class piece of reporting and it caused an immediate explosion in Brent Walker's head office. George Walker remembers the article well. 'I couldn't believe what I was reading,' he says. 'Goldcrest was a good money maker for us but it was a very small part of the operation. It had about a hundred employees out of nineteen thousand on Brent Walker's payroll and so I tended to leave it alone. Now here was a suggestion that somebody in the film division was up to no damn good.'

Walker felt he had no choice but to act quickly. Not only would the article undermine confidence in the share price but, worse still, it could destroy the rights issue he was putting together to fund Brent Walker's further expansion. 'I obviously needed to know what had really happened,' he recalls. 'I called in KPMG, the

accountants, along with Simmons & Simmons, the law firm. I told
them that I wanted them to go in and tear Goldcrest apart and find
out what was really going on.'

The internal review took two weeks to complete; then, on 16
September 1988, a press release was put out to the Stock Exchange
confirming that the two payments under review were indeed
genuine and had been properly transacted. But despite this assurance, matters didn't end there. In December, the Serious Fraud
Office announced that it too was going to investigate the allegations
made against Brent Walker.

The company immediately re-engaged KPMG and Simmons &
Simmons to co-ordinate its response to the SFO. None the less, the
SFO still decided to take full statements from both John Quested
and Donald Anderson, Goldcrest's finance director. Quested and
Anderson told the SFO exactly what they had told Brent Walker's
internal inquiry: the *Independent* story was wrong and the film sales
were legitimate. However, unknown to KPMG, Simmons &
Simmons or the SFO, Quested and Anderson were lying and had
falsified evidence to prevent the truth from coming out. Initially
the deception was successful, and on 23 October 1990 the SFO
announced that it was discontinuing its inquiries.

But Brent Walker hadn't stood still during the two years it had
been under SFO investigation. In 1989 George Walker had taken
his biggest gamble to date, paying £685 million for William Hill
and Mecca Bookmakers, thus making Brent Walker the owner of
one of the largest chains of betting shops in the world. Given the
signs of impending recession, this was always going to be a high-
risk purchase and it plunged Brent Walker even further into debt,
but George Walker was convinced that the £30 million cash flow
produced by the shops would ensure that the company survived the
downturn.

What Walker hadn't reckoned on, however, was the two body
blows his company received during 1990. The first was the
withdrawing of a £150 million Japanese bank loan which had
already been verbally agreed. The second was that William Hill's
warranted profit figure of £55 million annually was deeply inaccu-
rate. 'We were in big trouble,' Walker recalls, still indignant at what

happened. 'The collapse of the Japanese deal meant we couldn't renew our short-term loans, and then I found out that we'd been given false figures for William Hill. It was actually only making £40 million a year and so I said that we weren't prepared to pay the £50 million that was still owed for the company. Of course, everyone immediately said "Brent Walker's got money problems" and that caused even more problems.'

Brent Walker's forty-seven bankers, led by Standard Chartered, made it clear that they were not prepared to lend the beleaguered company any more money. Walker was told forcefully that the only way forward was for the company to organise its own bond issue. This meant Brent Walker persuading investors to buy interest-bearing promissory notes, redeemable at a specified date in the future. This type of bond issue was particularly popular at the time as banks had become extremely nervous about over-exposing themselves to any type of risk.

George Walker knew that a bond issue was the only thing that would stop the banks pulling the plug on the company he had spent twenty-five years building up, and so he did everything possible to ensure its success. He persuaded Michael Smurfit, the Irish industrialist, to invest £25 million; British businessman Tiny Rowland agreed to contribute another £5 million. But, even with all of Walker's considerable bargaining skills, he could still only raise £60 million, and the banks were adamant that £100 million was the minimum needed to ensure Brent Walker's survival.

Matters came to a head in early November 1990 when the Standard Chartered Bank invited Walker to dinner at its prestigious City offices in Aldermanbury Square. During the sumptuous meal, the bank made its position crystal clear. It was prepared to accept the bond issue raising less than £100 million, but the Walker family would have to commit its entire fortune to the success of the company. 'It was agreed,' says Walker bitterly, 'that I would put every penny I had into the bond issue, which was just under £3 million. It was also agreed that I would invest my children's entire trust fund, which came to about £27 million. In total, we would put in £30 million on top of the £60 million that I had already raised. The banks would lend the rest.'

George Walker remained concerned about one aspect of the deal, and on 26 November 1990 he wrote to Malcolm Williamson, the Standard Chartered director handling the deal, to seek clarification. 'During the evening,' said Walker in his letter, 'a discussion alighted upon the fact that possibly I could be removed as chairman and chief executive. As you know, I have always agreed to accept a suitable non-executive chairman. I do not believe, however, that I could accept the idea of not being chief executive unless I was executive chairman. I can't put this amount of money into a company and not control its future. I just want to make this clear before we go ahead.' The contents of the letter seem unambiguous. George Walker wanted Standard Chartered's assurance that he would remain as either chairman or chief executive of Brent Walker before he invested his family's money.

Malcolm Williamson's reply was equally straightforward. His letter first of all said: 'I do not believe that the suggestion that you should be removed as chairman and chief executive arose in any circumstances other than the possible failure of the Bond Issue.' He then went on to outline the banks' plans for the company if the bond issue were successful, and made it clear that the banks wanted a new chairman, a new finance director and several new non-executive directors. At the end of his two-page letter, he returns to Walker's central point. 'I do realise', says Williamson, 'that you are putting a lot of your own money into a company that you have both built and run for a long time. The above issues summarise what I believe to be important factors on which the banks and shareholders will judge the running of a public company over the coming years and are meant to strengthen your position rather than weaken it.'

George Walker was reassured by the letter and particularly by its claim that the proposed changes of senior personnel were intended to strengthen rather than weaken his position. He therefore decided to go ahead with the plan that had been agreed and invested almost £30 million in the Brent Walker bond issue. Six months later, he was ousted as chief executive in a boardroom coup inspired by Standard Chartered Bank.

The board meeting that ended up sacking George Walker was held on 31 May 1991. It was meant to have begun at 7.30 p.m. but, as the directors assembled at Brent Walker's offices in London's Trocadero centre near Piccadilly Circus, the company's new chairman, Lord Kindersley, telephoned and asked for the meeting to be delayed by several hours. He was, he said ominously, still with the company's bankers. After a brief discussion, the other directors including George Walker adjourned to one of Brent Walker's nearby casinos for dinner. At this point, nobody had any inkling of what was going to happen next.

The directors finally re-assembled at 11 p.m. and the chairman arrived soon afterwards, accompanied by Malcolm Williamson. George Walker was well aware that he had become a thorn in Standard Chartered's side. The bank wanted to sell William Hill to reduce the company's debt, but Walker refused to countenance such an idea. The price Brent Walker was being offered was substantially less than it had paid for the bookmakers just two years earlier, and anyway, said Walker, it was William Hill's cash flow that was keeping the company alive.

It didn't take long for the reason why Malcolm Williamson was attending the Brent Walker board meeting to become clear. He gave each of the directors a letter saying that the company would continue to have the support of the banks only if the chief executive was immediately fired. 'Well, you can imagine this was a bit of a shock,' says George Walker in something of an understatement. 'The other directors quite rightly said that we need to stop the board meeting, get legal advice and reconvene tomorrow. But Williamson said "No. If you get up from this table without firing George Walker I will put the company into receivership and I've got two men waiting outside ready to do it."'

The board spent over five and a half hours discussing what to do before finally putting the matter to the vote at 4.30 the following morning. Three directors backed Walker and three abstained, but four directors plus the chairman voted that he should go. 'The meeting broke up just before five,' recalls George Walker. 'There were tears, there were directors crying, the whole lot. This had been a very, very tough meeting and, to give Malcolm Williamson his credit, I'd never met a tougher banker. He rammed it home to them and they were terrified.'

George Walker was completely stunned by this sudden turn of events. He felt that the meeting had been improperly conducted and that he had personally been betrayed by the Standard Chartered Bank. 'I think what the bank did was diabolical,' he says, still angry at events now more than five years past. 'They had entered into a written agreement with me and broken it. They had sat in on a public company's board meeting, threatened the directors and made them fire the chief executive. It's unheard of for a public company board meeting to run from eleven o'clock at night until five o'clock the following morning. Some of the directors were in their seventies. How the hell are they going to think responsibly about sacking their chief executive under those circumstances?'

But these charges are absolutely rejected by Standard Chartered. Sources close to the bank point out that Brent Walker's financial condition had substantially deteriorated since Malcolm Williamson's letter was sent out and that urgent action was needed to redeem the situation. They also say that the letter was not a contract and never promised to guarantee George Walker's position. Finally, they emphasise that the bank has a duty to behave responsibly not only towards Brent Walker but towards its own shareholders as well.

George Walker may have been battered by this onslaught, but he wasn't beaten. He used his huge shareholding in the company to repel an attempt to throw him off the board of directors altogether and then began a series of legal actions to establish that the company had indeed behaved improperly. It was at this stage that the SFO again became involved in the affairs of Brent Walker.

Two months after the acrimonious board meeting that brought about Walker's departure, Lord Kindersley and the new Brent Walker board contacted the SFO and asked for a meeting. According to a senior SFO insider, 'We met them on 23 August 1991. They had fifteen areas of concern and, as they talked, it became clear that we needed to take another look at Brent Walker.' The company itself said later in a press release that it had requested that the SFO 'investigate certain aspects of the affairs of the group and its associated companies and the SFO had decided to do so'.

Tricia Howse, a blonde, chain-smoking former Customs and Excise lawyer, was the case controller for the SFO's second Brent Walker investigation. Howse has been with the SFO since it was first set up and was renowned for her energetic and committed approach to fraud investigations. 'The first thing I did,' she says, 'was to sit down with KPMG and go through their interim report line by line. Then I organised a series of section 2 interviews with the relevant Brent Walker management in order to gather as much information and evidence as possible.' Finally, the SFO raided Brent Walker's offices and removed what was described at the time as a van-load of documents.

In many ways the allegations that had been made by the Brent Walker board were similar, if not identical, to those which had previously been investigated. Most of them related to the film division and suggested that Goldcrest had used Brent Walker's money to make it appear that sales had been made when nothing had actually happened. Once again, the *Worlds Beyond* series was at the centre of the maelstrom.

George Walker was furious with Brent Walker's new directors for bringing in the SFO. 'These were old allegations,' he says. 'They had already been investigated by KPMG, Simmons & Simmons and the SFO. Now they had dusted off the same old files and bought the SFO back in. The one thing it did was discredit me and undermine my attempts to get my company back.' It's a view shared, to an extent, by George Walker's lawyer, Michael Coleman of Harkaveys. He is also suspicious of the board's motives for re-involving the SFO. However, he does accept that the SFO had a job to do. 'It is right that allegations of dishonesty are properly investigated,' he says. 'But I'm not sure that the SFO went in with a completely open mind. The allegations were a relatively minor issue within one division. Yet the SFO seems to have started out with the idea that this was something very big and would result in a major prosecution.'

This assertion is utterly rejected by Tricia Howse, who insists that 'the evidence we assembled showed that there was a strong prima facie case of fraud at Brent Walker and it seemed to us at the time that George Walker was at the heart of it.' Howse's belief was partly based on the discovery, two months into her investigation, of file 1913, which became known as 'the plotters' file'. This showed that Brent Walker's film division had indeed self-funded much of its declared profits and, more importantly, that a number of senior people had always known what was going on. Furthermore, according to an SFO insider closely involved with the case, Wilfred Aquilina, Brent Walker's former finance director, later confirmed this during his section 2 interview. But, as the SFO investigation progressed, it began to look at more than just the old false accounting allegations. The SFO also started to examine several new accusations involving George Walker personally.

The first of these related to £7.5 million which, on 26 May 1989, had been transferred from Brent Walker's account at Standard Chartered Bank in London to Goldcrest's account at the Arab Banking Corporation in New York. From here, the money went to an offshore trust company based in Hamilton, Bermuda. According to the SFO, these transfers were made on the instructions of George Walker and Donald Anderson, Goldcrest's finance director, and were not for any legitimate company business.

The second allegation involved a sum of £5 million which was transferred from Brent Walker's account at Standard Chartered on 24 August 1989 to Goldcrest's Los Angeles bank account. From here, the money was wired to an offshore trust in Nassau, Bahamas. Once again, said the SFO, this was done at the behest of George Walker and Donald Anderson and was not for any legitimate company business.

George Walker himself aggressively denied any wrongdoing and said that he could answer all points raised. He told the SFO that he had written to the Arab Banking Corporation weeks before the £7.5 million transfer request had been made, instructing it to move monies above £50,000 only on receipt of a written letter signed by himself and followed up by a telephone confirmation. Despite these instructions, ABC had transferred the £7.5 million with just a faxed authorisation. Why, argued Walker, would he have given ABC these instructions if he intended to move money illicitly by fax?

In respect of the £5 million transfer allegation, Walker claimed that he would never have given approval for such a large sum of money to be moved offshore. Furthermore, said Walker, Goldcrest's Los Angeles bankers had made this transaction only after being shown a board minute which apparently authorised a number of senior executives, including George Walker, to approve this type of money transfer. But investigations had revealed that this board minute was bogus. Why, said Walker, would he have been party to the forging of a board minute which only gave him the power to do that which he could do already?

It was a good point but, to Walker's intense frustration, the SFO did not accept it, and on 8 January 1993 he was charged with the theft of £12.5 million. He was also charged, along with Wilfred Aquilina, the former Brent Walker finance director, on two counts of false accounting. Together, it was alleged, they had conspired to commit a fraud on the creditors and shareholders of Brent Walker involving a total of £164 million.

John Quested, the former managing director of Goldcrest, was separately charged with lying to the SFO during a section 2 interview that he had given to the office during its first investigation into Brent Walker. This came to court in December 1993 and Quested was convicted of giving the SFO false and misleading information. However, the outcome of this case was kept secret to prevent it prejudicing the upcoming trial of Walker and Aquilina.

The one man initially missing from the Brent Walker proceedings was Donald Anderson, the New Zealand national who had been the finance director of Goldcrest during the period of the alleged fraud. He had fled the country in July 1992 during a round of interviews with the SFO and couldn't be found to be extradited. Anderson did, however, return to the United Kingdom of his own volition shortly after Walker and Aquilina's trial had finished and was later prosecuted himself.

The SFO's decision to bring charges against George Walker came as a surprise to the former boxer. Walker claims that the evidence was always against his being involved in the fraud and that the SFO knew this. He now believes that his prosecution was primarily motivated by the SFO's need for a high-profile conviction during its nightmare years. 'The SFO had just lost Blue Arrow and one of the Guinness cases had collapsed,' he says. 'It was getting a lot of stick in the press and I think if they had nailed me, an East Ender and an ex-boxer, it would have been seen as a real feather in its cap. I think no matter what the evidence was, they were determined to convict me and I guess they thought if they could get me into court, their barristers could make me look guilty even though I wasn't.'

Walker also believes that there was another, more insidious force at work behind his prosecution. 'Some powerful people wanted me tied up with a Serious Fraud Office investigation rather than fighting to win back my company. They told the SFO that I was guilty and the SFO wanted it to be true. The fact that the evidence pointed in another direction wasn't an issue.' Not surprisingly, this is a claim that is forcefully denied by Tricia Howse. She says: 'We investigated this case without fear or favour. We carried out our own very thorough investigation and prosecuted on the basis of the evidence we assembled.'

Interestingly, George Walker also claims, like some of the Blue Arrow defendants, that the police working on the case took a very different view from the lawyers. 'One of the policeman said to me,' recalls Walker, '"We've got nothing." And I said to him, "Well, that's because there isn't anything to find." I think if the police had got their way, I would never have been prosecuted.'

Despite the apparent reservations of some of the police involved, the case against George Walker and Wilfred Aquilina opened at the Chichester Rents courtrooms in Chancery Lane on 2 June 1994. The SFO's case was that Walker and Aquilina, together with Quested and Anderson, had conspired fraudulently to inflate the profits of Brent Walker during the 1980s, using a complex network of offshore companies. The case, particularly against Walker, looked weak from the beginning. Within ten days of the trial starting, Peter Rook, the SFO's QC, had to concede that George Walker's signature had indeed been forged on several documents, a strange thing to happen to the alleged fraudster-in-chief.

However, everyone knew that the heart of this trial was always going to be the testimony given by George Walker himself, and no one was willing to take a final view until they had heard what he had to say. Eventually the time came for Walker to go into the witness box; he ended up giving evidence for a marathon eighteen days.

Walker remembers being tremendously apprehensive about the ordeal before it began. 'I was nervous and I was tired,' he says. 'But once it started, it became a contest, a fight. Peter Rook got the better of me several times and I realised that his job was to make me look bad. After one particularly bruising encounter, I turned to the jury and said, "He's very clever. He made me slip up. He's trained to do it. That's his job. But I'm not lying. I just made a mistake." And the jury believed me.'

One of the more unexpected facts to emerge from the trial was that one of Brent Walker's senior executives had being working for MI6, the British Secret Intelligence Service. Government officials confirmed to Michael Coleman, George Walker's lawyer, that George Kieffer had provided help on 'sensitive' matters when he travelled abroad for the company and that Walker had been supportive of his extra-curricular activities. The officials even offered to tell the judge in private of Walker's co-operation, should it be necessary to help mitigate a sentence.

When Roy Amlott QC came to sum up for the defence, he said that the SFO had used a 'blunderbuss' of a conspiracy charge when it was clear that the wrongdoing really involved only Brent Walker's film division. There had been no mention of the company's huge entertainments empire, which was where George Walker and Wilfred Aquilina spent the vast majority of their time. If they really had intended to perpetrate a fraud, suggested Amlott, it would not have been in the film division.

The jury, consisting of ten men and two women, were finally sent out to consider their verdicts on 18 October 1994. The trial had taken four and a half months and cost over £2 million. They spent seven days deliberating before announcing that George Walker had been found not guilty on all counts. 'I felt unbelievably relieved,' remembers Walker. 'But I also felt unbelievably angry. The SFO had put me through all this and for what? They knew they didn't have a case. I tell you this,' he adds, still reliving the experience, 'if it wasn't for my wife, I'd have done something unbelievably stupid after the trial had finished.'

Michael Coleman also doesn't believe that the Serious Fraud Office ever really had a case against Walker. He says: 'I don't think for a second that the SFO was either dishonest or incompetent. But I do think that it was massively over-ambitious. The SFO was diverted from the truth by its desire to prosecute a big name like George Walker. It was only interested in facts that went against Walker, not in facts that went for him.'

George Walker himself claims that the most unpleasant part of being involved in this type of trial is that even a not guilty verdict doesn't completely remove the taint. According to him, 'Even my own brother, Billy, still doesn't believe that I'm innocent. I remember on one occasion, he pulled me to one side and said, "You have got the money, haven't you?" And I said to him, "Billy, I put the money in. I didn't take any out." He looked at me in amazement. He still can't quite believe that I'm innocent. And neither does the rest of the world. But it's the truth.'

Walker's co-defendant, Wilfred Aquilina, was convicted on one count of false accounting, relating to a £4.5 million payment to an offshore company. Judge Geoffrey Rivlin told him that his false accounting had been a 'serious act' and that an 'aggravating feature' had been giving accountants a handwritten bank statement which he knew to be false. He then sentenced the former finance director to an eighteen-month suspended prison term and a fine of £25,000. It was all too much for Aquilina, who was suffering from clinical depression. He burst into tears and sobbed, 'I want to die.'

The final Brent Walker trial was brought in the autumn of 1996 when Donald Anderson went into the dock. He was convicted of attempting to pervert the course of justice by organising a wide-ranging cover-up of what was described in court as 'the Brent Walker profits fraud'. The jury accepted that Anderson had created a series of false documents between August 1988 and October 1990 to conceal the fact that £19 million of false profits had been invented by the company to mislead shareholders and bankers alike. Anderson was sentenced to two years' imprisonment and disqualified from being a company director for five years.

It's difficult to sum up the Brent Walker story. Bankers and shareholders, including George Walker, who had the biggest stake of all, lost over £2 billion. The film division's profits had clearly been artificially inflated and a concerted attempt had been made to conceal the truth from both the auditors and the Serious Fraud Office. Tricia Howse believes that the final outcome was a vindication for the SFO. 'We prosecuted a total of four people in the Brent Walker case,' she points out, 'and we got convictions against three of them. We also established that a serious fraud had taken place. To that extent, I think we did a good job.'

But it's the figure of George Walker that dominates this affair, just as he dominated Brent Walker, and he makes two powerful points. First, he says, the SFO was manipulated into investigating him; and second, he was prosecuted against the run of the evidence. For its part, the SFO claims that Walker had a case to answer and that it was right that these charges were put to a jury. In as much as the case was not struck out by the judge at half-time, the SFO seems to have a point. It is beyond doubt, however, that as far as the public were concerned, the outcome of the Brent Walker case pushed the Serious Fraud Office even deeper into the mire. It became a media myth that the 'Seriously Flawed Office' was facing disbandment by the government, although, in reality, it continued to enjoy a healthy conviction rate and retained the wholehearted support of Sir Nicholas Lyell, the Attorney-General. But the public's perception of the SFO was going to get even worse before it finally started to get better.

9

The Max Factor

PERHAPS THE MOST FAMOUS CASE of all those handled by
the Serious Fraud Office was its investigation into the events
leading up to the collapse of the Maxwell group of companies.
Robert Maxwell, the founder of the group, was a billionaire media
mogul who owned two huge public corporations, the Maxwell
Communications Corporation and Mirror Group Newspapers,
as well as a large number of smaller private companies. He
had accumulated his vast wealth over four decades and in the
face of massive hostility from both the British establishment
and the media. In the early 1970s a damning DTI report
proclaimed him unfit to run a public company, and doubts about
his business ethics continued up to his mysterious death on 5
November 1991.

It is generally thought that the Serious Fraud Office began its first
investigation into the Maxwell group just after Robert Maxwell
died, when the Swiss Bank Corporation reported that its £57
million loan had not been repaid and that the assets on which it had
been secured had apparently gone missing. But the SFO's first file
on Robert Maxwell, numbered MAX 001, was actually opened two
months earlier, following the transmission in September 1991 of
BBC *Panorama*'s six-month investigation into the tycoon's
finances. This programme, which I produced, revealed for the first
time that the Maxwell companies were virtually bankrupt and that
Robert Maxwell had secretly launched a share support operation to
prop up MCC's share price while he desperately tried to reduce its
crippling debt burden.

But it was Robert Maxwell's fall from his magnificent yacht, the *Lady Ghislane*, into the waters off the Canaries and the subsequent collapse of his business empire which finally led to the SFO's launching a major inquiry into the Maxwell group of companies. George Staple believes that it was probably the most demanding investigation ever undertaken by the office. 'It was not only one of the biggest cases we ever prosecuted,' he says, 'but it was also the most high-profile. We were investigating in ten jurisdictions and had over a hundred police, lawyers and accountants on the team. It was a huge undertaking by any standard.'

The man chosen to lead the SFO investigation was John Tate, who had previously been responsible for the Barlow Clowes inquiry which was now coming to a successful conclusion in the courts. Tate still laughs when he remembers how John Knox, the SFO's deputy director, first broached the subject of his handling the Maxwell case. 'John phoned me at home,' recalls Tate with a smile. 'He said how did I feel about taking on First Tokyo Investment Trust, which I immediately recognised as being part of the Maxwell empire. So I said to him that Barlow Clowes had taken its toll and that I really wanted a rather smaller case to run. He said, "Trust me, John, this will be." Famous last words.'

Following Robert Maxwell's death, his sons, Kevin and Ian, took over the running of the Maxwell group. They are both highly capable individuals who were bullied mercilessly by their domineering father. It was only Robert Maxwell's extraordinarily forceful personality that had kept the Maxwell group afloat for so long; by November 1991, most informed commentators knew that the companies were virtually bankrupt and that it was only a matter of time before the banks finally pulled the plug. The media's initial coverage of Kevin and Ian was fairly positive. According to Keith Oliver, Kevin Maxwell's extremely able lawyer, 'It was accepted by everyone that the group was in financial difficulties but they were still heralded in the press as the "young lions" who could bring the group around. However,' he adds ruefully, 'the discovery of missing pension fund assets changed all that overnight.'

The revelation that Robert Maxwell had used £400 million worth of shares belonging to his employees' pension funds to prop up various private companies horrified the world. On 2 December 1991, trading in Maxwell Communications and Mirror Group Newspaper shares was suspended by the London Stock Exchange and a day later Kevin and Ian Maxwell were unceremoniously forced to resign. Within months the SFO found itself investigating no fewer than six separate complaints, and John Tate and his team were hard pressed to keep up with the constant flow of new allegations being made about the wrongdoing that had occurred inside the Maxwell empire.

Tate's first move was to seize as many documents as he could from Maxwell House, the twenty-storey building in London's New Fetter Lane which Robert Maxwell had used as his international business headquarters. Detective Chief Inspector Graham Watson, the officer who had arrested Peter Clowes, was asked by Tate to lead the SFO raid. 'It was a massive task,' Watson recalls. 'By the time we'd finished, there were so many sacks of documents that it required a fleet of vans to remove them. Each document had to be properly numbered, logged and then put into the Serious Fraud Office's property room. I think it took well over a month before we could actually start looking at things.' But it wasn't just the sheer quantity of documents seized in the raid that caused the SFO problems. According to John Tate, 'We also had a number of difficulties with the defence solicitors who were present at Maxwell House. They virtually objected to us removing anything at all.'

As the documents were slowly logged, the scale of the task confronting the SFO gradually became more and more apparent. Detective Superintendent Ken Farrow, one of the new breed of high fliers in the police service, took over from Graham Watson, who was retiring, as the senior officer involved in the case. Farrow remembers being stunned at the amount of paper that had to be processed. 'Somebody suggested that I should go down and have a look at one of the accountancy teams sifting through the documentation,' recalls Farrow. 'I remember arriving and seeing seven or eight young accountants surrounded by large plastic bins, almost up to the ceiling, wading through these files looking for evidence. It was a colossal task.' Tate, too, remembers being almost overwhelmed by the amount of material that had to be examined. 'I think the documentation we seized on the first raid occupied a pile about sixty-five feet high,' he says. 'But that was only a drop in the ocean when you considered the additional material held by the liquidators which also had to be examined. That covered the space of several tennis courts.'

When Tate and his team eventually got to grips with the documentary evidence, a new story began to emerge from the chaos. What had originally looked like six separate complaints brought to them from people as diverse as the pension fund trustees, the banks and the liquidators, as well as the DTI, turned out, as the case progressed, to be closely linked. 'What we discovered', says Tate, 'was that the Maxwell empire, and particularly some of Robert Maxwell's private companies, were desperately short of money and that they were determined to find funds from wherever they could to ensure its survival. This included using money from the pension funds, money from the banks and money from the public companies. Each complaint was interrelated and was all part and parcel of one single enterprise, namely keeping the Maxwell group afloat.'

It was obvious to everyone involved that the two people most likely to know what had really gone on at Maxwell House were Kevin and Ian Maxwell and, in an unprecedented move, they were summoned by the House of Commons Select Committee on Social Security to answer questions about the missing pension fund assets. But, while they both turned up for the hearing, they repeatedly refused to make any substantive comments whatsoever, claiming that anything they said could prejudice their right to a fair trial. The select committee, for its part, argued that since no one had been charged, the matter could hardly be *sub judice*. However, the Maxwell brothers' caution was well founded. Less than six months later they were arrested, along with Larry Trachtenberg and Robert Bunn, two of their key aides, in a series of dawn raids at their homes.

The arrest of Kevin Maxwell provided one of the most memorable pieces of television news footage of recent years. At 6.35 a.m. on Thursday 18 June 1992, two police officers walked up to his palatial Georgian town house at Jubilee Place in Chelsea and knocked on the front door. As if on cue, Pandora Maxwell, Kevin's feisty wife, leaned out of the upstairs window and said, to the delight of the waiting media: 'Piss off, we don't get up for another hour.' Undeterred by the abuse, the police officers knocked again. 'I'll call the police,' threatened an increasingly irritated Pandora Maxwell. 'Madam,' replied one of the plain-clothes officers with barely disguised relish, 'we are the police.'

It might have been great theatre for the world's press but it made Keith Oliver, Kevin Maxwell's lawyer, absolutely furious. Oliver was acutely aware that his client had been pilloried in the media in a way that very few other individuals ever had, and he was convinced that a public arrest would only accentuate this negative image. Because of this, Oliver had taken the trouble to write to the SFO, saying that Kevin Maxwell would willingly present himself for interview or arrest at any time at a police station of the SFO's choosing. But his offer was ignored. 'They did exactly what I asked them not to do,' recalls Oliver, still angry at events now years past. 'They acted in a way that gave rise to a media circus. Had they acted in a proper and professional way, it could all have been avoided.'

In fact, the manner of Kevin Maxwell's arrest had been discussed at great length inside the SFO's Elm Street headquarters. 'There was a lot of deliberation by everyone involved in the case,' says Detective Superintendent Ken Farrow, whose officers carried out the arrest. 'But we finally took the view that this was someone who was suspected of having committed a serious criminal act of dishonesty and that we would normally go to his home, arrest him and search it. On balance, we thought it best to treat Kevin Maxwell in the same way as we would treat any other suspect.'

What Ken Farrow hadn't anticipated, however, was the enormous media presence outside Kevin Maxwell's home that day. Farrow knew that once it became known that the arrests had been made there would inevitably be a huge media scrum outside Snow Hill police station, where Kevin and Ian Maxwell would be taken, but it never occurred to him that news of the plan would leak out in advance. 'I couldn't believe it when I got a phone call from one of my inspectors saying that the press was already outside the house,' recalls Farrow. 'I had told my officers that the eyes of the world would be on them that day, but I hadn't expected people to be looking quite so soon.'

The public arrest of Kevin and Ian Maxwell had exactly the negative effect that Keith Oliver had so feared. News programmes around the world led with the interchange between Pandora Maxwell and the police officers, followed by the pictures of Kevin Maxwell being arrested and taken to Snow Hill. Alun Jones, the QC who eventually defended Kevin Maxwell in court, believes that this was all part of a deliberate strategy by the SFO to discredit his client. 'The arrest of Kevin Maxwell was a public disgrace,' he says. 'I think news of the arrest was deliberately leaked to show the world that the SFO was taking on these crooks and was going to bring them to book.'

The suggestion that the SFO has turned arrests into public relations stunts for the media has been made before, most notably by the Guinness defendants and Asil Nadir. However, on those occasions the allegations have not stood up to scrutiny. In the case of Kevin Maxwell, the accusation seems much harder to disprove. Yet even this, it turns out, is just another myth.

The man actually responsible for alerting the media to the imminent arrest of Kevin and Ian Maxwell was not an SFO officer at all but a freelance telephone hacker called Eddie, who used to make his living by intercepting communications from the emergency services and selling the information on to the media. Not surprisingly, given that he earned several thousand pounds from the Maxwell tip-off, he remembers the night of 17 June extremely well. 'I was driving through the City using electronic computerised scanning equipment,' he says, 'when I picked up a conversation about the arrest of someone called Maxwell which was due to take place the following morning. My equipment display showed me that the call had originated inside a City of London police station and so it was pretty clear what it was about. I pulled over and started phoning my contacts in the media.'

It may seem an unlikely scenario, but Eddie has given a sworn statement to the police about his involvement in these events and it confirms the story he told me. Even more convincingly, perhaps, various media organisations have now admitted that Eddie was the source of their information about Kevin Maxwell's impending arrest and have produced copies of pro forma invoices showing that they paid Eddie for his efforts. One of these invoices even has the words 'Maxwell tip fee – good info' written on it. Ken Farrow, for one, is pleased with the vindication of his team. 'The allegations that we had been the source of the leak hurt us all,' he says. 'We knew that it wasn't true but very few people believed us. It's good to put the record straight.'

As the investigation approached metamorphosis into a prosecution, it became clear that the SFO was prepared to deploy massive resources to keep this case on track. The man chosen to lead the prosecution was Alan Suckling QC, who had worked alongside John Tate during the Barlow Clowes investigation. But six other barristers were also employed by the SFO in bringing the Maxwell case to court, including Richard Lissack, one of the bar's brightest young stars. One of the things Lissack remembers most about the early part of the case was the enormous effort put in by almost everyone working on it. 'It virtually ran the lives of those of us involved in it,' recalls Lissack. 'It was work of an extraordinary order and intensity. We would often have to work right through the night and there were a number of occasions when we ended up sleeping on the SFO's floor. There was a tremendous team spirit and it was good to be part of it.'

The Maxwell case was finally transferred from the City of London Magistrates' Court to the Central Criminal Court on 19 July 1993. Six people were charged with a total of ten counts of fraud and false accounting. They were Kevin Maxwell, Ian Maxwell, Larry Trachtenberg, Robert Bunn, Michael Stoney and Albert Fuller. All had previously been employed in senior positions within the Maxwell empire. The SFO's case was that each defendant had played a part in dishonestly using assets, owned by or pledged to others, in an effort to help Robert Maxwell Group Ltd, Robert Maxwell's most important private company, stay afloat. All six pleaded not guilty to the charges.

As the legal proceedings developed, it became clear that it would not be practical for all the defendants to take part in one trial. It was therefore agreed relatively early on that the prosecution of Michael

Stoney and Albert Fuller could wait. However, even with the number of defendants reduced from six to four, the case still looked horrendously complex. Alan Suckling therefore suggested to Mr Justice Phillips, the trial judge, that the SFO reduce the number of charges from ten to four. These, he said, would be two counts of dishonestly using pension fund assets, one count of dishonestly using bank assets and one count of dishonestly using the public company's assets.

On the face of it, Alan Suckling's compromise seemed fair enough. George Staple believes the proposal simplified things without surrendering any of the key points. 'Our original scheme', says Staple, looking back, 'allowed us to show the jury the whole fraud in its various different aspects without it becoming overly detailed.' However, Mr Justice Phillips was still not convinced that the case had been cut back enough. He wanted the SFO to bring just the two charges relating to the pension funds which, he said, was where the greatest public concern was anyway. John Tate, for one, was very disappointed with the judge's decision. 'I wasn't happy,' he recalls. 'I thought that we had presented a very sound argument for trying the four counts together. It's difficult to say the judge was wrong, but I'd certainly have preferred it if we had been allowed to prosecute the four counts that we had asked to bring.'

In fact, Mr Justice Phillips' insistence that the SFO proceed only with the two pension fund counts was actually a much greater blow than it has ever publicly admitted. Unknown to anyone outside a very close-knit group, Robert Bunn, one of the most senior members of the Maxwell empire, had admitted in a police interview to behaving dishonestly in relation to both the banks and the public companies. Bunn's confession was the SFO's ace; but it couldn't be played if the prosecution was only allowed to proceed with the pension fund allegations.

Robert Bunn's statement, which has never been made public before, was taken by two City of London Police officers, Detective Inspector Stephen Morgan and Detective Sergeant Philip Carson, on Tuesday 6 October 1992. It was a crisp autumn day and the interview was conducted in Snow Hill police station's rather austere Interview Room 1. Also present was Robert Bunn's lawyer,

Ian Burton of Burton Copeland, and his assistant, Lynette Smith. The interview began just after 11 a.m. with Detective Inspector Morgan pointing out to Mr Bunn that this was not a section 2 interview. 'We must make it clear to you,' said Morgan, 'that this is a police interview. It's not being done under the terms of section 2 of the Criminal Justice Act. Anything you say today is admissible in evidence against you in any proceedings that should subsequently be brought against you. In view of this, I'll formally caution you and tell you again that you do not have to say anything, unless you wish to do so, but anything you do say may be given in evidence.'

So far, nothing out of the ordinary; but what was to come next would make this interview the stuff of legend. As Morgan knew well, Robert Bunn had been the deputy finance director of Maxwell Communications Corporation, a director of MCC's pension fund and a director of Robert Maxwell Group Ltd, the private company which was suspected of causing all the problems. Bunn was, without question, someone who had been at the very centre of the web and was as likely as anyone to know what the spider had been up to.

As the interview progressed, Robert Bunn's testimony made it increasingly clear that serious criminal wrongdoing had occurred in the Maxwell empire. He told Detective Inspector Morgan that another defendant had asked him to sign a large number of stock transfer forms relating to shares in Berlitz, which were owned by the Maxwell Communications Corporation, but that he had refused this request. 'He told me that Robert Maxwell wanted me to give them to him,' said Bunn. 'So why did you refuse to sign them?' said Morgan, pretending not to understand the answer. 'Because', replied Bunn patiently, 'if they were MCC's, it would have been a breach of the loan agreement.' He then went on to explain that MCC had already pledged its Berlitz shares to the banks and that these shares could not therefore be lent to any third parties. But, as Morgan pointed out, the Berlitz shares had been lent anyway. 'So this would amount to an illegal use of the Berlitz shares?' he asked. 'That's correct,' came the unambiguous reply.

Robert Bunn then went on to outline what had happened next. He said that he had told another senior member of the company

that 'the Berlitz shares owned by MCC couldn't have been collater-
alised. It was a breach of the loan agreement. He said that I had to
leave it with him and the following day I received a phone call from
Robert Maxwell. He told me that they were Robert Maxwell Group
shares, private side shares, and when I said that I didn't think that
was correct and that they were MCC's, he told me that MCC was
nothing to do with me.' Morgan quickly recapped on what Bunn
had said, knowing from bitter experience that the devil was almost
always in the detail. 'So he's telling you that they're private side
shares,' said Morgan. 'But you know yourself that they're not?' 'I
believe they were MCC's,' replied Bunn firmly.

As the interview went on, Bunn gave more and more examples of
how Robert Maxwell's private company, Robert Maxwell Group
Ltd, had used assets it didn't own in a desperate last-ditch effort to
stay afloat. At one point Bunn outlined how, in October 1991, he
and a number of others had deceived the Toronto Dominion Bank
by falsely pledging Berlitz shares to secure a loan of $3.75 million. 'I
was called up,' said Bunn, 'and told that there was a loan which had
been negotiated between Maxwell Communications and the
Toronto Dominion Bank. It was secured by Berlitz shares.' I asked
who owned the Berlitz shares. He was told, he said: 'Robert
Maxwell Group.' Detective Inspector Morgan shook his head
slowly, realising that this statement could not be true. 'Of course,'
said the policeman, 'the world now knows and I suspect you knew
then that what was being used to secure the loan was Maxwell
Communications shares. Was that your belief at the time?' He
looked directly at Bunn. 'That was my belief,' said Bunn, nervously
returning his stare. 'Although you had been told that they were
Robert Maxwell Group?' pressed Morgan. 'My belief was that they
were Maxwell Communications,' replied Bunn. 'You were, in
effect, deceiving the Toronto Dominion Bank?' said the policeman,
summing it up. 'Yes,' said Bunn.

'On the face of it,' said Detective Inspector Morgan as he began to
draw the interview to a close, 'you've been involved here in
deceiving banks by imputing to them, or in some cases allowing
them to think, or actually telling them, that shares that you believed
were owned by MCC are in fact owned by the Robert Maxwell

Group. Is that right?' Morgan again looked directly at Robert Bunn. 'That's right,' came the reply. 'And you'd accept that you've acted dishonestly on those occasions?' asked Morgan. 'Yes,' came the reply.

There was silence all round the room as the enormity of what had been said that morning slowly sank in. Robert Bunn, the former deputy finance director of the Maxwell Communications Corporation, a FTSE 100 company, had finally admitted to what so many had previously suspected but couldn't prove. There was serious criminal dishonesty at the heart of the Maxwell empire.

For John Tate, then, Mr Justice Phillips' decision to allow the SFO to proceed only with the two pension fund charges was a body blow from which the prosecution never really recovered. He knew that, since Bunn's confession related solely to the banks and the public companies, it could not be introduced into a court case involving only the pension funds. 'I can understand why he made that decision,' says a still despondent Tate, 'but I do think it was the turning point in the case.'

There was one further question which needed to be resolved before the court case could finally begin. Keith Oliver remained convinced that Kevin Maxwell had been subjected to so much public opprobrium that it would be impossible for him to get a fair trial. Oliver therefore instructed Alun Jones QC to bring an abuse of process application before Mr Justice Phillips, arguing that the trial should not go ahead.

Jones told the court that the SFO's behaviour had been unfair from the start, and laid out Kevin Maxwell's grievances one by one. He began with the SFO's first raid on Maxwell House, from which, he claimed, far more documents had been removed than was either fair or reasonable. He then told Mr Justice Phillips about the media circus which had taken place during Kevin Maxwell's arrest and about his client's written offer to surrender himself to the police at any time. Finally, he said that the SFO had not attempted to stop the publication of numerous hostile articles about Kevin Maxwell, despite having a duty to do so. The consequence of all this, said Jones, was that any jury would be automatically prejudiced against Kevin Maxwell and that he would not be able to receive a fair trial.

The judge listened impassively as Jones laid out the case, but even the Maxwell camp knew that the defence counsel was unlikely to carry the day. In his summing up, Mr Justice Phillips examined each of the complaints in turn before concluding: 'Mr Jones has not persuaded me that adverse publicity has rendered impossible a fair trial for his client. It is my belief that at the end of the trial the jury will reach its verdict in relation to Mr Kevin Maxwell on the evidence before it, uninfluenced by the publicity that has preceded the trial. For that reason, the application to stay does not succeed.'

There was, however, one positive outcome for the Maxwell camp as a result of its abuse application. Mr Justice Phillips decided that a rigorous jury selection process should be applied to ensure that everything possible was done to get an impartial jury. This involved creating a jury questionnaire designed to spot prejudice in potential jurors. It was the first time that this type of questionnaire had been used in Britain since the trial of the Kray twins back in the late 1960s.

The questionnaire listed forty-one questions and was put to seven hundred and fifty potential jurors. Some of the questions were obviously relevant, such as: 'Do you know anyone who has lost money as a result of the collapse of the Maxwell group of companies?' But some were slightly more curious, such as: 'Have you heard of "Maxwell the Musical"?' and 'What happened to the production?' The defence is adamant that the questionnaire was designed only to weed out prejudice. But some of the questions do seem more likely to identify avid newspaper readers than potentially biased jurors. Having read the questionnaire a number of times, one is tempted to conclude that a subtle attempt was being made to dumb down the jury. However, if there was it doesn't seem to have succeeded, since a number of the jurors during the trial asked some extremely pertinent questions.

Members of the SFO – which, it should be said, agreed the questionnaire with the defence – now talk in code whenever they discuss the jury selection criteria. Richard Lissack, the SFO's junior counsel, believes it created an unusual phenomenon. 'The consequence of this very lengthy questionnaire', he says, choosing his words with even more care than usual, 'was that the jury were acutely aware that they had been chosen, not just selected, but chosen because it was thought by everybody that they would try the case fairly and this placed upon them, either consciously or unconsciously, in my judgement, an additional burden.' But Lissack's view, with its implicit suggestion of bias, is totally rejected by Keith Oliver. '"Chosen" is an unfair and singularly inappropriate term to use,' he retorts. 'Had this "chosen" jury convicted Kevin Maxwell, then their critics would now be extolling their virtues.' It is, of course, a fair point to make; but it still doesn't explain those rather bizarre questions.

The Maxwell trial finally started at Chichester Rents on Wednesday 31 May 1995, some three and a half years after Robert Maxwell's death. Kevin Maxwell, who was accused of playing a larger role in the alleged fraud than his three co-defendants, faced two charges of conspiracy. The first claimed that he and his father had conspired to defraud Maxwell pensioners over dealings in shares worth £100 million in Scitex, an Israeli company. The second alleged that he had conspired with his co-defendants, Ian Maxwell, Larry Trachtenberg and Robert Bunn, to defraud pensioners over dealings in shares worth £22 million in Teva, another Israeli company.

Alan Suckling opened the prosecution for the SFO by sketching out the background to the charges. 'This case', he said, 'concerns the misuse of the assets of the Maxwell pension funds. In the second half of 1991, the group of companies controlled by the late Robert Maxwell was in debt and in increasing financial difficulties. They were finding it harder and harder to pay their bills.' Robert Maxwell and Kevin Maxwell, alleged Suckling, decided to use the Scitex shares, which belonged to the pension funds, to help the privately owned Maxwell companies pay their bills. The pension funds were never repaid. 'The agreement to use the Scitex shares in this way', he concluded, 'was dishonest and a fraud upon the pensioners.'

Suckling then turned his attention to the alleged Teva fraud. In November 1991, he said, after the death of Robert Maxwell, the position of the Maxwell companies had become desperate. The Teva shares, which were also owned by the pension funds, were used to borrow money from the National Westminster Bank in an attempt to prevent the collapse of.the group. 'All four defendants agreed to use the shares in this way,' said Suckling. 'This, too, was dishonest and a fraud on the pensioners.'

The prosecution case ran for just over four months before Alan Suckling finally sat down on 10 October 1995. During this time, he called sixty-nine witnesses to give evidence. John Tate, the case controller, was generally pleased with the way things had gone. 'I think the prosecution ran as well as one could expect in any major enterprise involving human beings,' he says. 'We didn't have any major surprises and, given that we were using real-time transcripts, computer graphics, CD-ROMs and transatlantic satellite links, it all worked out very well indeed.' But there was at least one setback for Tate and his team: Robert Bunn was discharged by the judge on grounds of ill health.

John Tate's view that everything had gone as well as could be expected wasn't shared by everyone watching the case. Most of the journalists covering the trial felt that Alan Suckling was nowhere near as impressive as he had been during the Barlow Clowes prosecution. John Steele, the *Daily Telegraph*'s court reporter, was just one of those who thought that Suckling's delivery lacked impact, and he said as much in print. 'I found his performance mundane,' remembers Steele. 'At times it almost seemed like he was verifying entries in the telephone book. There were whole days when he did little more than plod through the paperwork with the witness, asking things like, "Is that accurate?" and "Does that reflect what went on at the meeting?" It was certainly not a sparkling performance.'

This view of Suckling's presentation is shared by Alun Jones, the QC representing Kevin Maxwell. But Jones doesn't believe that Suckling's apparent lack of panache necessarily had a negative impact on the trial. 'I don't think Suckling would dispute that he is a pedestrian advocate,' says Jones. 'But I think that journalists find this more frustrating than the jury.' However, even Jones accepts that a lack of drama can sometimes have a detrimental effect in court. 'I suppose it's fair to say', he concedes, 'that, in a long fraud trial, this type of style can make people a bit comatose and cause attention to wander just a little.'

Unfortunately for Suckling, his downbeat courtroom performance became an even greater issue during the second half of the trial, with questions eventually being raised about his very leadership of the prosecution case. The process began when Suckling started to prepare for his cross-examination of Kevin Maxwell, the only defendant willing to go into the witness box and give evidence. It was obvious that this was always going to be the most important part of the trial and Alan Suckling asked Richard Lissack, who had himself just been made a QC, to cross-examine the other defence witnesses while he concentrated on the task of cross-examining Kevin Maxwell. According to John Steele, 'Richard Lissack's style was noticeably different from that of Alan Suckling. He was more energetic, more ebullient and probably regarded by those on the defence side as more aggressive. His cross-examination was therefore much livelier than Suckling's and I personally thought more effective.'

Lissack's more upbeat style, coupled with a number of rumours that had started to circulate around the courtroom, focused attention on Suckling's position as lead counsel for the prosecution. The rumours suggested that the SFO's legal team had been bitterly divided on a number of issues even before the case had come to court. One senior SFO lawyer closely involved with the case has privately admitted that he questioned whether Suckling should be lead counsel; he didn't feel that his style was sufficiently aggressive, nor did he think he was enough of a team player. Another SFO lawyer has claimed that there was a huge row over exactly which charges to bring against Kevin Maxwell. These divisions eventually became so serious that Kevin Maxwell's defence team got to hear about them. 'People were telling us from within the prosecution camp that they disagreed with the way things had been done,' says Alun Jones, with obvious relish. 'It was clear from quite early on that there was very serious dissension within the SFO team.'

These tensions may well have contributed to the general souring of the atmosphere within the Maxwell prosecution team; but no one has ever suggested that they affected the outcome of the case. Without question, the most significant factor within the trial itself was the testimony of Kevin Maxwell, and on this point there is complete unanimity on the part of both prosecution and defence: Kevin Maxwell's testimony was brilliant.

Kevin Maxwell gave evidence for a total of twenty-one days, so no one can fairly claim that the issues were not properly examined. The defence case was simplicity itself. On the first charge, Kevin Maxwell told the court that his father had shown him a document confirming that the ownership of the Scitex shares had been trans-ferred from the pension fund to one of his private companies. This, said Kevin Maxwell, convinced him that it was legitimate to use the shares in the way he had done. While the document has never been found, it became very clear during the trial that the SFO hadn't looked for it particularly hard. As to the second charge, Kevin Maxwell said that it was common practice within the Maxwell group to move shares between the pension funds, the public companies and the private companies, and that this extraordinarily casual way of treating assets had been repeatedly approved by both lawyers and accountants. If it had been in any way dishonest, they would have objected. According to Alun Jones, 'If Robert Maxwell had been in the dock during this trial, he too would have been acquitted and on exactly the same points.'

Kevin Maxwell's testimony was the pivotal point in the trial. He conceded that he had repeatedly lied to at least one bank as he fought to prevent the Maxwell group from collapsing, but claimed that he and his father were generally honest. He also said that his training in the 'one group' culture of the Maxwell empire had blinded him to the obvious conflicts of interest that arose in using pension fund assets to prop up his father's private companies. It was, by all accounts, a masterly performance. According to Richard Lissack, 'Kevin Maxwell was probably the most remarkable witness I have ever seen in court. He was the master of the setting and the situation. He was composed, unfailingly courteous and human. I think over the course of his evidence he displayed every emotion and I sat a few feet away from him and I don't think those emotions were feigned or put on. He was the consummate witness.'

It was a view shared by John Tate, the man who had spent five years preparing the case against him. 'If I was marking him, I think I'd give him a triple A starred,' says Tate with a grim smile. 'He was first rate. He was fully familiar with all the facts of the case. He was as familiar, I think, as anyone in that court including both prosecuting and defence counsel. When we came to the cross-examination, on some days we held him to a draw but on other days he was undoubtedly ahead of us. In my twenty years involved in the courts, I've never come across such a good witness.'

Lord Justice Phillips began his summing up on 3 January 1996. He also identified Kevin Maxwell's testimony as the single most important part of the trial. 'Kevin Maxwell was in the witness box for over twenty days,' the judge reminded the jury, 'and I doubt if there have been many criminal cases where jurors have had a better opportunity to study the demeanour of the witness. You will have formed individual views and maybe a collective view of whether or not Mr Kevin Maxwell gave the impression of speaking the truth. Impressions are important. One of the great merits of the jury system is that twelve citizens with a wide variety of experience are much better placed to form an impression than a single judge.'

Yet another five days still had to pass before the seven men and five women who were ultimately responsible for deciding the defendants' guilt or innocence were at last allowed to retire and consider their verdicts. They spent eleven nights cocooned at a secret hotel discussing the evidence, eventually deliberating for a total of forty-eight hours and seventeen minutes: the longest jury retirement in British legal history. Then, at five minutes to two on Friday 19 January 1996, they finally returned to the courtroom and announced that they had reached a verdict. For Kevin Maxwell, Ian Maxwell and Larry Trachtenberg, the moment of truth had come at last.

John Tate remembers the moment extremely well. 'I was at the top of Gray's Inn Road', he says, 'eating a curry when my mobile telephone rang. I was told the jury was coming back in and asked to present myself immediately at the court. Typically, I couldn't find a cab so I hared off down Gray's Inn and Chancery Lane and arrived red-faced and rather out of breath. Then the foreman stood up and announced that all the defendants had been found "not guilty". There was absolute uproar in the court with dozens, if not hundreds, of journalists trying to get out with their mobile phones and ring their respective news organisations. I think everyone was slightly stunned by the verdict. I was still trying to get my breath back and I think that slightly blunted my sense of drama, but the fact is that sometimes there are acquittals and prosecutors should not get too worked up about it. It's part of the job.'

Most people at the SFO seem to share the same view, although, not surprisingly, human factors also come into play. Richard Lissack was told of the verdict on the telephone. 'I will never forget that call from one of the SFO's law clerks,' he says. 'She told me the verdict and then hung up, clearly very upset. Not because she was driven by some sort of spite but because years and years of work had apparently come to nought.'

But for Kevin Maxwell and his co-defendants, it was the moment they had been dreaming of for five long years. As soon as the verdicts were announced, Kevin Maxwell ran over to the jurors and shook hands in turn with each of them. His brother, Ian, sobbed with relief. Even Keith Oliver remembers being affected by the emotion of the moment. 'I think one's immediate reaction was a moment of reflection,' he says, 'and then a realisation that a fair-minded jury faced with an extraordinarily complicated case had examined all of the evidence and determined it in favour of Kevin and the others. Then there was this dawning realisation that all of the work and the heartache and the agonising that goes with a case of this complexity had been worthwhile.'

But the not guilty verdicts left the SFO with a huge dilemma. No one disputed that, on the two pension fund charges at least, Kevin Maxwell and the others had been fully exonerated; but the fact remained that the SFO had originally wanted to bring ten charges in relation to the collapse of the Maxwell empire and so far only two had been heard. More than this, the SFO had told Mr (now Lord) Justice Phillips, when he had originally insisted on allowing just two counts to go forward, that it would later seek to introduce the remaining charges. After all, said the SFO, the Court of Appeal had made it clear following the Blue Arrow case that large trials should be broken up into a number of smaller segments in order to make them more comprehensible to the jury. Against this, the SFO was also aware that Kevin Maxwell had lived under a cloud for five years and that he had already given evidence for a staggering twenty-one days. It knew that a decision to move for a second trial might look punitive. It could also look like sour grapes.

Lord Justice Phillips gave the SFO just one week to decide what it wanted to do next. Richard Lissack, who had taken over from Alan Suckling as the SFO's lead counsel immediately following the verdicts, remembers those seven days particularly well. 'It was quite unforgettable,' he says. 'It was a week which eclipsed even the hours of hard work that had gone before and during the case, and that is saying something. It was a week of intensity which I'm sure I'll never experience again in my professional life.'

The decision whether or not to move for a second Maxwell prosecution was probably the most difficult ever taken by the Serious Fraud Office. Strangely, the SFO had not been pilloried as much as it had feared over the Maxwell acquittals. Since the verdicts had been delivered on a Friday afternoon, most of the critical comments had gone into the newspapers on Saturday, journalistically the least important day of the week. Furthermore, while some commentators had made reference to both the infighting and Alan Suckling's lack of courtroom flair, it was generally accepted that the case had been properly presented. Finally, the SFO's success with the Davie Report, the BCCI investigation and a whole raft of less high-profile cases was starting to shift the media's perception of the SFO towards a more favourable assessment. But, as everyone involved in the Maxwell prosecution was acutely aware, this case still had the potential to do the office enormous damage.

This shared fear led to an unprecedented meeting taking place at Elm House just three days after the not guilty verdicts were announced. On the morning of Monday 22 January 1996 George Staple, the director of the Serious Fraud Office, was approached by several of his assistant directors and asked to call a meeting of the senior staff so that they could collectively discuss the second Maxwell prosecution. 'It was perhaps the most important case that the office had,' recalls Staple. 'Understandably, they wanted to feel that their views had been heard.'

The meeting took place later the same day in the director's office on the ninth floor of Elm House. Chris Dickson remembers it particularly well. 'We all knew that this was a decision which was going to be of enormous importance to the Serious Fraud Office,' he says. 'And since we were all going to have to live with the decision, whatever it was, it was important that we all had owner-ship of it. Pleasingly, this was a view that George shared and he didn't object to the meeting at all.'

Ten of the SFO's most powerful lawyers attended the meeting and, by all accounts, the discussion was extremely frank. Staple asked each of them in turn for his or her views on the matter and it soon became clear that there were two schools of thought. According to Chris Dickson, 'On the one side were those who said that, since the judge had reduced the number of charges from ten to four to two, it was important that there was a second trial. After all, there was evidence on which a jury might well convict after hearing the case. On the other hand, there were those who thought that the SFO was simply not going to succeed in having a second trial and that it was best to draw a line in the sand.'

John Tate also remembers the meeting extremely well. He was sceptical of its value at the time and hasn't changed his view. 'I didn't think it was desperately helpful, frankly,' he says, shaking his head at the memory. 'My colleagues were not in a position to know the strengths and weaknesses of the additional counts which were yet to be tried. To be fair to them, I think they were concerned about the wider issues such as its possible impact on the public. And I do accept that they were entitled to have their opinions on those points. But I'm afraid I disagreed with them, even on that.'

By the end of the meeting it was clear that at least two of the SFO's most senior lawyers were implacably opposed to moving for a second Maxwell prosecution, and several others were ambivalent. But there was no doubt that the majority still favoured going ahead and, while everyone accepted that the eventual decision would be taken by George Staple alone, this made the latter outcome much more likely.

John Tate was, perhaps understandably, the most passionate advocate for pressing on. He had always resented the way the original case had been truncated and was determined that at least some of the remaining charges should be put to a jury. 'What we had already prosecuted was a fraud on the pension funds,' he says, still utterly convinced that he is right on this issue. 'What we sought to prosecute amounted to a fraud on the banks. The banks were just as much victims as the pension funds. The banks were entitled, I think, to have their case properly prosecuted and to have the protection of the criminal justice system. It's important to remember that there was more to this case than that which had been heard at the first trial. There were also a number of defendants who had never been before a court, despite the fact that they had been charged with very serious criminal offences. And we are not talking about penny charges, we are talking about accounts which had an order of about £100 million. That's big, by anybody's standard.'

George Staple knew that John Tate's arguments unquestionably had merit; but so did those of his staff who opposed him. Staple therefore turned to the Attorney-General and asked for a meeting to discuss the matter further. 'It was absolutely right that the Attorney-General, who superintends the director, should be consulted on something as important as this,' says Sir Nicholas Lyell, the Attorney-General at the time. 'George Staple, Richard Lissack and John Tate all came over to see me and we spent some time thrashing out the issues involved.'

This meeting took place three days after the Elm House discussion, on Thursday 25 January, at the Attorney-General's rooms in the House of Commons. The SFO team sketched out the arguments both for and against going ahead and Sir Nicholas Lyell listened attentively for several hours. Then he turned to John Tate. 'I can remember the Attorney-General saying to me, "Well, what do you want to do?"' recalls Tate with a smile. 'And I can remember getting a very sick feeling in the pit of my stomach and saying: "Go on." Then he went round the rest of the room and I think, to a man, we all said the same thing: "Go on." Then he turned to George Staple and said: "Well, George, it's your decision, but whichever way you decide, I will support you."'

It's a meeting that has also stayed deeply etched in George Staple's mind. 'I didn't really need to be reminded that it was my decision,' says Staple. 'But it was good to know that whatever I decided it would have his support.' The meeting finally came to an end at about 7 p.m. and the SFO team climbed into a taxi for the trip back to Elm House. Everyone knew that George Staple now had less that eighteen hours to make up his mind; but he didn't need any more time. According to John Tate, 'I think that George took the final decision in the back of that taxi. Certainly by the time we reached Elm House, we all knew what we were going to tell the judge the following morning.'

At 11 a.m. on Friday 26 January, Richard Lissack QC stood up at Chichester Rents and told Lord Justice Phillips that the Serious Fraud Office wanted to continue with five of the original counts against Kevin Maxwell, Larry Trachtenberg, Albert Fuller and Michael Stoney. It did not wish to continue against Ian Maxwell or Robert Bunn, in view of the latter's continuing ill health. Lissack told the judge: 'We have considered the position of the defendants and the burden that will be placed upon them if we were to proceed further. We have applied the twin tests of merit and public interest in the case of each count and each defendant in each count.' The final decision, concluded Lissack, had only been reached 'after the most painstaking reflection and care'.

Kevin Maxwell's lawyer, Keith Oliver, was furious with the SFO for what he saw as an oppressive decision. 'I think it was particularly unfortunate and ill-informed,' he says, still angry at the unfairness of it. 'It was taken in the heat of the moment and without proper consideration of the facts. If the SFO had properly analysed the case and reflected upon the fact that Kevin Maxwell had given evidence for twenty-one days and that the central issue was the question of his honesty, then they would have seen that this case did not require a second trial.' But Oliver believes that there was something potentially even more worrying underpinning the SFO's action. 'While I accept that this decision may have been taken in good faith,' he says, 'the perception was that the Serious Fraud Office and the government did not accept the jury's verdict.'

Keith Oliver immediately instructed Alun Jones to bring another abuse of process application, this time in front of Mr Justice Buckley who had just taken over from Lord Justice Phillips as the Maxwell judge. Jones argued that it was unfair and unreasonable for the SFO to bring further proceedings in the light of what had gone before. 'We felt', says Jones, 'that this second trial would amount to double jeopardy. A man should not be tried for the same crime twice.' Richard Lissack, for the SFO, replied that the remaining charges were quite distinct from what had gone before. He also said that, if the prosecution were prevented from proceeding with the counts which had been severed, a defendant might 'have 80 per cent of his offending free'. Finally, he pointed out that if these proceedings were stayed, 'there would be no public examination of the Berlitz area of the case.' This was, of course, a veiled reminder to the judge of Robert Bunn's earlier confession of dishonesty.

Mr Justice Buckley listened carefully to both sets of arguments before coming down unambiguously on the side of Alun Jones. In his 29-page ruling, the judge first made it clear where he stood on the question of whether or not the SFO was trying to charge Kevin Maxwell and the other defendants with the same crime twice. 'The factors that have influenced me most', he wrote, 'are that the essential criminality of the prosecution's case was before the jury in the first trial. The defendants' alleged dishonesty was the central issue.' Having taken this view, Buckley then remorselessly followed its logic. 'In the circumstances of this case,' he says, 'to launch another long trial at enormous public expense would, in my judgement, run a grave risk of suggesting to the public that the authorities did not accept the verdict of a jury. I do not propose to take that risk.'

But it was Mr Justice Buckley's final point that attracted by far the most press attention. 'As I mentioned earlier,' he says, almost as an aside,

Mrs Pandora Maxwell gave evidence before me. Her obvious distress was, I am convinced, entirely genuine. She described the agony of trial and the days waiting for the verdict with the prospect of a significant prison sentence in the balance. She told me of problems with her children. In particular, their son who had been told by schoolmates that his father was going to prison for a long time. Whenever her husband goes out, she is now repeatedly asked, 'Will daddy be coming home again?' I can understand the expectation that built up in the family's mind

that an acquittal would be the end of the matter. Mrs Maxwell's
bewilderment and anger at the decision to proceed to another
trial was not feigned. I cannot be over-influenced by such
matters but no one could have been unmoved by her evidence.

It is, of course, an excellent thing that judges are compassionate and
appreciate the degree of suffering that accompanies the judicial
process. But, as many commentators pointed out at the time, surely
any defendant's spouse would make the same points, yet few are
quoted by a trial judge at quite such length.

Mr Justice Buckley's order, on 19 September 1996, to stay the
second Maxwell prosecution finally bought the Maxwell case to a
close. It had run for almost five years and cost over £25 million.
Kevin Maxwell used the opportunity to launch a blistering attack
on the Serious Fraud Office within hours of Buckley's decision
being made public. He told the *Independent* newspaper that the
SFO was 'fixated with the desire to secure a conviction'. According
to him, the SFO was 'determined to clean up the city and was
willing to use terror and every other weapon at its disposal'. If you
look at the SFO's annual report, he went on, 'how do they measure
themselves? We live in the age of the chartermark, where hospitals
and schools publish league tables. But what is their measure? It is
solely their conviction rate. They have a dual role as both the investigator and the prosecutor. It is not the prosecutor's role to secure
convictions. It is the prosecutor's role to present the case to the jury
and that is all.'

Kevin Maxwell's outburst was not, perhaps, surprising. He had
preserved a remarkable degree of restraint in the face of massive
provocation for many years. But, for many people, there still
remained the question of who was responsible for the £400 million
fraud on the pension funds. Alun Jones, who knows the story as
well as anyone, says: 'There was fault across the whole group but I
don't think it was criminal. Bankers, auditors, lawyers and accountants all looked at these things and they didn't think anything was
wrong. Frankly, an awful lot of people found it very easy to go
along with Captain Bob, collecting their audit fees and their
interest charges.'

This answer, like the outcome of the Maxwell affair itself, isn't really satisfactory; but it's hard to see what more could be done. The SFO had mounted a huge investigation and bought a number of people to trial. It had tried to proceed with four counts showing the full scale of the alleged fraud, but had been told that two was the maximum possible. Later, following the acquittals, it had tried to re-introduce the missing counts and the evidence, including Robert Bunn's extraordinary confession, which supported them. Mr Justice Buckley's eventual decision to stay the proceedings was both humane and just; but that is not to say that the SFO was wrong to try to go on.

The close of the Maxwell case also brought an end to the nightmare on Elm Street. While there was some hostile press coverage, most informed commentators recognised that the SFO had done all that could reasonably have been expected of it. It had fought to get its best case before the jury and it had kept on fighting. Indeed, the SFO gained a tremendous amount of respect for its decision to try to press on with a second trial. It wasn't just about the Maxwell case; it was sending out a warning to all would-be fraudsters. It was saying that the Serious Fraud Office didn't like to back off. It had finally recovered its nerve.

Part III

Fraudbusters

10

The Biggest Fraud of All

T HE STORY OF THE WORLD'S BIGGEST FRAUD finally ended at 10.30 a.m. on Thursday 20 November 1997 in Court 12 of the Old Bailey, when Abdul Chiragh was sentenced for his part in dishonestly providing information to Price Waterhouse, the external auditor of the Bank of Credit and Commerce International. Chiragh, a small, smartly dressed man in his mid-fifties with gold-rimmed glasses and a dark moustache, was the last of the BCCI conspirators to be prosecuted and he had aggressively denied the charges against him, despite the almost overwhelming weight of evidence assembled by the Serious Fraud Office. Now, having been convicted, he seemed extremely nervous about what was to happen next.

Even though this was the sentencing hearing, the courtroom itself was still strewn with the hi-tech equipment that now characterises a major fraud trial. Large computer terminals were everywhere so that counsel could call up documents at literally the touch of a button. There was also sophisticated video and projection equipment enabling witnesses to give evidence by satellite from virtually anywhere in the world. It had all been installed at the insistence of Chris Dickson, the man who had been the SFO case controller for all six of the BCCI prosecutions, and who firmly believes in using the latest technology to aid the jury whenever possible.

Dickson himself arrived for the hearing just seconds before the judge entered the court. As he hurriedly removed his winter overcoat and red check scarf, the clerk of the court stood up and gave the order: 'All rise.' Dickson had actually left the SFO three weeks earlier to start a new job with the Joint Disciplinary Scheme of the Accountancy Standards Council, but he knew that this was going to be the last day of the last trial of the biggest fraud case the world had ever seen, and he wanted to be there.

Leading the prosecution for the SFO was Anthony Hacking, one of the bar's most distinguished QCs. He had worked with Chris Dickson on several of the previous BCCI prosecutions and so knew the case particularly well. Now it was his job to remind the court of the seriousness of the BCCI fraud and of Abdul Chiragh's part in it. Hacking's glasses, perched on the end of his nose, lent him a scholarly air as he stood up and began to sketch out the details of the Crown's case one last time.

Chiragh, said Hacking, had played a key part in deceiving the auditors about BCCI's real financial position. Chiragh was a chartered accountant with a small practice in Tooting, south London. He had been asked by a senior BCCI employee to prepare fraudulent accounts for a number of bogus companies showing that they had received over $400 million in loans from BCCI which were being successfully serviced. In fact, BCCI had lent this money to other companies which had then gone bankrupt, and none of it was now recoverable. Had it not been for men like Chiragh concealing the truth, said Hacking, it might have been possible to have stopped the BCCI fraud a great deal earlier than was actually the case.

Having put Chiragh's wrongdoing into some sort of context, Hacking then reminded the court what Lord Lane had said about the way white-collar criminals should be treated. 'Professional men', said Hacking, quoting from the voluminous law book in front of him, 'should expect to be treated at least equally, if not more harshly, than people from other backgrounds.' Finally, at the request of Judge Ian Davies, Hacking went through the list of all the other BCCI defendants who had been convicted in Britain and the sentences they had received. He ended, ominously, with the conviction of Abbas Gokal, by far the most important fraudster ever prosecuted in this country. Mr Gokal, said Hacking, had received fourteen years' imprisonment and been fined £3 million.

If this list made Abdul Chiragh feel even more uncomfortable with his predicament, he didn't show it. His own QC, David Evans, rose as soon as Hacking sat down and began putting forward arguments as to why the judge should be lenient towards his client. He first made the point that Chiragh had only 'a relatively small and short involvement in the BCCI fraud' and hadn't actually made much money out of it. Then he said that Mr Chiragh now faced total 'personal and financial ruin' and would clearly be unable to work in the financial services area again. Finally he said, with some force, that Abdul Chiragh wasn't in the same league as Abbas Gokal and it wasn't fair to suggest that he was. It was a good attempt at mitigation, and it might have been effective – had it not been for the fact that, just before the jury trial began, it was discovered that Mr Chiragh had tried to persuade his former secretary to destroy evidence and then perjure herself on his behalf. This revelation had clearly hardened Mr Justice Davies' attitude towards Mr Chiragh and, after the briefest pause, he handed down a sentence of five and a half years' imprisonment with a fine of £20,000.

Chris Dickson left the court surrounded by a posse of reporters asking about the fact that the SFO had now brought six prosecutions against people involved in the BCCI fraud, all of which had been successful. As Dickson sat sipping a celebratory cappuccino in a coffee shop just opposite the Old Bailey, he expressed considerable satisfaction with the outcome of the trials. 'This was a crime with an enormous number of victims,' he said. 'Most of them were small depositors who entrusted their savings to this bank. And, between them, they lost vast amounts of money. I'm pleased that the people who caused this suffering have been punished and that justice has been done.' For Chris Dickson, that final sentence marked the end of six years' hard work; but the BCCI story goes back even further.

The Bank of Credit and Commerce International was founded in September 1972 by Agha Hasan Abedi, a Pakistani businessman with a background in international banking. Abedi's dream was to establish a first world bank for the third world, and he persuaded a number of newly oil-rich Arabs, particularly from Abu Dhabi, who wanted a safe home for their petrodollars, to support the project. They capitalised the new bank at a modest $2.5 million, but it soon began to grow at an astonishing rate. Within three years, BCCI had

$113 million of capital and assets of $2.2 billion. By the early eighties, it had no fewer than 146 branches in thirty-two countries, including forty-five in the UK where it quickly established itself as the largest foreign bank.

But it was BCCI's move into the United States which gave the first hints that this was a bank not to be trusted. BCCI wanted to buy a number of US banks and the Federal Reserve Board, which controls the US banking sector, made it clear that it was unlikely to sanction such a move without knowing much more about BCCI. Undaunted, BCCI started purchasing US banks anyway, secretly using nominees to act as front men for the company. In this way, BCCI eventually acquired four US banks including Financial General, the biggest bank in Washington and the one which held the personal accounts of many of the most powerful figures in the United States. As an inside joke, BCCI later renamed the bank First American.

It took the Federal Reserve over fourteen years to assemble enough evidence to move against BCCI, but suspicions about the ultimate ownership of First American and the other acquisitions were present almost from the outset. The Central Intelligence Agency, which later admitted using BCCI to fund some of its agents and covert operations, discovered the truth as early as 1985 and prepared a report confirming BCCI's secret and illegal control of First American. Astonishingly, it failed to tell the Federal Reserve of its findings.

BCCI's biggest problem was that most regulators knew that it wasn't really possible prudently to develop a bank at this frenetic pace. BCCI didn't have the capital resources or the management infrastructure in place to grow safely at such speed. Even given the fact that many Muslims wanted to use BCCI rather than the western banks for cultural and political reasons, the bank was growing too fast; and rumours were rife as to how this was being accomplished. Initially, BCCI simply bribed the world's rich and powerful to join it. As one former employee told the *Financial Times* in 1991, 'This bank would bribe God.' It offered potential customers expensive presents, prostitutes or anything else that would persuade them to open up a deposit account. But, as time went on, even these novel sales techniques failed to produce sufficient results and BCCI was forced to move downmarket in its relentless hunt for wealthy new customers. By the end of the eighties, BCCI had recruited far more than its fair share of the world's leading drug dealers, terrorists and gangsters.

There were pressing reasons for BCCI's urgent pursuit of new depositors. During the eighties, it had secretly lost a fortune through over-ambitious acquisitions, poor trading and bad loans. Now it was technically bankrupt. The only way it could stay in business was to bring in fresh money. To prevent the truth from coming out, the bank deliberately made itself harder and harder to regulate. BCCI's registered offices were in Luxembourg but its largest number of branches were in Britain. It also set up a large subsidiary in the Cayman Islands, which was where it kept most of the really incriminating files. The fact that it had so many entities made auditing BCCI difficult and supervising it virtually impossible. BCCI was widely recognised as being a bank without a lender of last resort – it didn't have a national government standing behind it – and it should have been more closely supervised than its rivals. But, despite the best efforts of an international College of Regulators set up to monitor BCCI, the opposite happened and the bank escaped scrutiny for far too long.

The files that needed to be studied most closely related to the Gulf Shipping Group, a huge international company run by Abbas Gokal and his two brothers. Gokal had been one of BCCI's first customers and his close personal friendship with Agha Abedi, the bank's founder, allowed him to borrow hundreds of millions of dollars without adequate security. While the Gulf Group's business thrived, this didn't matter; but a prolonged recession in the shipping industry meant that, by 1984, the Gulf Group was insolvent and it was the bank rather than the company that was in trouble.

Agha Abedi knew that the loans made to the Gulf Group were so large that to call them in would destroy BCCI, and so he and his senior managers secretly worked out a plan which would allow both the bank and the shipping group to survive. Abbas Gokal set up a series of offshore companies, apparently unconnected with him, which were designed to move funds clandestinely from BCCI to the Gulf Group and back to BCCI again. In this way, it was possible to give the appearance that the Gulf Group was solvent and that business was continuing as usual. By the time the fraud was finally discovered, this deception had cost BCCI over $1.2 billion.

Price Waterhouse was the auditor initially taken in by this elaborate charade; but it was down to its efforts alone that the truth began to emerge. By 1990 Price Waterhouse had become so concerned about the relationship between BCCI and the Gulf Group that it set up a special task force to investigate. The results of this investigation were finally given to the Bank of England, effectively BCCI's lead regulator, on 2 July 1991.

The Price Waterhouse report, code-named 'Sandstorm', was dynamite. It had been prepared under section 41 of the 1987 Banking Act and it showed that BCCI's balance sheet was rotten to the core. Many loans were bad, and depositors' accounts had been plundered to keep the bank going. According to Price Waterhouse, as well as the $1.2 billion secretly lent to the Gulf Group, there were additional losses of $663 million caused by BCCI's poor treasury trading. Furthermore, said the report, BCCI had spent $364 million on its unlawful purchases of the four US banks and another $500 million buying its own shares from shareholders who wanted to leave the company before it finally collapsed. Taking all these elements together, there was over $2 billion missing from the bank, plus the massive additional costs of keeping these losses secret. In all, said Price Waterhouse, the fraud had cost BCCI's depositors over $4 billion, and it was highly unlikely that this money would ever be recovered.

The Bank of England was stunned by the report. Not even in its worst nightmares had it ever thought that the situation could be as bad as this. The Bank was left with just three options. The first was the simplest. It could shut BCCI immediately. This would secure BCCI's remaining assets and maximise the chances of seizing evidence for later court action. However, it would also cause a political crisis and a media storm. The second option involved slowly winding down BCCI. This would be less dramatic, but would give those responsible for the fraud an opportunity to destroy the evidence and conceivably fly the coop. The third option was to approach the one man who might be willing to bail out BCCI: Sheikh Zayed bin Sultan al-Nahyan, the majority shareholder and the ruler of Abu Dhabi.

The last option initially looked the most appealing – until Price Waterhouse told the Bank of England that it suspected that the Abu Dhabi authorities had known about BCCI's problems for more than a year and had kept them secret. This was a charge categorically denied by the Arabs, but it meant that option three was effectively ruled out. On reflection, the Bank of England decided that the only course of action open to it was to close down BCCI. Immediately.

The Bank of Credit and Commerce International, a bank supposedly with assets of over $20 billion and with branches in sixty-nine countries, was shut for good at 1 p.m. on Friday 5 July 1991. It was an unprecedented move and provoked an outcry across the world. Everyone wanted to know how it had happened and who was responsible. And somebody was going to have to come up with an answer.

Barbara Mills, then director of the Serious Fraud Office, was contacted by the Bank of England just before it shut down BCCI and warned that she was about to receive the biggest case of her life. Three hours later, the Bank formally asked the SFO to launch an investigation into the collapse of BCCI. 'It was obviously going to be an enormous case,' says Mills, reflecting on a day that shook the financial world. 'We didn't know the full ramifications at the time, but it turned out to be the first worldwide banking fraud. I immediately rang Chris Dickson and told him that he was to stop working on all his other cases because we needed to move very fast on this one.'

Chris Dickson also vividly remembers the dramatic telephone call from his boss. 'Friday 5 July 1991 is a day I'll never forget,' he says. 'I was at home mowing the grass when Barbara rang. She told me that BCCI had gone into provisional liquidation, which didn't altogether surprise me, given the rumours I'd been hearing. Then she told me that the Serious Fraud Office had been asked to mount an investigation, which again didn't really surprise me. Then she said that she wanted me to drop all my other cases and lead the investigation. Now that did surprise me.'

Dickson's first move was to go over to BCCI's palatial London headquarters in Leadenhall Street and see the scale of the task for himself. As he entered BCCI's sealed offices, he remembers being almost overwhelmed by what lay ahead. 'It was like the *Marie Celeste*,' he says. 'The employees had simply been told to pick up their personal effects and go. Everything else had been left out. There were working papers on desks and literally thousands of filing cabinets full of papers. And, of course, this was just one branch, albeit a very important one. As I looked round it, I can remember thinking that our investigators were going to have to travel around the world to get to the bottom of this mess, to places where people had different views of the criminal process and different views about banking secrecy. The more I thought about it, the more obvious it became that there were going to be enormous legal as well as logistical problems. Frankly, it was a daunting prospect, but it was also a very exciting one. The main reason I'd joined the Serious Fraud Office was to investigate an enormous fraud like this.'

The Bank of England's decision to shut down BCCI predictably aroused enormous anger among the distraught depositors. Most of the losers were Asian businesspeople and they were horrified when they realised that it would be months before they would get their money back, if indeed they ever saw it again. In the meantime, many of them stood to lose their businesses and their homes. Investors from around the country soon formed a national pressure group along the lines of the Barlow Clowes Investors Group and began lobbying the government for compensation. The suspicion was growing that the Bank of England had known that BCCI was in trouble long before it moved against the bank and yet had given no warnings at all.

This suspicion was fuelled by a number of full-page advertisements taken out in the British press by the Abu Dhabi authorities and headlined 'A statement by the majority shareholders'. The advert claimed that 'The majority shareholders of the BCCI group were shocked by the abrupt action taken by the Bank of England

and other regulators to freeze the assets of the BCCI and close its operating branches.' It went on to say: 'In October 1990, as a result of the disclosure of various irregularities, the President and Chief Executive Officer resigned. At the request of the majority shareholders an internal inquiry into these irregularities was instigated shortly afterwards and is continuing. The majority shareholders believe that they took effective steps in mid-1990 to prevent the occurrence of new irregularities.' It was clear from the adverts that the UK authorities must have known that there were problems with BCCI much earlier than the public had previously realised.

Norman Lamont, the Chancellor of the Exchequer, asked Lord Justice Bingham, an appeal court judge, to launch an inquiry into the way the British authorities had handled the BCCI crisis. His report, published in October 1992, was critical of the Bank of England in as much as the Bank could have done more than it actually did. Bingham said that he thought 'the Bank was rather easily deterred' and that it did not pursue matters with the 'resolute action' the situation demanded.

Infighting between the regulators, the liquidators and the various pressure groups made the SFO's job even more difficult than usual. Everyone was jockeying for position and seeking to make capital out of new information as it emerged. The liquidators were particularly concerned that the SFO was going to exercise its section 2 powers and seize all the documentation, thus making their job virtually impossible. However, following discussions with Chris Dickson, it was agreed that they could keep all the paperwork, providing the SFO could get instant access.

After about four weeks of intensive work, Dickson and his team finally managed to put together a position paper outlining exactly what would be needed, in terms of personnel, resources and costs, to complete the investigation. This paper made it clear just what a large undertaking the BCCI case was going to be for the SFO. 'This was a blockbuster case,' recalls George Staple, who took over from Barbara Mills as director of the SFO in April 1992. 'It was big in terms of the money lost to investors, it was big in terms of the number of jurisdictions involved and it was big in terms of the number of documents that were going to have to be examined.'

In these circumstances, it was inevitable that the SFO would assemble the biggest team it could, and eventually over sixty people were working directly on the BCCI investigation. According to Dickson, 'Our colleagues in the City of London Police immediately came forward and offered a huge dedicated team of police officers to help with the investigation. We also interviewed three account-ancy firms before eventually appointing Coopers & Lybrand to supply the accountancy investigation teams. Finally, because of the size of the operation, we moved everyone out of Elm House into much larger premises in Finsbury Square.'

Initially, there was some tension between the SFO and the police officers involved in the investigation. According to one SFO insider, 'The City Police thought, because they were putting in a lot of people, that they should be running the show. And that's not the way it's meant to work. The Serious Fraud Office was set up to run major fraud investigations. This point took a little while to sink in.' Another SFO lawyer attached to the case says that there was a lot of disagreement about whom to prosecute and whom to use as witnesses. 'The SFO wanted to prosecute the big fish,' says the lawyer; 'the police wanted to prosecute everyone. The difficulty with their view was that there would be no one left to tell the jury what had happened. Professional prosecutors know that documents can't do it all.'

Chris Dickson himself believes that the tensions between the SFO and the police have been slightly exaggerated. 'I think relations between the two of us were very good,' he says. 'I think you have to realise that this was the biggest thing that either we or the City of London Police had ever taken on and there were clearly going to be some difficulties at the early stages defining what our respective roles were. But generally speaking, I was overcome with admiration for the really first-class police officers that were seconded to us. They did a marvellous job.'

As the SFO inquiry gathered momentum, Dickson and his team found themselves spending more and more time in the Cayman Islands. This was where BCCI had kept its most sensitive documents and it was from here that the fraud could be most clearly understood. The SFO wanted to know why Price Waterhouse,

BCCI's auditors, had signed off BCCI's Cayman Islands accounts when the documentation seemed to raise so many questions. However, following a very full investigation which involved scrutinising a number of unusual payments as well as interviewing several local women about their relationships with the bank, the SFO decided to bring no charges.

One of the more unusual stories to emerge about the Cayman Islands part of the investigation involved a group of US law enforcement officers who wished to examine the same documentation as that seen by the SFO. The Cayman Islands authorities decided that this would be acceptable as long as the Americans, like the SFO, agreed to join the special volunteer police force for the duration of the visit. This involved swearing a short oath of loyalty to the Queen. The US officers spent some time discussing this among themselves before finally going ahead with the pledge. In front of three very curious SFO officers, they stood up, crossed their fingers and swore allegiance to the British Crown. As their senior officer later explained over a drink, the crossing of the fingers would clearly render the oath 'non-binding' in the eyes of the US government.

The first man to be prosecuted by the SFO for his part in the fraud was Syed Ziauddin Ali Akbar, who had run BCCI's treasury department in London. Syed Akbar was a central figure in BCCI and knew a great deal about its criminal activities as well as its more unusual political contacts. It was widely rumoured that Akbar was paid over £20 million by BCCI in 1988 in return for his continuing silence about the bank's activities, but this allegation has never been examined in a court of law.

Syed Akbar was arrested in France on 3 September 1991, but it took almost eighteen months for the SFO to get him extradited back to the United Kingdom. He was finally brought to Bishopsgate police station in the City of London on 27 April 1993, to be charged with twenty counts of false accounting. At his subsequent trial, Syed Akbar was described by the judge as 'the chief engineer of BCCI' and sentenced to six years' imprisonment. When he was released from Brixton prison some three years later, Akbar found himself facing another extradition warrant, this time brought by the US authorities, who wanted to send him to New York to face extortion charges. But, because of an administrative bungle, Akbar managed to avoid this fate and has since left the country of his own volition.

One little-known aspect of the Syed Akbar case is the part played by Mark Braley, a 25-year-old accountant who had been seconded to the SFO from Coopers & Lybrand. Braley used his privileged position at the SFO to steal a series of confidential documents relating to the Akbar investigation and then asked his friend, Bernard Lynch, to try to sell them to Michael Barratt, Mr Akbar's solicitor, for £200,000. Braley's plan was frustrated when Barratt went to the police, who secretly recorded the subsequent meetings on tape. Once the police had established exactly what was going on, Braley and Lynch were arrested and prosecuted. According to Chris Dickson, 'It was obviously an embarrassment for everyone concerned, but it was one of those things and the people involved were dealt with appropriately.'

The next person to be prosecuted by the SFO's BCCI team was Mohammed Abdul Baqi, the 66-year-old former managing director of Attock Oil. Mohammed Baqi was arrested on 3 February 1992 on his way to Heathrow airport and taken to Bishopsgate police station, where he was held overnight before being questioned the following morning. Baqi, a long-standing BCCI customer, was charged with conspiring to furnish false audit confirmation slips to Price Waterhouse, BCCI's auditor. These slips appeared to show that Attock Oil owed BCCI sums totalling $76,517,952. In fact, this was untrue and no such sums were owed; but the false documents enabled BCCI's corrupt management to give a plausible explanation as to where at least some of the depositors' money had gone. Mohammed Baqi was later convicted and fined £120,000.

Probably the most high-profile person to be charged by the SFO as a result of its inquiry into BCCI was Nazmudin Virani, the 42-year-old chairman and chief executive of Control Securities plc. Virani, who had come to the United Kingdom in 1973 following Idi Amin's expulsion of the Ugandan Asians, was one of the Asian community's most respected business leaders and had previously won the coveted title of 'Asian Businessman of the Year'. In less than twenty years, Virani had managed to build up a £650 million hotel and leisure business which employed over 3,500 people. The SFO's raid on his company's headquarters on 17 October 1991 and subsequent arrest of Virani the following March put an end to this glittering career.

The SFO alleged that Nazmudin Virani, like Mohammed Baqi, had provided false audit confirmation slips to Price Waterhouse and charged him with no fewer than fourteen separate offences. Virani pleaded not guilty to all the charges but kept his defence secret from the SFO right up until the trial itself. Then, out of the blue, he claimed that he was dyslexic and hadn't known what he was signing. This came as a shock to the prosecution team; they immediately asked Virani to take a number of tests with an independent expert, who concluded that he could indeed read and write. The SFO also managed to trace a number of Virani's old school reports which showed that, while he might not have been a star scholar, he was perfectly capable of reading English. Nazmudin Virani was eventually convicted on six charges of providing false information and one of false accounting, and sentenced to thirty months' imprisonment. However, the trial judge felt sufficiently well disposed towards Virani to say, just before passing sentence, that 'I believe, on your release, you will resume an honest and useful life in the business community.'

The fourth person to be prosecuted by the SFO for his part in the BCCI fraud was Imran Iman, a former BCCI account manager. Iman was initially charged with two offences, the first relating to the overcharging of management fees worth over $74 million and the second to the concealing of loan guarantees worth $105 million. Both these offences had been committed as part of BCCI's attempt to conceal its enormous losses. Iman's trial began on 26 April 1994; at the end of it, he was sentenced to three years' imprisonment.

Interestingly, just before the trial started, Iman alleged that he had been a victim of an abuse of process. He told Judge Henry Pownell that he had been misled by the SFO into believing that he was only to be a witness in the proceedings and would not be prosecuted. Two American lawyers confirmed that they had had several meetings with Chris Dickson at which they had stressed the help that Iman had given to the American inquiry. They had also told Dickson that they planned to use Iman solely as a prosecution witness and urged him to do the same. Finally, they told the judge that they had given Dickson a number of documents in the belief that he did not intend to prosecute Iman. However, under cross-examination, both men admitted that Dickson had never actually said that Iman would not be prosecuted. Dickson, for his part, acknowledged that he was aware of their views but did not feel that it was in the interests of justice to set the record straight. Mr Justice Pownell ruled that, since all the witnesses agreed that no promises or undertakings had been given by the SFO not to prosecute Iman, there had been no abuse of process.

So far, the SFO had prosecuted four people as a result of its BCCI investigation and secured four convictions. But there was a growing feeling in the media that the really big players had managed to avoid capture. This, however, was about to change. Two years earlier, in April 1992, and unknown to anyone outside a very small circle of people within the SFO, City of London Police officers had discovered a safe deposit box. In this box was a document signed by Abbas Gokal, the head of the Gulf Shipping Group, showing that his company secretly owed a staggering $1.2 billion to BCCI. It also showed that the Gulf Group had borrowed this money through a complex web of offshore companies in order to avoid Price Waterhouse, BCCI's external auditor, finding out the true scale of BCCI's lending to the company.

As the SFO immediately recognised, this was an extraordinary find and it pointed towards the biggest fraud of all. But, as everyone involved in the case also knew, Abbas Gokal had fled to Pakistan, which had no extradition treaty with the United Kingdom. None the less, George Staple decided that this find was so important that it could not be ignored, and he ordered that a huge investigation be immediately launched into the role of the Gulf Shipping Group in the collapse of BCCI.

Detective Sergeant Douglas Reeman was given the job of leading the SFO investigation. Reeman soon discovered how the Gulf Group, once an extremely successful shipping and trading conglomerate, had suffered dramatically in the recession of the early 1980s and threatened BCCI with bankruptcy. It was at a meeting on 15 June 1984 between BCCI's top management and Abbas Gokal at United House, the Gulf Group's headquarters in Switzerland, that the plan was hatched to set up a number of companies through which money could secretly be passed from BCCI to the Gulf Group, thus enabling the latter to continue trading and the former to tell its auditors, Price Waterhouse, that its loans to the shipping group were steadily being reduced. Four years later, BCCI's auditor believed that the Gulf Group owed the bank just $300 million. In fact, as the documents found in the safe deposit box showed, the real figure was over four times this amount.

Having seized the papers in the safe deposit box, Detective Sergeant Reeman and his team turned their attention to Switzerland and raided United House. Here they found thousands of documents chronicling the fraud and showing how Gokal and some of BCCI's most senior management had misled Price Waterhouse by secretly switching the Gulf Group's borrowing to nominee third parties. 'It was a clear agreement between the two parties to embark on a fraudulent course of action which would enable them to both stay in business,' says Reeman, looking back at the Swiss documents. 'I thought it was also very significant that BCCI had gone to such lengths to keep these documents away from the auditor.'

By early 1994, the SFO was ready to prosecute Abbas Gokal; but he still hadn't surfaced from his bolt hole in Pakistan. It was starting to look as if the gamble taken by George Staple two years earlier wasn't going to pay off. 'It would be fair to say that a fair amount of disillusionment had started to creep into the investigative team,' recalls Reeman. 'We all knew that the investigation could be terminated at any time.' But Reeman claims that he personally always remained optimistic that Gokal would eventually come out into the open. 'I never lost sight of the fact that Abbas Gokal had travelled extensively throughout his business life,' he says. 'He was not, in my view, the kind of person who was likely to stay in Pakistan for ever.'

Doug Reeman's confidence was finally rewarded on Thursday 14 July 1994, when he was telephoned by the New York District

Attorney's office. 'The New York DA told me', says Reeman, 'that they were expecting to interview Mr Gokal in New York on 18 July and, if we had any questions for Mr Gokal, they would gladly put them to him. I was a bit surprised by the telephone call but I thanked him for his offer and said that, under the circumstances, it would be inappropriate for them to put any questions on our behalf.'

The New York District Attorney had originally planned to interview Abbas Gokal in Pakistan, but this would not have allowed him to testify in front of a Grand Jury. He therefore decided to offer Gokal immunity from prosecution if he would go to New York and give evidence there. This offer incensed the SFO, even though it knew that Gokal had told the US authorities that he was willing to answer questions on both US Senate corruption and Pakistan's nuclear weapons programme.

Detective Constable Stephen Joels, Doug Reeman's junior officer, was given the task of finding out how Abbas Gokal intended to travel to the United States. Despite the fact that Gokal had booked under his middle name, Kassimali, it was quickly established that he and his wife intended to fly to New York via Frankfurt on a Pakistan International Airways flight. This meant that, for about one hour, in Germany, Abbas Gokal would be within reach of British justice.

The SFO team investigating BCCI knew they had very little time to lose if they were going to snatch Gokal off the plane at Frankfurt airport. The first thing that needed to be done was to clear the operation with George Staple. 'We met with George,' recalls Chris Dickson, 'and explained to him what had happened. He then very quickly took the decision to mount an arrest.' According to Staple, the likely American reaction wasn't a significant factor in the debate. 'We weren't under any obligation to the United States not to arrest him if we had the opportunity to do so,' says Staple forcefully. 'And, in my opinion, it was very strongly in the public interest that Gokal should be arrested. So that was the decision I took.'

Doug Reeman obtained the arrest warrant from the City of London Magistrates' Court on Friday 15 July and immediately asked Interpol for assistance in the arrest of Abbas Gokal at

Frankfurt airport the following Monday. But it wasn't until Sunday 17 July that he finally got his answer. 'Time was very tight,' says Reeman, 'because our request had been sent just before the weekend and it had to go through the judicial process. But I finally heard on Sunday night that the German authorities had agreed to act on our warrant and that they wanted me to attend the arrest for identification purposes.'

Reeman got on the first plane from Heathrow to Frankfurt and arrived in Germany just ahead of Gokal himself. He then waited with the German border police for the PIA jet to land. After it taxied up to the gate, the German police instructed all the passengers to leave the plane one by one. Fifteen minutes later, the plane was empty but there was still no sign of Gokal. 'I was confident I hadn't missed him,' says Reeman, anxiously re-living the moment. 'Not unless he had changed his appearance substantially. So the German police asked one of the PIA stewards to recheck the plane and he did. But, after a a short while, he came back and said, "The plane is empty."'

By now, Doug Reeman was getting very worried indeed. 'The German police asked me to go on the plane and check for myself. As you can imagine, I was very apprehensive as I walked down the gangway and entered the plane. I thought, this is it. He's either here or he's not. Then I looked into the first-class cabin and there he was, sitting with his wife, surrounded by stewardesses. Frankly, I felt extremely relieved.' It was an indication of Abbas Gokal's still considerable powers that he was able to persuade a PIA steward to lie on his behalf and the cabin crew to let him and his wife remain on board when every other passenger had been ordered to leave.

Doug Reeman's relief at finding Gokal was shared by most of the other people working on the BCCI inquiry. 'I, for one, was absolutely elated,' remembers Chris Dickson. 'I was thrilled for Doug Reeman who had put so much work into it, thrilled for George Staple who had backed such a high-risk investigation and thrilled for the Serious Fraud Office who had arrested one of the most important players in the BCCI fraud.'

Abbas Kassimali Gokal's trial began on 11 September 1996 at the Old Bailey in London. He was charged with two counts of conspiracy to defraud. The indictment said simply that Gokal, along with others, 'concealed the fact that the Gulf Group owed the BCCI group a sum of money in excess of one thousand two hundred million United States dollars ($1,231,192,699), well knowing that there was no realistic likelihood of the Gulf Group ever discharging this liability to the BCCI group'. It was the biggest sum of money ever alleged to have been defrauded in a British court.

The trial lasted for 125 days before Abbas Gokal was found guilty on both counts in April 1997. The trial judge, Mr Justice Buxton, said before passing sentence that Gokal was 'an intelligent, sophisticated and unscrupulous man who put the interests of himself and his family before all else and certainly before any obligation to conduct his business affairs with honesty and straightforwardness'. The fraud, he went on, 'had created a serious threat to the integrity of the whole international banking system', and Gokal had shown not the slightest 'apology or remorse for the damage and loss he had caused to many thousands of innocent people'. Mr Justice Buxton then sentenced Abbas Gokal to fourteen years' imprisonment and fined him £3 million. It was the longest sentence ever given at the end of a British fraud trial.

Looking back, Chris Dickson is clear why the BCCI prosecutions were so successful. 'In the BCCI cases', he says, 'we had a single defendant in each trial and I think that was of enormous value. We also worked extremely hard in refining the evidence and cutting it down to the absolute minimum necessary for the jury to understand the case. It seems to me these are two of the main reasons why we did so well.' But the BCCI prosecutions did much more than just come up with a winning formula for serious fraud trials. They also changed the public's attitude towards the Serious Fraud Office.

'I think the Gokal case was a turning point,' says Chris Dickson with a smile. 'I think that people are now starting to accept that the SFO has done some excellent work in the past and that serious fraud is not something that is going to be tolerated in this country.' Certainly, the media coverage of the Gokal trial would suggest that Dickson is right when he says that there has been a shift in attitude. For the first time in five years, the press was almost universally complimentary about the SFO's handling of a case and the vast majority of the papers even reported Mr Justice Buxton's very complimentary closing remarks. Now, with the additional conviction of Abdul Chiragh, the six BCCI prosecutions stand as the jewel in the SFO's crown. They have tilted the balance of public opinion back in favour of the Serious Fraud Office.

11

The Other Side of Elm Street

I T MAY HAVE TAKEN until the end of the trial of Abbas Gokal in April 1997 for the British media to reassess their view of the Serious Fraud Office, but the British government had decided that the SFO was doing a good job over two years earlier. On 31 January 1995, Rex Davie, a senior civil servant, published his report into the Serious Fraud Office and recommended not only that the SFO should continue in its present form but that its caseload and budget should be increased. His report was welcomed by Sir Nicholas Lyell, the Attorney-General, and went on to receive all-party support in the House of Commons.

For George Staple, who had fought long and hard to persuade the government that the statistics rather than the headlines told the true story about the Serious Fraud Office, Davie's conclusions were manna from heaven. 'I think the publication of the Davie Report was the most important moment of my five years as director of the SFO,' he says now. 'There had been a lot of speculation as to whether or not the SFO should continue as a free-standing organisation or be subsumed back into the Crown Prosecution Service. This report emphatically answered that question. The SFO was here to stay.'

Rex Davie's report was the culmination of a two-year debate about the future of the Serious Fraud Office. It had begun in July 1993 when the Royal Commission on the Criminal Justice System called for a feasibility study into the merger of the Serious Fraud Office and the Fraud Investigation Group of the Crown Prosecution Service. The FIG, as it was known, had been established in 1985 under the aegis of the DPP and is considered the forerunner of the SFO. It pioneered the multi-disciplinary approach to fraud investigation which the SFO later adopted so successfully. However, there were some significant differences between the two organisations. The FIG didn't have the SFO's section 2 powers; the cases it handled were generally less complex, and it had many more of them on its books. Even the FIG's multi-disciplinary approach was based on a much more informal relationship between the police, lawyers and accountants than that which existed at Elm Street.

Sir Nicholas Lyell, personally a great supporter of the SFO, knew that he couldn't simply ignore the Royal Commission's suggestion. He therefore asked John Graham, who had previously worked for the SFO as its principal establishment and finance officer before joining the Treasury, to form a small committee and examine the issue in detail. But the Graham team's terms of reference were vague to say the least: 'in the light of the recommendation of the Royal Commission on Criminal Justice that a feasibility study be conducted into the possibility of a merger between the SFO and the Fraud Investigation Group of the CPS, to review the arrangements for the investigation and prosecution of criminal fraud cases in the SFO and CPS and to make recommendations'. The Graham team was also asked to examine the relative workloads of the FIG and the SFO and to assess the criteria for allocating cases between the two departments.

George Staple knew that the Graham Report could easily sound the death knell of the Serious Fraud Office. The fact was that 1993 had been a bad year for the SFO, with Asil Nadir fleeing the country and Roger Levitt receiving his derisory 180-hour community service sentence. The media was out for blood. 'I was certainly conscious of a huge amount of speculation that we might not survive,' admits Staple. 'But I personally remained convinced that the right way to investigate serious fraud was by means of a small, specialist unit and not as part of some huge bureaucracy.'

John Graham and his colleagues spent seven months considering the evidence before finally publishing their report in March 1994. It began by outlining a number of important findings. First of all, it claimed that over 40 per cent of the Fraud Investigation Group's work did not involve serious or complex fraud at all and suggested that this should be handled locally by the Crown Prosecution Service. Next, it said that there was an overlap between some of the FIG's larger cases and the SFO's smaller ones. According to the Graham Report, this was 'anomalous' since it meant that 'different approaches are brought to bear on what in many instances are very similar cases.' Finally, it claimed that, with the SFO's fall in caseload over the last eighteen months, there was bound to be an 'increasing margin of spare capacity' at Elm Street.

On the surface, the Graham Report's findings seemed to favour the Serious Fraud Office. Its recommendation to reduce the Fraud Investigation Group's work by 40 per cent was obviously a body blow for the FIG. And pointing out that the SFO had spare capacity while observing that similar frauds were not being investigated in similar ways seemed tantamount to inviting the SFO to cherry-pick the FIG's most important cases. But the report's final conclusions were not as comforting for the SFO as the introductory paragraphs seemed to suggest.

The Graham Report did accept that an expanded SFO handling the top tier of the FIG's cases was one possibility for the future. However, it also outlined another one. 'We are convinced', wrote the Graham review team,

that there is a sound case for establishing a new organisation including the SFO's caseload and all the serious or complex cases dealt with at FIG. This would allow Section Two powers to be exercised over all serious or complex cases and, if carefully managed, it would allow a better allocation of resources to cases. Wherever the organisation is located it needs to deal with its largest cases on the same basis as the Serious Fraud Office currently operates.

Once again, there were some crumbs of comfort for the SFO; but the suggestion of a new organisation sounded ominous indeed. The Graham Report acknowledged that it could be established under the auspices of the SFO, but said that it might be cheaper to base it within the CPS. For Sir Nicholas Lyell, the Attorney-General, the report crystallised a concern that had being growing for some time. 'There was a serious question as to whether or not the CPS should swallow up the SFO,' he says, looking back on the debate. 'We needed to know if we would get better value for money by going that route.'

But the Graham Report, having identified the two options, resolutely refused to state a preference. It clearly felt that the SFO's caseload should be merged with the FIG's most serious and complex cases. But it didn't say whether or not this should be done as part of an enlarged Serious Fraud Office or as part of the Crown Prosecution Service. George Staple thought that this failure to take a view meant that the report missed the mark. 'It was a report which went into a good deal of detail on how the SFO worked,' he says. 'But it never seemed to me to come to quite the right conclusion.' For Sir Nicholas Lyell, there was nothing else for it. He set up another inquiry, this time chaired by Rex Davie.

Unlike John Graham's team, Rex Davie's committee was given one very specific task and its terms of reference were extremely clear: 'to consider the merits and feasibility of merger between the Serious Fraud Office and the Fraud Division of the Crown Prosecution Service', the Fraud Division being the new name for the old Fraud Investigation Group. Besides Rex Davie himself, the committee included representatives from the SFO, the CPS, the Association of Chief Police Officers, the Home Office, the Treasury and several other government agencies. It was a particularly high-powered group and everyone knew that the government would be hard pressed to ignore its recommendations.

The Davie Committee took six months to come to a view and then published a report which ran to forty-six pages and five appendices. It began by spelling out the practical difficulties involved in any sort of merger between the SFO and the CPS. First of all, said Davie, such a merger 'would introduce investigation into an organisation which otherwise is concerned solely with prosecution and would therefore need to be ring fenced. The CPS could do this but the ring fencing would reduce any savings which might be expected to accrue from a merger.' Secondly, said the report, 'abolition of the

SFO would mean that there was no longer an organisation whose *raison d'être* was the investigation and prosecution of serious fraud.' Finally, said Davie, a merger would require primary legislation because of the way in which Parliament had established the section 2 powers.

It was clear, even from a cursory reading, that the Davie Committee had effectively ruled out any idea of collapsing the SFO into the CPS. But a number of other outcomes were possible, and the Davie Report considered each of them in turn. By far the most interesting was a police proposal that the CPS should set up a quasi-autonomous Serious Fraud Unit, with the police being solely responsible for its investigations. For this to work, said the police, the SFO's section 2 powers would need to be transferred to them. Once again, however, this idea was roundly rejected by the Davie Committee, which said that 'it represented a return to the position pre-Roskill.' None the less, they did agree that the role of the police in SFO investigations needed to be much better defined, and recommended that a memorandum of understanding be drawn up between the director of the SFO and the various chief constables as a matter of urgency.

Having eliminated the alternatives, the Davie Committee began to examine the case for preserving the status quo. 'The Serious Fraud Office', it said,

> has developed a specialism which needs to be preserved and not diluted. The mere fact that two organisations are involved in the prosecution of fraud in this area is not, of itself, a conclusive reason for change. There have been a number of developments since the establishment of the SFO, and indeed a number of improvements in both the Fraud Division and the SFO since the Graham report. The Group believes there is scope for building on these and for introducing further changes in order to meet the requirements identified.

The most urgently required change, said Davie, related to the relatively unstructured way in which cases were assigned between the SFO and the CPS. If the SFO had a full workload, it would generally only accept the biggest cases. If the SFO were not busy, it would take on quite small cases. The Davie Report made it clear that this ad hoc approach was unsatisfactory and needed to be addressed quickly. It therefore proposed a new set of criteria, including the lowering from £5 million to £1 million of the SFO's financial threshold, to be used when assessing if a case was suitable for the Serious Fraud Office. The Davie Report also suggested strengthening the role of the Joint Vetting Committee, whose job it was to monitor cases coming to the SFO, to ensure that the office did not try to cherry-pick the most interesting investigations and pass the others on to the FIG.

The Davie Report was a massive endorsement of the work of the Serious Fraud Office. It single-handedly buried the idea that the SFO should be merged back into the CPS and instead said that its workload should be significantly increased. George Staple was delighted with the outcome. 'Essentially, it was a vindication of the SFO,' he says, with real enthusiasm. 'It recommended that the office should stay in business. It was saying what I had been saying privately for many years. We needed a small, free-standing organisation that wasn't overly bureaucratic to deal with the very difficult area of serious fraud.' Sir Nicholas Lyell was also pleased with Rex Davie's conclusions. 'It was a very important report,' he says. 'If it had come down in the opposite direction, it is possible that the Serious Fraud Office might have been dissolved and that, in my opinion, would have been a grave error. The truth was that the SFO had been making very good progress and the Davie Report simply reflected that fact.'

Lyell's pleasure at the conclusions of the Davie Committee was reflected in his statement to Parliament on 31 March 1995, when he accepted the report on behalf of the government. 'I should emphasise', he told the Commons, 'that despite the often misguided criticism to which the prosecuting agencies have been subject, the Serious Fraud Office and the fraud division of the CPS have made real advances since they were set up in the eighties. In its seven years of existence to date, the Serious Fraud Office has brought to trial 141 major cases involving 309 defendants, of whom 191 have been convicted. More significantly, in over 75 per cent of cases brought to trial by the SFO at least one person has been convicted, usually the principal defendant.'

Nor was it just the government side that accepted the Davie Report. John Morris, the shadow Attorney-General, also conceded that it was better to keep the SFO and the CPS separate rather than bring them together. It wasn't, however, a ringing endorsement. 'I welcome the Davie Report and the Attorney-General's conclusions,' he said. 'While I would not necessarily have devised the Serious Fraud Office and maintained a fraud division of the Crown Prosecution Service at the same time, a shotgun marriage now is not the best way to proceed.' It might have been grudging; but there was now genuine cross-party support for the Serious Fraud Office.

Much of the credit for this parliamentary success belongs to George Staple. Under his stewardship, a quiet revolution had taken place at Elm Street, a fact that went unnoticed by the vast majority of the media. Staple is not, by his own admission, a dyed-in-the-wool prosecutor; but his years as a senior partner at Clifford Chance, one of Britain's biggest law firms, have made him an exceptional manager. The structural changes he implemented at the Serious Fraud Office made a huge difference to its overall effectiveness and probably ensured its survival.

When George Staple took over as director in April 1992, he found that the SFO was divided into divisions of lawyers, accountants, financial investigators and law clerks. Investigative teams were formed from these divisions on an ad hoc basis to deal with cases as they came in. However, as Staple soon realised, this structure was inflexible and divisive, and certainly did not allow for the most efficient use of resources. 'I was concerned that we may not have been getting as much out of the SFO as we could,' he reflects. 'Because the office was organised into divisions of professionals, it wasn't always possible to assemble a properly weighted team and there wasn't any synergy between the various groupings. I thought we could do it rather better.'

Staple therefore came up with a plan to alter things dramatically. 'I was in no doubt that change had to take place,' he says, 'but I wanted to get everyone's support for it. So I took the whole senior management team away for the weekend and explained my ideas to them. By the end of two days, I think everybody was in no doubt that this was the right way to go.'

Staple's plan was to create five action divisions, each run by an assistant director, plus a sixth policy division. Staple wanted each division to be located on a separate floor in Elm Street and include several lawyers, financial investigators, accountants and law clerks. Each division would then be assigned a number of cases and, because everyone in the team was working in close proximity, it should be possible to process the cases far more efficiently than before. As an additional bonus, Staple hoped that the assistant directors, who would now be personally responsible for every case in their division, would take a more hands-on approach to the supervision of their junior staff. Finally, Staple wanted each of the new divisions to be responsible for liaising with a given number of police forces around the country, thus improving the traditionally poor communications between the SFO and the police service in general. 'It seemed to me', says Staple, 'that having a mix of professionals within a division would encourage the multi-disciplinary approach and make us far more flexible. Each division would be able to carry between fifteen and twenty cases and the fact that we now had a mechanism for building closer working relationships between ourselves and the various police forces was another plus.'

It took over two years for Staple's reforms to work through the system, simply because of the nature of the SFO's business. It just wasn't possible for people to drop cases they had been working on and immediately switch to cases within their new divisions. But, as new cases came in and old cases finished, the re-organisation slowly took shape and eventually proved every bit as successful as George Staple hoped. 'I thought it was terribly important to get these changes through,' recalls Staple. 'I owed it to the Attorney-General and to everyone else who had supported the SFO to make it as effective as possible. It was also very important in terms of our relationship with the police to ensure that each force had an easily identifiable point of contact.'

While there is no doubt that relationships between the SFO and the police service have steadily improved over the years, this remains a sensitive area. George Staple believes that an element of residual friction is perfectly understandable. 'You've got to remember that the SFO was set up to do something that the police had previously done themselves,' he says. 'So, in the early days it was important to try and build up trust between the police and the SFO and I know that my predecessors, John Wood and Barbara Mills, worked very hard at this. But I think it was inevitable in some cases that the police would take a slightly different view to the SFO as to how an investigation should be pursued and I don't blame them for expressing that view because they are very experienced in this field. However, over the years, I think that things have changed and the police now accept that the SFO has developed a real expertise in this area.'

Detective Superintendent Ken Farrow, who led the police side of the Maxwell investigation, also says that many of the early problems have been resolved. 'I think it's true to say that there were some tensions,' he admits, 'but I don't think they exist any more. Originally, some police officers thought that they were doing most of the work and then being excluded from the decision-making process. I think that feeling has gone, and it's now accepted by everybody that we are equal partners at the table when cases are being discussed.'

None the less, while both sides seek to minimise the problems in public, what they say in private is slightly different. Police officers still resent the fact that the final decision, even in the investigative phase of a case, rests with the lawyers at the SFO rather than with the detectives working on the ground. They also say that it is a flaw in the system that they cannot interview people using the SFO's section 2 powers. For its part, the Serious Fraud Office has never really come to terms with the fact that the police officers attached to it answer to their chief constables first and can technically be pulled off a case at any point. To get round this, the SFO has recently started recruiting more financial investigators, some of whom are retired police officers, in an attempt to reduce its dependence on the goodwill of the police. Discussions on this issue with a large number of people on both sides of the divide leave no room for doubt that divisions between the police and the SFO remain; but it is equally indubitable that the confidence-building measures undertaken over the years have considerably reduced the tensions.

Unfortunately for George Staple, his reforms never really attracted the public attention that they deserved. But this is not the only area of the SFO's work that fails to get the media attention it warrants. One of the most important contributions it makes to the fight against fraud is the work it does for overseas prosecutors. With fraud becoming increasingly international in scope, this is a growth area for the SFO, yet it is seldom reported in the newspapers.

Tricia Howse, the Brent Walker case controller, was involved in the SFO's first major joint investigation with a foreign prosecutor. The case began in 1989 shortly after Ferranti, the UK electronics company, merged with a US rival called International Signal and Control. A few months later, Ferranti was bankrupt and its shares were suspended. According to Howse, 'it was obvious that something had gone seriously wrong and so John Wood, the SFO director at the time, announced that he was going to find out exactly what had happened and assigned me to the case. Then he received a telephone call from the USA and two gentleman from America asked if they could fly over and see him. They told us that the FBI, the Department of Defense, the Internal Revenue Service and various other agencies had been investigating International Signal and Control for over two years and everyone was working under the aegis of the Federal Attorney in Philadelphia. I think they were terrified that we would do something to queer their pitch.'

However, as they talked, it became clear that the US investigators were more than willing to share the information they had assembled with the Serious Fraud Office, and it was agreed that the best way forward was for both sides to launch a joint investigation into the fraud. Witnesses were interviewed by both US and UK investigators to prevent duplication, and a case was quickly assembled against a number of people. But, as Howse remembers, not many of them were British. 'It became pretty obvious from very early on that most of the potential defendants were American and that the heart of the fraud was at the Pennsylvania headquarters of International Signal and Control. In the circumstances, we thought it was quite right that the charges were bought in the US courts and the whole thing was done and dusted in about three years. The main individual pleaded guilty and was sentenced to fifteen years' imprisonment.'

The successful outcome of the Ferranti case helped the SFO develop its relations with a whole number of US law enforcement agencies. And, pleasingly for the SFO, the US authorities never tried to hide the importance of the British end of the investigation. Indeed, they even went so far as to highlight it in a series of press releases. But despite their willingness to share the glory, the Ferranti case attracted virtually no UK media attention. 'We had very little publicity here,' recalls Howse with a wry smile. 'It was sad in a way, because it was a jolly good story. But at least we had the satisfaction of knowing that we had played a major part in a very successful investigation and obtained a very just result.'

The Ferranti case was not the only example of the Serious Fraud Office carrying out an investigation and then deciding that the case should be prosecuted in a foreign jurisdiction. An identical pattern occurred in the case of Nick Leeson, the rogue trader who single-handedly lost over £700 million and destroyed Barings, one of Britain's oldest merchant banks. This case did, however, manage to attract a large amount of positive publicity for the SFO before the file was finally passed on to the Singapore authorities.

The SFO investigation into Barings Bank began in February 1994 when Nick Leeson fled Singapore and flew to Frankfurt, only to be arrested by the German police. The SFO had to decide fairly quickly whether Leeson was simply a dishonest trader out of his depth or part of an organised conspiracy which had made money from his enormous losses. Detective Inspector Andrew Noad, one of the SFO's most experienced police officers, was assigned to the case. In September he flew to Germany with two colleagues and spent a total of nine days over two weeks cross-examining Leeson at the Hoechst gaol in Frankfurt. Noad found Leeson to be a person-able enough man but soon discovered that he had virtually no scruples whatsoever. When Noad asked him about the effects of his actions on the bank's bondholders and employees, Leeson simply shrugged his shoulders and replied tritely, 'Shares go up, shares go down.' Later he said contemptuously: 'It's not something I'm proud of, but I can't do anything about it.'

Nick Leeson may have lacked conscience but he was desperately keen to return to the United Kingdom, where he was convinced he would get a less severe sentence and where the prison conditions would be better than in Singapore. He therefore confessed everything to Noad, hoping that this would persuade the police officer to take him back to Britain. Interestingly, during the weekend break from questioning by the SFO, Leeson allowed himself to be interviewed by Sir David Frost for a television special. According to the SFO officers, Frost's non-confrontational interview technique allowed Leeson to put himself across in a far better light than he actually deserved. The Frost programme was, according to the investigators, little more than a PR stunt for Nick Leeson.

Leeson's admission that he had behaved dishonestly in sending false statements from Singapore to London in order to suck out ever larger sums of money from the bank was enough to ensure a conviction in either jurisdiction. But Leeson had also said that he was the only person involved in the fraud and, as the evidence pointed in the same direction, Noad found himself thinking that this case should be heard in Singapore. After all, that was where most of the evidence was, and that was where the offence had been committed. Acting on Noad's recommendation, the SFO decided not to apply for Leeson's extradition to the United Kingdom and instead turned over the transcript of his confession to the Singapore authorities. Leeson was subsequently sent back to Singapore where he is currently serving a six-and-a-half-year sentence.

The SFO has always aspired to play a major international role in the fight against serious fraud, but initially things did not go well. For the first three years of the SFO's life, the UK government refused to sign the Special Protocol on Fiscal Matters to the European Convention on Mutual Assistance in Criminal Cases. This protocol was designed to provide a legal gateway enabling Europe's police forces to gather evidence on each other's behalf, and while Britain remained a non-signatory the SFO found it very difficult to get any foreign assistance. According to Tricia Howse, 'We had to live for three years without belonging to the principal international evidence-gathering club. I remember we had to grovel every time we wanted help.'

The SFO did what it could to get round the problems caused by the government's reluctance to sign the protocol. John Wood launched a charm offensive with his opposite numbers in all the countries where the SFO was likely to need help and supported any international investigations that came his way, hoping this would create some goodwill among his foreign counterparts. However, it wasn't until 1991, when the United Kingdom finally signed the protocol, that the SFO was at last able to begin to develop its international role.

Probably the most important of the innovations introduced by the SFO in the fight against international fraud was the Mutual Legal Assistance department. The MLA unit, as it is better known, is based at Elm Street and acts on behalf of foreign investigators seeking evidence of fraud in the United Kingdom. The investigators make a formal written request for assistance to the Home Office which is then passed on to the SFO. It is the MLA unit's job to obtain the evidence required and pass it back to the country that made the initial request. The unit now has the reputation of servicing foreign requests for assistance more quickly than any of its European counterparts.

One reason for its ability to move so fast is a piece of legislation passed by Parliament in February 1995 which allows the director of the Serious Fraud Office to use the section 2 powers granted in the Criminal Justice Act to help overseas regulators investigating financial crimes. According to Chris Dickson, who ran the MLA unit until he left the SFO in October 1997, 'once a request is received, we would normally talk to the overseas prosecutors to get it clear in our minds what it is they want. If it's a search, we would normally ask one of their representatives to be present, not to do the searching, but to identify any material which might be relevant to their investigation. Of course, the great thing from their point of view is that once the request has been accepted, we can use all the powers of the SFO to ask questions and obtain documents in exactly the same way as we would do for a domestic case.'

The MLA unit has dealt with over 100 requests since this latest power came on to the statute books and it is growing faster than any other part of the Serious Fraud Office. One of the most important cases it has handled recently related to the Italian police inquiry into Silvio Berlusconi, the media magnate and former prime minister of Italy. The Italian authorities wanted the SFO to obtain documents from a leading City solicitor as well as a major bank, both of whom fought aggressively to protect their client's confidentiality. The case eventually went to the House of Lords, which ruled that the SFO was wholly justified in its actions, and the documents were despatched to the Italian authorities shortly afterwards. According to Chris Dickson, 'the documents we seized were extremely important to the prosecution and we like to think that we played a major part in the eventual success of the case.'

The difficulty for the Serious Fraud Office with the MLA unit, as with its international work generally, is that it consumes a lot of resources without being particularly visible. The SFO gets no credit for being part of an investigation that reveals serious fraud overseas, although it is convinced that this is an extremely worthwhile use of its limited resources. But, to its intense frustration, very few other countries have an MLA unit of their own, which means that the SFO's requests for assistance can take months to be answered while other countries asking Britain for help are often serviced in a matter of weeks.

Over the years, a few very high-profile cases have dominated discussions about the overall success of the Serious Fraud Office, while it has not been able fully to communicate the importance of its international work or to demonstrate the skill with which it handles its more run-of-the-mill cases. Now the Staple reforms have put the SFO on an even keel and the Davie Report has more or less guaranteed its survival. The six successful BCCI prosecutions have even given the office something to brag about. All that remains is for Ros Wright, the latest SFO director, to avoid any banana skins and communicate the bigger picture to media that would far rather be reporting bad news about the Serious Fraud Office than joining in the congratulations.

12

The Gentle Touch

R OS WRIGHT'S FIRST DAY as director of the Serious Fraud
Office didn't begin particularly well. Accompanied by a BBC
film crew, she drove to Elm House for a prompt 8 a.m. start. But,
to her surprise, when she arrived at the building, she found
herself almost alone. An IRA bomb scare at all the major London
railway stations had derailed most of her staff's travel arrangements and frustrated their attempts to be in early to welcome their
new boss.

Some people might have been irritated by this unfortunate beginning, particularly given the presence of television cameras to record
the event for posterity. But one of Ros Wright's great strengths is
her sense of humour and, realising what had happened, she
immediately laughed it off. This ability to defuse potentially
embarrassing situations with charm and good grace should, hopes
the SFO, help to diffuse some of the residual hostility of its still
plentiful critics.

But Ros Wright was certainly not selected for the tough job of
SFO director simply because of her personality alone. She was
called to the bar in 1964 and has been involved with fraud all her
working life. Between 1983 and 1987, Wright was head of the
DPP's Fraud Investigation Group and her team prepared and
prosecuted many of the major fraud cases in the London area,
including work on the Guinness case before it was taken over by the
SFO. Subsequently she worked on the regulatory side of law
enforcement with the Securities and Futures Authority, rising to
the post of senior lawyer and general counsel.

Even though Ros Wright's credentials made her particularly well suited for the position of SFO director, it didn't actually occur to her to apply for the job until she was telephoned by a government head-hunter. 'Initially I said that I wasn't interested because I was perfectly happy at the SFA,' recalls Wright with a wry smile. 'But then he rang me again and this time he was very insistent. He persuaded me that it certainly wouldn't be a bad thing for me to send in my CV, which is what I did. I then instantly regretted it, of course, and thought it had been a very silly thing to do. Later, I realised that director of the Serious Fraud Office was actually one of the most exciting jobs in the Civil Service, if not the whole of the legal profession.'

Ros Wright started her £108,192 per annum job as boss of the SFO on 21 April 1997. She said at a press conference to announce her appointment: 'I am coming back to my roots. I regard myself principally as a prosecutor and, for a large part of my career, a fraud prosecutor.' While Wright might have been disappointed to discover that the SFO was not at this point handling any cases as high-profile as Maxwell or Polly Peck, her in-tray must have made interesting reading none the less. Top of the list of files to read was probably the one concerning Morgan Grenfell and Peter Young. A decision on whether or not to prosecute Young for putting tens of millions of pounds of private investors' money into high-risk offshore companies will need to be taken by Wright before long, and getting it wrong could be a costly mistake. Almost as high-profile is the SFO investigation into how the huge Japanese company Sumitomo came to lose $2.6 billion in the copper market. Interestingly for Wright, she already has a file on the potential defendants from her days at the Securities and Futures Authority. And there are a number of other cases which she will also need to watch carefully, including the SFO's investigations into accounting irregularities at Wickes, the building materials chain, and Andrew Regan's bizarre deals with the Co-operative Wholesale Society.

One of the first tests for Ros Wright came with the referral of a case involving the National Westminster Bank, which had lost over £90 million as a result of futures and options dealings by one of its traders. The Bank of England was sufficiently worried about what had happened to ask NatWest for a report to be drawn up under section 39 of the 1987 Banking Act. This report was then sent over to the SFO for its consideration.

Robert Wardle, the SFO's vetting officer, was the first to see the report when it arrived at Elm House. It was his job to read it and make some initial enquiries about its contents. Wardle knew from the outset that this was a particularly difficult case to assess. 'It involves the very complicated futures and options market,' he said at the time. 'It's not an area where jurors would have had much experience.' Wardle also sent the NatWest report to two senior police officers attached to the SFO. They too scrutinised the document and made a number of discreet telephone calls. With NatWest's losses leading on the BBC's *Nine o'Clock News*, there was no doubt in Wardle's mind that this was going to be tricky.

When the initial checks were finished, Wardle organised a meeting between himself, the police officers and Ros Wright. Their job was to brief the director about what they had discovered and offer their views on the subject. Wright, who had also read the files herself, then had to decide whether or not formally to accept the case for investigation by the SFO. The meeting was held on 18 July 1997 in the conference room on the tenth floor of Elm House; it revealed a surprising amount about the new director's views on the relationship between the regulatory authorities and the SFO.

Wardle began the meeting by checking that Wright had received notes from both himself and the police officers outlining their provisional thoughts on the case. Then he quickly brought his boss up to date on the latest situation. 'I've now had an opportunity to look at the report,' said Wardle, 'and I've also had a look at the interviews with some of the players. Plainly this case fits our vetting criteria in as much as the losses are over £1 million, there's been a good deal of public interest and it involves a highly specialist market. Furthermore,' he said, 'I'm reasonably sure that we will need our section two powers if we are to get to the bottom of it.'

As Wardle and the police officers sketched out their thoughts on the case, it became clear that they all favoured launching an investigation into NatWest's extraordinary losses. While none of them explicitly said so, they clearly thought that there had been serious criminal dishonesty at the bank and that the SFO was best placed to find out what had really happened. However, Ros Wright was not persuaded by what she heard. 'It's quite interesting to go through the criteria one by one,' she said, when her three colleagues had finally finished speaking. 'If you look at the first block, it says that "there must be a high level of public concern"; well, that is certainly present. Then it says: "A serious dishonesty on the part of the main potential defendants". Well,' said Wright, looking round the room, 'I think that there is no question that this is dishonest in a criminal sense.' But the third criterion is "whether urgent action is needed and is best taken by the prosecutor". Now I think that is probably not satisfied.'

All three men looked surprised at her comments. The director of the Serious Fraud Office had acknowledged that there was criminal dishonesty in a complex market, but she still did not intend to launch an investigation. Wright clearly believed that this was one case best left to the regulatory authorities for which she used to work. And, in some ways, she was probably right. If the SFO had decided to prosecute the case, a jury might well have failed to comprehend the crime, thus leading to another embarrassing acquittal. But, on the other hand, a Serious Fraud Office which is reluctant to tackle serious fraud because of the complexities involved undermines its own *raison d'être*.

Ros Wright herself does not accept that her decision might in any way suggest to the City that she is soft on complex fraud. 'On the contrary,' she says, 'I think the message is that we, in partnership with the regulators, have got a very firm system of government here. Where the conduct concerned is bordering on criminality and the regulators have the ability to deal with the situation, it can be safely left to them. After all, they also have some very serious powers at their disposal.'

Besides deciding which cases to take on, the director of the Serious Fraud Office also has to spend a good deal of time developing relations with her foreign counterparts. Fraud is increasingly international in scope and the SFO is committed to developing a multinational approach to fraud investigation. Not surprisingly,

Switzerland, with its stringent rules on banking secrecy, is one of the countries that figure most prominently in many of the SFO's cases, and in June 1997 Ros Wright decided to join Gordon Dickinson, one of her assistant directors, on a trip to Berne and Zurich. Dickinson was hoping to persuade the Swiss authorities to speed up the delivery of some important documents that he needed for the upcoming Butte Mining case, and Wright thought it would be a good opportunity to meet her Swiss opposite numbers.

Both Dickinson and Wright left the United Kingdom with high hopes for the trip. They knew that the SFO's Mutual Legal Assistance department was working well and swiftly servicing requests from all parts of the world. They thought the Swiss might have already benefited from this service and would therefore take a sympathetic view of the SFO's own request for help. Unfortunately for the Serious Fraud Office, things didn't quite work out like that.

To Ros Wright's dismay, it soon became clear that the Swiss considered the British to be extremely slow when it came to handling requests for assistance. Rudolph Weiss, a senior officer with the Swiss federal police, explained the position with some relish. 'We have a little bit of a problem with regard to Great Britain,' he said, looking straight at Wright. 'We hoped that when the UK joined the European Convention on Mutual Assistance the problem would be solved. But, as a matter of fact, we would say that this is not the case. Things may be going better now but it still takes a very long time.' Wright was initially taken aback by this allegation but she gradually realised that the Swiss police were confusing the UK's general response to requests for assistance with the SFO's much quicker service.

'You've got to remember', Wright said later, looking back on the meetings, 'that the SFO is not the only authority in Britain that handles requests for co-operation from the Swiss authorities. In all the cases that the Swiss raised with us, none of the requests had been made to the Serious Fraud Office. They all involved crimes which were dealt with by other agencies. I obviously don't know what the truth is behind the alleged delays, but I said that I will make enquiries when I get back to the United Kingdom and I will.' Wright's offer of help did go some way towards reducing the tension, but the Swiss attitude to the British in general soured the rest of the trip.

Despite these problems, Dickinson's attempt to acquire material for the Butte Mining trial seemed to meet with some success, as a package turned up at the SFO some six weeks later containing a number of documents relating to Swiss bank accounts. However, Dickinson suspects that the arrival of these papers had as much to do with his previous correspondence as with the trip itself. 'We received at least some of the documents that we talked about with the Swiss authorities,' he says. 'But I think this is probably in response to the letters of request that we sent to the Swiss almost two years ago. Still,' he added, not wanting to look churlish, 'I'm quite pleased to have them.'

Ros Wright's other main preoccupation over the early summer of 1997 was the publication of the SFO's ninth annual report. The report itself serves two functions: it fulfils the director's statutory requirement under the 1987 Criminal Justice Act to submit an annual report to the Attorney-General; and it gives the SFO an opportunity to tell the wider world of its successes over the last twelve months. Wright was determined that her first report was going to make an impact. 'This is our only publication,' she said, looking through an early mock-up. 'It's the public face of the Serious Fraud Office and I want it to deliver a good strong message.'

One of Wright's big ideas was to make the annual report more case-related. The SFO had prosecuted many fascinating cases and it was clear that this was what interested most people. Wright hoped that, by highlighting this side of the SFO's work, the report would become more accessible and would reinforce the idea that the office was convicting defendants on a regular basis. To strengthen this impression, Wright also wanted the report to contain far more pictures of convicted defendants than had previously been the case. 'There is no point in having a library picture of anonymous people pretending to be defendants when we have got pictures of convicted real ones,' she said to James O'Donoghue, the SFO's head of information. 'People who are convicted of fraud have to realise that their pictures are going to be plastered all over the press

and I don't think that the annual report of the SFO should be any
different. If we're going to have pictures, we might as well have real
ones.'

In many ways, the SFO's ninth annual report succeeded beyond
Wright's wildest dreams. She ended up doing over twenty media
interviews and the tone of the reporting the following day was
overwhelmingly supportive. The report showed, for the first time,
that the SFO's conviction rate had now reached 86 per cent and
seemed set to go even higher. 'I'm very pleased with the annual
report,' said Wright when she had finished the last interview of the
day. 'Every single case that we have taken before the criminal courts
in the last twelve months has resulted in at least one defendant
being convicted, usually the principal defendant. It's a very positive
message to put over.'

But Wright's pleasure in what looked like being a great public
relations triumph didn't last long. Just a few days later a High Court
judge ruled that one small section of the report had broken a court
order prohibiting the publication of certain information about an
upcoming SFO case. It left the office with little option but to write
to hundreds of recipients asking them to 'take note' of the judge's
decision and to pulp all the remaining copies of the report. But the
judge wasn't willing to leave matters there. He also launched an
attack on what he said was the report's emphasis on conviction rates
and its triumphalist tone.

Ros Wright accepts that the SFO made a mistake when it
breached the court order, but she doesn't feel that the judge's more
general attack was justified. 'We measure success', she says forcefully, 'as an investigation that's properly mounted, a prosecution
that's fairly brought and a trial that's effectively run. I think it's
unfair to look at one particular aspect of the report and to say that it
created a misleading impression. I also think that to say the statistics in themselves, and in particular the conviction rate, which last
year happened to be rather high, was triumphalist was a rather
strange and perhaps unfortunate criticism of the office.'

Many journalists present in the court when the judge delivered
his criticisms of the SFO's annual report also thought he had gone
too far. Like it or not, public relations is now an important part of

the work of any government department, and the Serious Fraud Office would be foolish not to maximise opportunities to present a positive message. However, the judge did not turn victory into defeat for the SFO. Having finished his 45-minute attack, he immediately ruled that the reason why the SFO was in contempt of court should be kept secret until the trial finished. To the relief of the entire office, Wright's error was not to be reported.

By the end of summer 1997, Wright was clearly starting to feel confident in her new job and she turned her attentions to more strategic issues. Ever since it was set up, the SFO had continually hinted that it favoured the abolition of jury trials for serious fraud cases. This idea was first floated in 1985 by the Roskill Committee, which had also recommended the establishment of the Serious Fraud Office, and it has long been regarded by the SFO as the missing ingredient in the recipe for successful fraud prosecution. Now Wright was ready to lend her weight to the argument, although, like her predecessors, she was reluctant to make an explicit call for change.

Wright's chosen platform was a speech to the members of the Finance and Leasing Association. She began by explaining to a surprised audience that the jury debate was now back on the agenda. 'Roskill', she said, 'advocated replacing the lay jury in complex fraud trials by a panel of seasoned market professionals directed by a legal assessor. But this idea was rejected twelve years ago. Now it's being reconsidered by government policy-makers and it certainly has some things to recommend it. The proceedings would be shorter and less expensive and there is no doubt that a panel of market experts would be able to grasp the complexities of the transactions without having them explained at interminable length. On the other hand,' she went on, determined to give the appearance of neutrality, 'the traditional views about the merits of trial by lay juries are very deeply entrenched indeed.'

Wright's approach to this issue has become more sophisticated as she has become more involved in the debate. She now points out that the lack of research in this area makes it almost impossible for anyone really to know what goes on in the jury room. 'I want to see proper academic research done into the way juries determine the issues in a complex fraud case,' she says, 'and then we can go from there. At the moment that's not possible and so I think we need to change the law. Then we can review the situation from a position of knowledge.' It's a compelling point; but it wasn't her view back in March 1997. According to the *Lawyer* magazine, Wright told them then: 'If you really want to see justice done, I don't think juries in fraud are the way to achieve it.' It may be that the new director of the Serious Fraud Office has really become agnostic on the subject, but it seems more likely that the responsibilities of office have forced her to adopt a neutral public position.

The crowning glory of Ros Wright's first nine months as director has undoubtedly been the results in the courts. Between April and December 1997, the SFO did not lose a case and, while Wright isn't claiming any particular credit for the string of successes, it has further shifted people's perceptions of the office. More important still, a number of the cases prosecuted by the SFO in this period were relatively large, high-profile cases where the outcome was considered to be anything but certain

Perhaps the biggest case brought by the SFO during this time was that of Landhurst Leasing. This company was founded by Ted Ball in the early 1980s and arranged lease finance on classic cars such as Aston Martins and Ferraris. By the end of the decade it was a thriving multi-million-pound business and had expanded its activities to include a number of new markets, such as seating at the London Docklands Arena. The money provided to Landhurst customers under the lease agreements came from a syndicate of banks, who made available a facility of £121 million.

One of Landhurst's most important clients was MGL, the company which owned the Brabham Formula One team. MGL had failed to find sufficient sponsorship to keep Brabham going, and it became totally reliant on Landhurst for its funding. Landhurst eventually lent MGL a total of £7.2 million, although it only had assets worth about £1 million. This unsecured lending, which breached the terms of Landhurst's own borrowing facility with its banks, was finally exposed when Landhurst went into receivership in August 1992. Brabham, one of the most famous names in motor racing, collapsed shortly afterwards.

The SFO alleged in court that Ted Ball and David Ashworth, Landhurst's finance director, had only agreed to finance Brabham because they had received over £420,000 in corrupt payments. Initially, both men bitterly denied the charges; but then Ashworth changed his plea and accepted that he had corruptly received £60,000 from Brabham at a motorway service station. He threatened to incriminate Ball, who also changed his plea to guilty. Both men were imprisoned after Tim Langdale, the SFO's QC, told the judge that 'Ball and Ashworth took full, dishonest advantage of their controlling positions at Landhurst for personal gain. It was plain and simple old-fashioned greed.'

The Landhurst result, coupled with the successful outcome of the last BCCI trial and a whole host of less high-profile convictions, has left the Serious Fraud Office at the beginning of 1998 in a better position than at almost any time in its history. Ros Wright is confident that the SFO has turned the corner once and for all. 'I think there was a perception, primarily among the ignorant, that the Serious Fraud Office has never won a case,' she says. 'Statistically that was wrong, and our recent results will hopefully nail that lie for good. This is a seriously good office and I think we're doing an important and successful job.'

This is a view shared by Sir Nicholas Lyell, the former Attorney-General, who shepherded the Serious Fraud Office through many of its darkest moments. He says the SFO has provided an important addition to the UK's crime-fighting arsenal. 'It was absolutely essential that we set up the SFO ten years ago because, before that, it simply wasn't possible to bring these long cases. Obviously, the SFO has had its difficulties over the years but I think it's got a very creditable record and it has proved its worth time and again.'

Even Monty Raphael, the senior partner at Peters & Peters and the doyen of defence lawyers, is surprisingly supportive of the Serious Fraud Office. 'We have generally found the SFO to be a fair and professional organisation,' he says, 'and, bearing in mind the battering that it's received from the media, it's been extremely resilient and has done quite well. But I do think that it may have set its horizons too low. I'd like to see Ros Wright doing a bit of empire building and taking on a lot more serious and complex fraud cases.

I'd like to see the SFO having a series of regional offices and fraud as a whole given a much higher priority in our criminal justice system.'

But Raphael isn't completely sanguine about the workings of the office. He points out that it is virtually impossible to assess the SFO objectively, and that this prevents any final verdict being delivered. 'We need reliable, published, objective criteria so that we can measure the performance of the SFO properly,' he says. 'We need to know that it's efficient, that its procedures are effective and that the public is getting good value for money. It seems a pity that, ten years after the SFO was set up, we still haven't got any performance indicators in place.'

In the absence of such indicators, one is forced back on observation, anecdote and discussion. The records show that the Serious Fraud Office has been unfairly pilloried in the past. It has made mistakes, but it never really deserved the poor reputation it acquired. The high-profile nature of the SFO's work means that it remains vulnerable to media attack, but Ros Wright's communication skills may enable it to handle such problems more effectively in the future. Under her leadership and with George Staple's reforms now fully in place, the fraudbusters of the SFO can probably look forward to a less traumatic second decade.

The Final Score

THE SERIOUS FRAUD OFFICE does not think that a crude statistical analysis of its conviction rate can show whether or not it has done a good job. And it is probably right to hold this view. But the fact remains that the media have fastened on to the SFO's conviction rate as a way of measuring its success, and the figures do tell an interesting story.

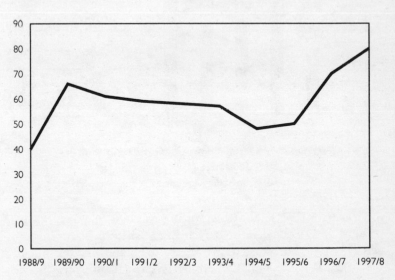

Figure 1: SFO caseload by financial year, including all cases accepted and prosecutions brought (1997/8 year to date)
Source: Serious Fraud Office figures.

According to the SFO, as at 12 January 1998 it had taken part in 165 trials involving 381 defendants and managed to secure 248 convictions. This gives it a healthy 65 per cent conviction rate over the first ten years of its life. It will be interesting to see what happens when the higher caseload, which is a consequence of the Davie Report and is shown in Figure 1, finally starts feeding through into the statistics.

The trouble with the figures issued by the Serious Fraud Office itself is that they are cumulative totals. They do not lend themselves to an examination of the SFO's year-on-year 'progress', for want of a better word. For historical comparisons of the SFO's conviction rate, one has to look at Figures 2 and 3.

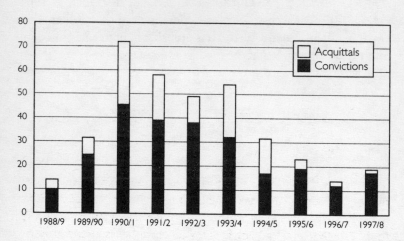

Figure 2: SFO conviction rate expressed in numbers
of defendants tried (1997/8 year to date)
Source: Based on Serious Fraud Office annual reports.

These two charts show that, during the first four years of its life, the SFO's conviction rate remained fairly constant. In percentage terms, it fluctuated between the low sixties and the middle seventies. Then, in mid-1992, things started to go badly wrong. Over the next two years, the SFO's conviction rate plummeted from 75 per cent to just over 50 per cent. It is noteworthy that this period almost exactly mirrors the Serious Fraud Office's nightmare years.

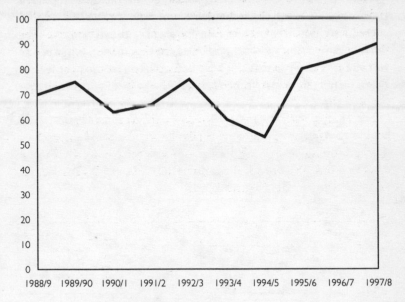

Figure 3: SFO conviction rate expressed as a
percentage of defendants tried
Source: Based on Serious Fraud Office annual reports.

The nightmare was caused by the negative reporting of a small number of very high-profile cases; but it is clear that the SFO's overall conviction rate went into a deep decline at much the same time. Whether one had any bearing on the other is almost impossible to say, but it is an intriguing notion that the persistent media attacks on the SFO may have actually undermined its ability to prosecute cases successfully.

The Serious Fraud Office began a spectacular recovery from its low point in mid-1994. Since then, it has driven up its conviction rate from just over 50 per cent to its present level of over 95 per cent. This figure is acknowledged by the SFO to be unsustainable and reflects the relatively low number of cases being tried by the SFO. However, such a high conviction rate poses another question. Has the SFO been cherry-picking its cases to ensure convictions and silence its critics?

The Serious Fraud Office categorically denies this and says that it prosecutes so few cases that statistical anomalies may arise without there being a sinister strategy of some sort in operation. But, if the current conviction rate is maintained, an explanation will need to be sought. The SFO may not have been as bad as some people have claimed, but it is not perfect either.

Index

INSIDE TERRORISM

Bruce Hoffman

'Gripping – and alarming'   *Economist*

'In his stated aim – to focus on "the most salient and important trends in terrorism . . . as a means to explain why terrorists 'do what they do' as well as to shed light on likely future patterns and potentialities" – the author has succeeded brilliantly. His predictions for the future are hardly comforting, but they should be heeded by all governments with an interest in world peace'   Saul David, *Sunday Telegraph*

The face of terrorism is changing. New adversaries, new motivations and new rationales have emerged in recent years to challenge many of our most fundamental assumptions about terrorists and terrorism. Radical leftist organizations and longstanding nationalist and separatist movements are being superseded by groups with less comprehensible ideological and nationalist aims who pose a far greater and more lethal threat.

In INSIDE TERRORISM – updated for this paperback edition to take account of the American embassy bombings in East Africa and the terrorist bomb at Omagh in August 1998 – Bruce Hoffman, one of the world's leading experts on terrorism, provides an incisive anatomy of its nature, evolution and future.

£7.99   0 575 40126 5

INDIGO

COLLAPSE OF STOUT PARTY

Julian Critchley & Morrison Halcrow

'As anyone who has sat next to him at dinner will know, Critchley in full flow is always worth it'   William Waldegrave, *Daily Telegraph*

'Sir Julian Critchley and Morrison Halcrow show in their highly entertaining book, which well describes and accounts for the Conservative debacle, that the Conservative transgressions were not just venial or presentational: they were real and, as it turned out, mortal. Critchley has long been easily the wittiest Conservative politician and writer, a reputation which this book consolidates'
Ian Gilmour, *Literary Review*

The reverberations from the Tories' cataclysmic defeat at the 1997 general election lingered long. William Hague may have replaced John Major, and the new Labour government may have started to wobble following its prolonged honeymoon period, but still the Conservatives were not viewed as an effective opposition. In this Indigo edition of their acclaimed account of the Tories' collapse, updated to include the first year of William Hague's leadership, Julian Critchley and Morrison Halcrow provide another wonderfully witty and wise chronicle of one of the most spectacular political obliterations of the century.

£7.99   0 575 40168 0

*IN*D*IGO*

A BRUTAL FRIENDSHIP
Saïd K. Aburish

'Aburish is fast becoming an icon. To some Arab states, he has proved an author more traumatizing than Salman Rushdie . . . Keep on writing, Aburish'   Kathy Evans, *Observer*

'The value of Aburish's dashing and highly readable revisionism is to remind us that most Arabs have been ignored in their desire for democracy, human rights and even-handedness in their relations with the West'   Andrew Lycett, *Sunday Times*

The Middle East is the world's powder keg. Throughout the region terrorism, rebellion and unrest lurk at every corner. Young Islamists and disaffected liberals are challenging the authority of the king of Saudi Arabia and his family. Iraqi children are starving to death, while Kuwait is in the middle of a massive identity crisis. Lebanon is riven with civil strife. The social and economic gap between the haves and the have-nots grows unbridgeably wider.

In A BRUTAL FRIENDSHIP Saïd K. Aburish, long acknowledged as one of the world's leading authorities on Arab affairs, traces the origins of the present turmoil to the way in which the Middle East establishment has, since the First World War, subordinated the welfare of the average Arab to its conspiratorial alliance with the West. In explaining how current events in the Middle East represent a backlash against decades of collusion and conspiracy, A BRUTAL FRIENDSHIP provides an essential primer to the most volatile and dangerous area of world politics.

£8.99   0 575 40099 4

INDIGO

Out of the blue...

*I*ND*I*GO
the best in modern writing

FICTION

Sylvia Brownrigg *Ten Women Who Shook the World*	0 575 40150 8
Geoff Nicholson *Bleeding London*	0 575 40056 0
Nick Hornby *High Fidelity*	0 575 40018 8
Joe R. Lansdale *Bad Chili*	0 575 40134 6
Neil Ferguson *English Weather*	0 575 40061 7
Mameve Medwed *Mail*	0 575 40133 8
Alan Moore *Voice of the Fire*	0 575 40055 2
Julian Rathbone *Blame Hitler*	0 575 40094 3
Tim Earnshaw *Helium*	0 575 40115 X
Christopher Whyte *The Warlock of Strathearn*	0 575 40122 2

NON-FICTION

Julian Critchley and Morrison Halcrow	
Collapse of Stout Party	0 575 40168 0
Saïd K. Aburish *A Brutal Friendship*	0 575 40099 4
Robert Twigger *Angry White Pyjamas*	0 575 40124 9
Nicola Baird *The Estate We're In*	0 575 40156 7
Nick Hornby *Fever Pitch*	0 575 40015 3
Carole Morin *Dead Glamorous*	0 575 40035 8
Gary Paulsen *Eastern Sun, Winter Moon*	0 575 40069 2
Geoffrey Haydon *John Tavener: Glimpses of Paradise*	0 575 40191 5
Matthew Engel *Tickle the Public*	0 575 40083 8

*I*ND*I*GO books are available from all good bookshops or from:
>Cassell C.S.
>Book Service By Post
>PO Box 29, Douglas I-O-M

*I*ND*I*GO